The Beginnings
of Communication
Study in America

The Beginnings of Communication Study in America

A Personal Memoir

by Wilbur Lang Schramm

Edited by

Steven H. Chaffee
Everett M. Rogers

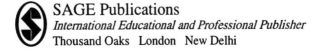

SAGE Publications
International Educational and Professional Publisher
Thousand Oaks   London   New Delhi

For information address:

SAGE Publications, Inc.
2455 Teller Road
Thousand Oaks, California 91320
E-mail: order@sagepub.com

SAGE Publications Ltd.
6 Bonhill Street
London EC2A 4PU
United Kingdom

SAGE Publications India Pvt. Ltd.
M-32 Market
Greater Kailash I
New Delhi 110 048 India

Printed in the United States of America

Library of Congress Cataloging-in-Publication Data

Schramm, Wilbur Lang, 1907-
    The beginnings of communication study in America: a memoir /
author, Wilbur Schramm; editors, Steven H. Chaffee and Everett M. Rogers.
        p.   cm.
    Includes bibliographical references and index.
    ISBN 0-7619-0715-7 (cloth).—ISBN 0-7619-0716-5 (pbk.)
    1. Communication—Study and teaching—United States—History.
    2. Communication—Research—United States—History.
    I. Chaffee, Steven H.   II. Rogers, Everett M. III. Title.
    P91.5.U5S37   1997
    302.2'07'073—dc21   96-51268

This book is printed on acid-free paper.

97 98 99 00 01 02 10 9 8 7 6 5 4 3 2 1

Acquiring Editor:	Margaret Seawell
Editorial Assistant:	Renée Piernot
Production Editor:	Astrid Virding
Production Assistant:	Denise Santoyo
Typesetter & Designer:	Andrea D. Swanson
Indexer:	Trish Wittenstein
Cover Designer:	Candice Harman

Contents

Editors' Foreword

On December 27, 1987, Wilbur Schramm died while sitting at home watching television with his wife. When friends came to sort through his effects a few weeks later, they found in his personal computer the manuscript for a book he had titled *The Beginnings of Communication Study in America.* Obviously in first draft form, it included six chapters and a table of contents outlining a seventh chapter yet to be written. There were no footnotes or citations to be found, either in the computer files or elsewhere in the papers that he left.

No one has ever been better qualified to write on the subject Schramm chose for this book. One of the most remarkable academic innovators ever known, he had been the central figure in the process embodied in his title. In this manuscript, as in some earlier papers, he focused on the four inspirational social scientists that he counted as the "forefathers" of the field of communication research: Harold D. Lasswell, Paul F. Lazarsfeld, Kurt Lewin, and Carl I. Hovland. Although they were in different disciplines, Schramm found in their theories and methods the intellectual material from which the new academic field of communication was built in the decades following World War II. His unfinished manuscript was intended to acknowledge in perpetuity their seminal contributions.

This book represents our attempt to complete what Schramm had begun, to the best of our ability. We undertook this task at the request of his widow, Elizabeth Schramm (who followed him in death in 1988) and their daughter, Mary Schramm Coberly. The manuscript was provided, on diskette as well as on paper, through the efforts of Schramm's longtime associates Lyle Nelson of Stanford University and Godwin Chu of the East-West Center. Mariko Jitsukawa at Stanford University assisted us greatly, poring over sources in the Stanford University Library to find missing references. We, with additional help from Stacey Frank and Stephanie Craft, located the remaining fugitive citations over a period of several years while collaborating on further studies on the history of the communication field.

With one unavoidable exception, plus an enormous one, we have preserved here what Schramm had written with only necessary editing. Part I of this book contains essentially his manuscript with citations added. Chapters 1 through 5 are the first five chapters that Schramm had drafted. Knowing him to be the most careful of craftsmen, we have taken the liberty of correcting the few errors that we spotted. Chapter 6 in Part I is the summing-up that Schramm had written as his final chapter for the book (planned by him as Chapter 7).

We have made two chapter-long exceptions to simply publishing Schramm's book as it stood when he died. Those two chapters compose Part II here. First, we attempted, following the outline from his table of contents, to write our version of what would have been Chapter 6. It appears here as Chapter 8 and it describes how communication study, once begun, spread among U.S. universities. This addition to Schramm's manuscript is unavoidable if we are to honor his manifest intent.

In our Chapter 7, though, we have taken a far greater liberty in writing a chapter that Wilbur Schramm would never have considered: An account of *the founder* of the field. That was, of course, Schramm himself. Communication scholars today may debate just who their forefathers were, but no one disputes that Schramm was the founder. We wrote Chapter 7 so that readers will understand why there is such widespread agreement on his preeminence—and why we have gone to this effort to bring to publication the final work of this remarkable man.

A few features of our editing should be explained. Schramm wrote his chapters here from a personal perspective, and we subtitled this book *A Personal Memoir* to emphasize the first-person nature of many of his observations. He saw the history of the field as it occurred *to him*. We use a similar method in writing our Chapter 7 on Schramm. Later scholars have retraced other sequences in the development of communication study, but it is beyond the scope of this volume to provide a thoroughly Olympian view. We feel no need to try to improve on Schramm's history of the field. Accordingly, we let stand here some statements about the history of communication study to which we might take exception elsewhere. This is, we feel, *his* book.

Schramm's style of writing is highly personal and uniquely his own. We were tempted to formalize his references to universities but have decided for example to let Wisconsin be "Wisconsin" rather than to alter it to the formal "the University of Wisconsin—Madison." Similarly, we left his references to noted scholars as he phrased them, often on a first-name basis. Paul F. Lazarsfeld was "Paul" to Wilbur Schramm. Where we think there might be doubt regarding the identity of a person or institution, or where an affiliation noted by Schramm has become obsolete, we have added an Editors' Note. Very few explanatory words are interpolated in the manuscript, and these are marked off by brackets. Our hesitation in editing is not altogether a favor, we realize. Schramm's manuscript was a first draft, and Schramm would surely have edited his own wording severely. He always did (Danielson, 1989). Schramm was, after all, an accomplished professional writer who had won an O. Henry Prize for short story fiction before the field of communication had begun to take form in his mind. He was, in addition to being the greatest scholar in our field, its finest storyteller. We try throughout this book not to let ourselves get in the way of Schramm's story.

We have incurred many debts, intellectual and otherwise, in editing this volume. We acknowledge the support of our home institutions: for Dr. Chaffee, the Institute for Communication Research and the Department of Communication at Stanford University. For Dr. Rogers, the Center for Advanced Study in the Behavioral Sciences at Stanford, where he was a fellow during the 1991-92 academic year, prior to his moving from the Annenberg School for Communication at the University of Southern California to the University of New Mexico's Department of Communication and Journalism. We thank the many colleagues and students of Schramm's with whom we consulted at various stages in the preparation of this book, particularly Erwin Bettinghaus, Eleanor Blum, Henry Breitrose, Wayne Danielson, Mary Anne Fitzpatrick, Fred Haberman, William Hachten, Jack Hilgard, Nathan Maccoby, Howard Mackay, Maxwell McCombs, Lyle Nelson, William Paisley, Theodore Peterson, Donald Roberts, Charles Savage, and David Manning White. Stephanie Craft deserves special thanks for her role in finalizing the manuscript and reading the page proofs. Others are cited in appropriate places, particularly in Chapters 7 and 8.

Here, then, are Wilbur Schramm's final words to scholars in the field that he began.

Steven H. Chaffee
Stanford, California

Everett M. Rogers
Albuquerque, New Mexico

PART I

The Forefathers of Communication Study in America

Wilbur Schramm

The Forefathers of Our Forefathers

Many of the brightest chapters, the most significant insights, decisions, and inventions in the history of human communication are hidden in the mists of time and distance, and we can know very little about them. But this book is principally a story from our own time. It is about scholars who led a significant revolution in social research on communication in our own century. We knew them personally. Their memories and records are still fresh. Their students are all around us. Furthermore, four of them had such an impact that we have come to call them the "forefathers" of modern communication scholarship.

Our Forefathers

I am speaking, of course, of Harold D. Lasswell, Paul F. Lazarsfeld, Kurt Lewin, and Carl I. Hovland.[1] Each of them was extraordinarily prolific in the conduct of research and in the advancement of theory. Three of the four founded research and training institutes, and all four guided large numbers of students and exerted great influence on their colleagues. As many observers have said, they entered communication study at one stage of its development and left it at a new stage. More accurately, they entered the field before there was a field called communication research or communication study and they created one.

They would not have said that about themselves, for they were modest concerning their own accomplishments. Indeed, they were quick to point out that if they were "forefathers," then they *too* had forefathers, and more significant insights concerning communication had been arrived at before their time than by any achievement of theirs. I remember a talk I once had with Lasswell concerning Communication Past. He asked me how many humans had lived and died on Earth. I guessed 100 billion plus or minus 25% during the million years that humans, or something like them, had been on Earth. If one accepts the Creationist view that the world began about 6,000 years ago with a single family in the Garden of Eden and started off anew with Noah's family in the Ark on Ararat, then we might have to reduce the estimate to *50* billion plus or minus 15% or so. He chuckled and said he would go along with Darwin on the time estimate. But he was obviously taken with the figures and what they implied about the ideas that were lost to us because there was no way to store them. We had a wonderful talk about the insights that must have been arrived at by our forefathers, unknown to us, in the mists of prehistory.

Lasswell had read that in glacial times the entire population of the British Isles may have been only 250 persons, and he wondered what special meaning communication must have had for them in all that loneliness. I noted that even in early postglacial times there were probably more chimpanzees than humans on Earth, and we speculated whether human communication had a rather special significance when humankind was not the dominant species.

Then we got around to some of the really important insights that must have come to humans during those early years. For instance, who first had the idea that everything could have a name and that the name might be transferred in place of the thing itself? At what magic moment, in what place, did someone see that by adding a few other sounds or gestures it would be possible to relate an action to a name? Where did the insight originate that by a certain combination of sounds or gestures it would be possible to communicate about the future or the past as easily as about the present? All these insights must have come to humans in the very distant past, and compared to them, the kind of insights that are coming out of present-day communication research are trivial.

I have sometimes returned to that conversation and recalled Lasswell's modest evaluation of his own products. One could add others to the unanswerable questions that we raised. Who first looked at a bone or a rock or a lump of clay and imagined how it could be transformed into a statue of a human figure? Someone did, for 25,000 or so years ago our ancestors in southern Europe were producing tiny human figurines, thought to have some magical connection with increasing the population of the tribe. Who first looked at a cave wall and imagined colors spread over it to represent buffalo or mammoths or other animals that the tribe hunted? And what was the origin of that still more exciting insight—when humans first saw that not only was it possible to draw objects but, having accomplished that, the picture could be generalized in style and meaning and given a sound so that sound and sight could be transferred back and forth and meanings could be integrated both with pictures and sounds and used as written language? Who saw that this new "writing," which the Sumerians pressed on clay tablets and the Egyptians drew on papyrus, could serve as a memory for humans?

If we try to place our four distinguished forefathers in the long sweep of communication history, we realize, as Lasswell said the night of our first conversation, that they and all the rest of us who were born in the 19th or 20th centuries came into the world after the really fundamental communication questions had already been asked. The progress from the first writing—Sumerians pressing wedge-shaped figures into damp clay tablets—to the 20th century has been largely technological—from pictorial symbols to alphabets to paper, ink, and printing to pictorial recording and electronic recording and transmission. We know many of the talented artisans and inventors who brought about these changes—the Ts'ai Luns and Gutenbergs, the Daguerres and Bells and Edisons, Marconis, DeForests, and Zworykins—but for the most part these later contributions were stylistic rather than fundamental. That is to say, the invention of rag paper in China about A.D. 105 was a different order of discovery from the concept, achieved some unknown hundreds of thousands of years earlier, that every object could have a name. The electronic computer may yet prove to be a fundamental insight as well as a technological triumph, but we shall have to wait and see. Rather, the more fundamental insights in human communication since the invention of writing have probably been in the way humans have learned to talk about themselves and their world. They have learned to talk about things that could not be seen (Democritus on atoms) or things they could not touch (Aristarchus and Pythagoras, Copernicus and Galileo, Kepler and Newton, on the universe). They invented a way to talk about numbers and quantities—not only to count two or three buffalos but also to understand the concept of two-ness and three-ness, which could be applied to anything countable. They developed the subtle concepts of "zero" and "infinity."

These individuals were forefathers of modern communication as much as some of the other humans who developed alphabets, for example, and more so than some of the ingenious inventors of communication machines—for instance the skillful John Baird, who 70 years ago was the first person to demonstrate television in public (in London, on January 26, 1926).

The world of 2 or 3 thousand years ago was full of brilliant minds working in what we would today call philosophy, arts, and rhetoric, raising questions and setting standards for future communicators but seldom aware that they were studying communication. The Romans had their verb *communicare;* the Greeks had their noun stem *rhetor.* Cicero and Quintillian, Aristotle, the schools of the Sophists and the followers of Socrates, analyzed what they called "rhetoric" in terms of persuasion and explanation, with a degree of sophistication not equaled for a long time afterward. Plato wrote one of the classics of communication study in the *Allegory of the Cave.* Homer composed narrative poems absorbing enough to be preserved by word of mouth and at the same time penetrating enough as analysis of a culture to set a standard for Greece in its greatest years. Herodotus was not only a great narrative historian but also a seldom-equaled analyst of the cultures that he saw around him. Caesar has sometimes been called the "greatest war correspondent" of all time—an idea that might startle young people who studied his *Gallic Wars* in Elementary Latin classes. Some dramatists of those times—Aristophanes, for example—were sharp social critics, foreshadowing modern commentators and essayists as well as modern dramatists. None of the philosophers and "wise men" of those times would describe themselves as communication scholars, and yet many of them had something of importance to say about human communication. Confucius, for example. Aristotle. The authors of the Upanishads.

So recent scholars and teachers such as Lasswell, Lazarsfeld, Lewin, and Hovland, who will stand tall in later pages of this book, were far down the road of communication development. They were products of a new age, a new time in human history, which we call the Age of the Mass Media.

The Mass Media Set the Stage for
Modern Communication Study

The world had been trembling on the verge of mass media for centuries. The Romans established publishing houses in which an army of scribes produced books by hand and also circulated handwritten newsletters to distant parts of the Empire. When the Chinese learned how to inscribe letters on wood blocks, it became possible to produce ornately illustrated books such as the *Diamond Sutra* and a palace newsletter that endured from the 8th century until the early 20th century and was thus clearly the longest-lived newspaper in history. Town criers sounded suspiciously like modern radio newscasters. The Koreans and Chinese learned to make metal type letters a century before Gutenberg did, but it required the combination of new technology and a favorable economic and political climate—printing from movable metal type and the European Renaissance—before these faint stirrings evolved into organized media, carrying information and entertainment to a wide public.

When printing developed into news sheets and news sheets into newspapers and when print shops that were accustomed to marketing a few books a year gained the ability to circulate 20 million books in Europe by the early 16th century, human communication acquired a different order of prominence in society. George R. White, the Xerox engineer, calculated that an average person's cerebral store of information probably increased by an order of magnitude (10 times) after printing came into use, and the total store of information available to an individual probably grew by *two* orders of magnitude (100 times) after printing came into use. He estimated that when electronic media came into use at the beginning of the 19th century, the average individual's store of information increased *another* order of magnitude and the amount of information available from the media grew by another *two* orders of magnitude.

This new prominence for communication in social life raised a series of important questions. One of them concerned the freedom to publish. Most European governments in the 16th and 17th centuries viewed the free gathering and circulating of news as a potential threat to their security, and because they were authoritarian, they felt they had the right to tell their subjects what news their subjects ought to know. As a result, the first circulation of news was either by word of mouth or on single sheets without title or publisher's name. When the idea of a newspaper, to be published at regular intervals, by an acknowledged publisher, began to appeal to Europeans in the early years of the 17th century, governments typically required publishers to obtain a patent (license) to publish. The kind of patent they could obtain was at first usually for news from *other countries.*

This pattern characterized most *corantos,* the first regularly appearing newspapers in England and in other western European nations: It was safer to report the news from abroad than the news from home. But this content was less than most readers wanted, and the situation resulted in a great deal of thinking and discussion about the freedom to know, freedom of speech, and freedom of the press. From these tensions came some of the memorable writings aimed at defining the relation of human communication to political and moral freedom—such as Milton's *Areopagitica*: "Let [truth] and falsehood grapple, who ever knew truth put to the worse, in a free and open encounter?"

When wars of independence flamed over Europe and in some of the European colonies, in the 17th and 18th centuries, the new printed media speedily became involved with them, just as the European sovereigns had feared. This involvement led not only to a great deal of soul-searching on the part of newspapers and magazines but also to a line of writers who had good reason to consider the reaction of communication to politics. John Stuart Mill's *On Liberty* was one of the notable books that came out of this challenge. Machiavelli had long ago advised "princes" to take careful account of what people were saying and thinking about their government. Metternich also was much concerned over the state of public opinion. Rousseau predictably insisted that laws should be based on public opinion. Voltaire, Carlyle, and Karl Marx were thinkers deeply interested in the relation of politics to public communication and opinion.

In our own century, after the World War of 1914-1918 had introduced the great mass of people to propaganda, a few scholars such as Walter Lippmann, who was a practicing newsman, took the lead in introducing the mass audience to the importance of public communication. Lippmann's 1922 book *Public Opinion* is still one of the most useful books that modern communication students have inherited from an earlier generation of scholars. But the real impetus to public opinion study was the appearance of movies, radio, and television and the increasing need for advertising to pay for the electronic media. Not only had the influence of the mass media on public ideas and opinions become clearly evident, but the use of the electronic and pictorial media was more difficult to specify than that of the printed media, and both advertisers and broadcasters needed to know specific information about their audiences. Furthermore, observers of society were concerned with who controlled the media and what opinions and attitudes were being learned by mass audiences. Thus the scholarly tradition of communication study flowered both in system study and later in survey research to measure the distribution of public opinion and how it changes.

Beginnings of Communication Study in the Universities

Two strands of development in the universities must be considered when we try to fill in the background for modern communication study. One was scholastic, the other practical and professional.

More and more often, scholars who wrote about philosophy and history, politics and economics, found themselves writing about communication, although they did not always index their books under that name. Furthermore, thinkers and social scholars whose work bordered on communication found themselves being interpreted so as to be meaningful to communication thinkers. Darwin, for example. Later, Freud. This setting was the environment from which the four communication forefathers emerged.

One feature of communication scholarship that later readers sometimes forget is the extraordinary keenness and insightfulness with which a group of social scientists in the years just before, and the decades immediately after, 1900 were writing about communication. Some of them were even able to stand aside and analyze the shortcomings of their own communication scholarship and propose an outline for what it ought to be. The Frenchman Gabriel Tarde in 1895, for example, sketched out the kind of statistics that would be needed to study attitudes and opinions, although such statistics did not then exist. Max Weber proposed to the first congress of German sociologists that they band together in a quantitative analysis of the German press. This suggestion, too, was ahead of its time. But even in those dawning years of empirical social research, there were some noteworthy books on communication. Let us take three examples.

Example: Charles Horton Cooley

One American scholar immediately preceding our four chief actors was Charles Cooley (1864-1929). A remarkable passage that he wrote about communication but published under the title *Social Organization* in 1909, tells us about his relationship to the new scholarly field of communication:

> By communication is here meant the mechanism through which human relations exist and develop—all the symbols of the mind, together with the means

of conveying them through space and preserving them in time. It includes the expression of the face, attitude and gesture, the tones of the voice, words, writing, printing, railways, telegraphs, telephones, and whatever else may be the latest achievements in the conquest of space and time. All these taken together, in the intricacy of their actual combination, make up an organic whole corresponding to the organic whole of human thought; and everything in the way of mental growth has an external existence therein. The more closely we consider this mechanism, the more intimate will appear its relation to the inner life of mankind, and nothing will more help us to understand the latter than such consideration. (Cooley, 1909/1983, p. 61)

It is through communication that we get our higher development. The faces and conversation of our associates; books, letters, travel, arts, and the like, by awakening thought and feeling and guiding them in certain channels, supply the stimuli and framework for all our growth. (pp. 63-64)

In the same way, if we take a larger view and consider the life of a social group, we see that communication, including its organization into literature, art, and institutions, is truly the outside or visible structure of thought, as much cause as effect of the inside or conscious life of men. All in one growth, the symbols, the traditions, the institution are projected from the mind, to be sure, but in the very instant of their projection, and thereafter, they react upon it, and in a sense control it, stimulating, developing, and fixing certain thoughts at the expense of others to which no awakening suggestion comes. By the aid of this structure, the individual is a member not only of a family, a class, and a state, but of a larger whole reaching back to prehistoric man whose thought has gone to build it up. (p. 64)

Thus the system of communication is a tool, a progressive invention, whose improvements react upon mankind and alter the life of every individual and institution. . . . And when we come to the modern era, especially, we understand nothing rightly unless we perceive the manner in which the revolution in communication has made a new world for us. (pp. 64-65)

The man who wrote these paragraphs was the son of the first dean of law at the University of Michigan. He prepared, as a student at Michigan, to become an engineer and worked for a time as a draftsman. Cooley analyzed statistics concerning street railways for the U.S. Bureau of the Census in Washington by way of preparing for advanced study in political economy. His PhD dissertation, approved at Michigan by the Department of Economics in 1894, was titled *The Theory of Transportation.* But by that time he had moved rather far from the engineering that he had begun to study and even from economics, in which he had earned his doctorate. He had been deeply influenced by reading what Darwin had to say about the interrelated quality of life, the "organic whole" described in the earlier quotation. He had been impressed by James Bryce's analysis of the system of American democracy (see Bryce, 1900/1987, 1921). After reading William James, he was resolved to follow James in looking at new events (such as the effects of communication) without preconceiving what they might do. He also came away from James's books resolved to try to write as well as the master. He taught his first course not in economics but in sociology, and it is hardly surprising that he built his career in that field because of the central role he gave to the mind. What is more impressive is the importance he saw, and emphasized throughout all his writing and teaching, in the centrality to society of human communication.

Example: Robert Ezra Park

Robert Park (1864-1944) was born in the same year as Cooley, took his undergraduate work at the same university, and also worked in nonacademic positions before settling down to become an academic. He was influenced by some of the same people as Cooley—William James, for one. His chief teacher at Michigan was John Dewey, who, among other things, was responsible for introducing him to Franklin Ford, with whom Park planned to start a new kind of newspaper, *The Thought News,* to report changes in public opinion, just as other newspapers reported prices in the stock market. But the time was not ripe; polling and survey research would not be ready for this kind of development for another 30 years, and the newspaper never got started.

Throughout his life, Park encouraged younger scholars to go into the quantitative study of public opinion, but instead of becoming editor of his own paper, Park became a reporter on other papers. For 11 years in the 1890s he worked on dailies in Minneapolis, Detroit, Denver, New York, and Chicago. He then went to Harvard for his MA (studying with William James, Josiah Royce, and Hugo Munsterberg) and on to the University of Heidelberg for his doctorate in philosophy, which he received in 1904 with a dissertation on *Masse und Publikum* (Crowd and Public) that built on his earlier interest in public opinion. When he returned to the United States, he did not go into teaching. Instead, he became secretary of the Congo Reform Association, concerned with the Belgian atrocities in Africa. Park became friends with Booker T. Washington, the American Black leader, who encouraged him to study the condition of American Negroes in the South. He took a kind of secretarial position with Washington and is believed to have written much of Washington's 1912 book, *The Man Farthest Down.* His active interest in minority relations lasted for the rest of his life. In 1914, at the age of 50, a decade after receiving his PhD, he finally did what he had supposedly been trained for: He returned to academia. He joined in building the great sociology department at the University of Chicago, leading it during its golden era from 1915 to 1935. In his later years, he visited many of the frontiers of racial problems, including South Africa, India, Southeast Asia, and Brazil, and was a visiting professor in China. In what might have been his years of retirement, he lived and taught at Fisk University in Nashville, Tennessee.

Park was probably best known by university scholars for his *Introduction to the Science of Sociology,* written with Ernest W. Burgess and published in 1924. This book was for years the leading college text in sociology. Park wrote on many topics, reflecting his varied career. Some of his books, such as *The Immigrant Press and Its Control,* combined several of these interests—in this case, his newspaper years, his long interest in racial problems, and his broad knowledge of the city. Many social scientists of the time wrote about communication, but Park was one of the few who had been a news reporter and could speak incisively about news and newspapers.

Perhaps one of the best ways to illustrate the qualities of Park's thinking and writing is by means of a few samples from an essay on the sociology of news that he published originally in the *American Journal of Sociology* (Park, 1940) and later as a book chapter under the title, "News as a Form of Knowledge" (Park, 1955).

He suggested that there were three fundamental types of scientific knowledge: "Philosophy and logic, which are concerned primarily with ideas; history, which is concerned primarily with events; and the natural or classifying sciences, which are concerned primarily with things" (Park, 1955, p. 74). Park noted,

> It is obvious that news is not physical knowledge like that of the physical sciences. It is rather, insofar as it is concerned with events, like history. Events, because they are invariably fixed in time and located in space, are unique and cannot therefore be classified as is the case with things. (p. 77)

Park spoke of news and public opinion:

> News, as a form of knowledge, is not primarily concerned either with the past or with the future but rather with the present—what has been described by psychologists as "the specious present." . . . What is meant here by the "specious present" is suggested by the fact that news, as the publishers of the commercial press know, is a very perishable commodity. Different types of news have a different time span.

In its most elementary form, a news report is a mere "flash," announcing that an event has happened. If the event proves to be of real importance, interest in it will lead to further inquiry and to a more complete acquaintance with the attendant circumstances. An event ceases to be news, however, as soon as the tension it has aroused has ceased and public attention has been directed to some other aspect of the habitat or some other incident sufficiently novel, exciting, or important to hold its attention. (p. 78)[2]

The first [typical] reaction of an individual to the news is likely to be a desire to repeat it to someone. This makes conversation, arouses further discussion, and perhaps starts a discussion. But the singular thing about it is that, once discussion has been started, the event under discussion soon ceases to be news, and, as interpretations of an event differ, discussions turn from the news to the issues that it raises. The clash of opinions and sentiments which discussion invariably evokes, usually terminates in some sort of consensus or collective opinion—what we call public opinion. It's upon the interpretation of present events, i.e., news, that public opinion rests. (p. 79)[3]

Park had more to say on the nature of news:

If it is the unexpected that happens, it is not the wholly unexpected that gets into the news. The events that have made news in the past, as in the present, are actually the expected things that are characteristically simple and common-place matters, like births and deaths, weddings and funerals, the conditions of the crops and of business, war, politics, and the weather. These are the expected things, but they are at the same time the unpredictable things. They are the incidents and chances that turn up in the game of life. (p. 82)

Park commented on the relationship of news and science:

Although news is an earlier and more elementary product of communication than science, news has by no means been superseded by it. On the contrary, the importance of news has grown consistently with the expansion of the means of communication and with the growth of science. Improved means of communication have cooperated with the vast accumulations of knowledge, in libraries, in museums, and in learned societies, to make possible a more rapid, accurate, and thoroughgoing interpretation of events as they occur. The result is that persons and places, once remote and legendary, are now familiar to every reader of the daily press. (pp. 86-87)

Park concluded the article this way: "Ours, it seems, is an age of news, and one of the most important events in American civilization has been the rise of the reporter" (p. 88).

Would you think that these quotes come from a very thoughtful scholar in a modern school of journalism or from a sociologist at the University of Chicago (which has never had a school of journalism)? Were they written recently or in the early years of the present century, when there were only a handful of schools of journalism in existence anywhere?

There were very able scholars at the end of the 19th century and the beginning of the 20th century who were deeply interested in the study of communication. For most of them, it was a secondary interest, merely an illustration of their main discipline, and none of them approached communication in the quantitative way that we associate with modern social science. Cooley and Park were known as sociologists, although one of them was trained in engineering and took his PhD in economics and the other worked as a newspaper reporter for 11 years before he entered graduate school and worked on the practical solution of minority problems for 10 years *after* he received a doctorate in philosophy.

A Third Example: Edward Sapir

We also consider here an anthropologist who discovered the attraction of academic anthropology only when he took a graduate degree *in Germanics*(!) and later worked 15 years for the Geological Survey of Canada.

At least superficial similarities appear in these three scholars' preparation for their great careers. Each spent a substantial period in nonacademic work, an experience that provided material later for theoretical books. None of the three, while he was in college, knew where his career was heading. Each of the three discovered the importance of human communication when he delved into the center of his subject interest.

The anthropologist was Edward Sapir (1884-1939). He was born in Germany, came to America at the age of 5, and later impressed his teachers so much that he won a scholarship at Columbia University. He took a year of graduate work in Germanics. Not until the middle of his master's study did he meet Franz Boas, who excited him by outlining the potential of the anthropological study of language—something that hardly could have been farther from his ambitions a year earlier. But from then onward, he was a linguistic anthropologist.

Sapir was so bright that a doctorate in a new field caused him no special problems, and he was hired in 1910, at the age of 26, as chief of anthropology for the Geological Survey of Canada. This was a good position for studying ethnology and a good opportunity for scholarly writing, but there were few other anthropologists with whom to discuss scholarly interests.

Therefore, he welcomed an invitation in 1925 to join the faculty in anthropology at the University of Chicago. This was a rich opportunity intellectually, not only for him but also for a number of bright young scholars, including Harold Lasswell. But after 6 years, in 1931, Sapir was offered a Sterling professorship and the opportunity to found a department of anthropology at Yale University, where he remained until his death in 1939.

Sapir's colleagues, anthropologists well acquainted with his work, testify to the richness of his ideas and his skill in expressing them. An example of Sapir's ideas about communication are expressed in three paragraphs that he wrote for the *Encyclopedia of the Social Sciences:*

> While we often speak of society as though it were a static structure defined by tradition, it is, in the more intimate sense, nothing of this kind, but a highly intricate network of partial and complete understandings between the members of organizational units of every degree of size and complexity, ranging from a pair of lovers or a family to a League of Nations or that ever-increasing portion of humanity which can be reached by the press through all its transnational ramifications.
>
> It is only apparently a sum of static institutions; actually it is being reanimated or creatively affirmed from day to day by particular acts of a communicative nature which obtain among individuals participating in it. Thus the Republican Party cannot be said to exist as such, but only to the extent that it is being reanimated or creatively reaffirmed from day to day by particular acts of a communicative nature as that John Doe votes the Republican ticket, thereby communicating a certain kind of message, or that a half dozen individuals meet at a certain time and place, formally or informally, in order to communicate ideas to one another and eventually to decide what points of national interest, real or supposed, are to be allowed to come up many months later for discussion in a gathering of members of the Party.
>
> The Republican Party as a historic entity is merely abstracted from thousands upon thousands of such single acts of communication, which have in common certain persistent features of reference. If we extend this example into every conceivable field in which communication has a place, we soon realize that every cultural pattern and every single act of social behavior involve communication in either an explicit or an implicit sense. (Sapir, 1931, p. 78)

Carl Hovland was at Yale during some of Sapir's years there, but we do not know how close he was to the old master.[4] However, we do know something about Sapir's influence on another student of communication who became well-known, namely, Benjamin Lee Whorf (1897-1941).

Some of the scholars that we have been talking about took a very long time to earn their doctoral degrees; Whorf did not take a PhD. Some of the

others worked for periods in nonacademic jobs—Cooley, for example, as
a draftsman and a transportation statistician. Whorf never held an academic
position until 1937-1938 when for a year he was a lecturer in anthropology
at Yale. He was a businessman—a fire prevention inspector for the Hartford Fire Insurance Company and later an officer of the company. He did
these jobs as well as he did everything else: "In no time at all," said the
chairman of the board of the company, "he became in my opinion as
thorough and fast a fire prevention inspector as there ever has been"
(Kremer in Carroll, 1956, p. 4). This fire prevention inspector became
interested in language. It happened, he said, in about 1924. He became
interested in translation and in the theory of meaning. The real concern of
linguistics, he wrote, "is to light up the thick darkness of the language. . . .
Linguistics is essentially the quest for MEANING" (Whorf, 1941/1956, p.
73).[5] He developed ideas about the relationship of language to meaning.
Then, in 1931, he met Edward Sapir and enrolled in the first course that
Sapir gave when he came to Yale. This was a turning point, for Sapir had
done a great deal of thinking and reading about Whorf's central interest in
linguistics, and from that time until Sapir's death in 1939, Whorf—without
giving up his job with the Hartford Company (he could not afford to work
for an academic salary, he said)—collaborated closely with Sapir.

The idea of linguistic relativity has quite properly become known as the
Sapir-Whorf hypothesis, because the two minds shared in developing it. This
hypothesis essentially states that one perceives the world through the language
one has learned to use in thinking and communication. "The 'real world,' "
Sapir wrote, "is to a large extent unconsciously built up on the language habits
of the group. No two languages are ever sufficiently similar to be considered
as representing the same social reality" (Whorf, 1941/1956, p. 134).[6] What is
it that makes the notion of linguistic relativity so fascinating even to the
nonspecialist? Asked John B. Carroll in his introduction to the collected writings
of Whorf. He answered his own question: "Perhaps it is the suggestion that [in]
all one's life one has been tricked, all unaware, by the structure of language into
a certain way of perceiving reality. . . . [The] implication [is] that awareness of
this trickery will enable one to see the world with fresh insight" (p. 27).

As Carroll says, the validity of the Sapir-Whorf hypothesis (the principle
of linguistic relativity) has "thus far not been sufficiently demonstrated nor
has it been flatly refuted" (p. 27). But it is one of the bright flashes of insight
that were coming from social scientists who did not think of themselves as
communication scholars but who were contributing to such scholarship at
the time when the forefathers of modern communication scholarship were
coming into the field.

Importance of Professional Background
in Developing Communication Study

Some of the ablest social scholars in the early 20th century who were ostensibly sociologists and political scientists, anthropologists and historians and psychologists, were thus preparing the way for other well-trained social scholars to come into the field as students of communication. At the same time, there was another development of importance to the study of human communication: the introduction of professional schools into universities to prepare students for careers in the mass media.

When social scholars committed themselves to the study of communication in the 20th century, they typically became deeply interested in the mass media. I want to share with you a story that Paul F. Lazarsfeld told me about an incident in his own career. In the 1930s, shortly after Paul had established the Bureau of Applied Social Research at Columbia University, the bureau signed a contract with Iowa State University (then called Iowa State College) to survey its radio audience.[7] At that time, WOI at Iowa State was perhaps the leading educational radio station in the country. It was nonprofit and gave a considerable part of its air time to teaching by radio, but it supported itself by commercial advertising. Therefore, it needed reliable information on its audience and sought out the new bureau at Columbia to obtain that information. The study was designed, and research assistants from Columbia went to Iowa to supervise the audience interviews. Back at Columbia, the data were compiled, and at last the report was ready, with Paul Lazarsfeld prepared to deliver it personally.

When Lazarsfeld arrived in Ames, he was met by the president of Iowa State College. They rode in a long black sedan through the campus. Paul was nervous. It was one of the first studies the bureau had attempted outside of the New York area. He had never been in the Midwest and was not accustomed to being met by a college president in a black limousine. As they rode through the beautiful campus, Paul looked from building to building, asking what they were. Then, in absolute horror, he heard himself—nervously making conversation—say as he looked at a steel tower in the middle of the campus, "Oh, so you have a broadcasting station!"

Paul said he was ready to dissolve in shame—after all, this was the radio station that he had just studied—but President Friley took it as a joke, and the tense moment passed. Paul said he thought later about why he had said what he had. What was the Freudian explanation for this embarrassing slip? He concluded, he said, that radio as a medium was simply not *real* to him. The programs, the people sitting around their radios listening, the survey interviews—all these were real, but he did not actually connect the tower and the radio station with them. The only part of the broadcasting process that was real to him was what happened from the radio set onward. He had spent very little time thinking about how those programs got on the air and reached the radio audience.

Paul used this story to make a point. I had just started a communication research institute at a university,[8] and Paul was helping to dedicate it. "This is what we most envy you and your colleagues," he said. "Most of you have worked in the media. You know what happens inside a broadcasting station or a newspaper office. We have more experience than you in field research but don't really know anything about the media." He said to me in the fatherly manner of an experienced institute director to a new one, "Don't ever move too far from the media!"

This was remarkably generous and frank talk and typical of the man. I thought of it again and again in my years at communication research institutes. And I think of it now as I try to explain the importance to communication study of the schools of journalism and broadcasting that appeared on university campuses in the mid-20th century.

We shall speak in greater detail about this development in a later chapter.[9] The first U.S. journalism school was established in 1908, and by midcentury there were more than a hundred of them, all devoted to what their sponsors called professional, rather than trade, activity and conse-quently increasingly interested in research and advanced degrees. They wanted many of their chief teachers to have appropriate advanced training; many of their students were looking ahead to careers at least partly in research and teaching. Students and faculty alike looked at the kind of media studies being conducted by universities and institutes—studies of audiences and effects and media content—and inquired why such studies were not being done in the professional schools. Before long, they were indeed being done in these schools. Teachers in the professional schools acquired or brought with them research training. Students began to write research theses.

Another development of some importance took place in certain of the professional schools: They organized institutes of research and advanced studies. Illinois and Stanford, Wisconsin and Minnesota, and numerous others added such an institute to their professional journalism schools, staffed by well-trained research scholars and carrying out research and training parallel to what was being done in the top-ranked social science departments of many universities. These research institutes had several advantages, as European universities had found out earlier in developing new fields of academic study. For one thing, the research institutes made it easier for universities to circumvent the traditional patterns of academic departments; in the second place, the institutes attracted a number of the ablest students to advanced study and research; and the institutes made it easier for the journalism schools to develop a field of study that had not been traditional for the university—in this case, human communication.

Thus the new schools of journalism and broadcasting provided a place for social science-trained teachers who were centrally interested in the study of communication. They supplied a continuing flow of bright students to universities where the social sciences were distinguished, and these media-concerned students would not let the social science teachers forget that communication was an important part of their discipline. Cooperation between the professional schools and academic departments opened new opportunities for research on the mass media, controls on them, and their effects on society. The professional journalism schools and their research institutes kept the name "communication," and the idea of communication research became familiar within the scholarly community.

The growth of these schools and institutes is a story in itself. It was one of the currents sweeping through the academic and professional worlds early in the 20th century, helping to prepare the way for the four scholars we call the forefathers of modern communication study to exercise their great influence.

The Forefathers and the Beginnings
of a New Pattern of Study

What was new about the four men to whom we give the title of forefathers? For one thing, they emphasized the empirical approach to communication study more than did their predecessors. They borrowed from the intellectual tradition that had been growing up in the hard sciences and the social sciences. All of the forefathers studied human communication—rather than treating it merely as one element in, say, collective behavior or in minority problems. All of them were keenly aware of the relationship of mass media to the problems they were studying. And all of them were deeply interested in examining the effects of communication in life as well as in laboratories or in books.

The four were very different. Lasswell was perhaps nearest to Cooley and Park (Park was his contemporary at Chicago), although we can hardly imagine either of them writing a dissertation on content analysis or studying themes in wartime propaganda, as Lasswell did. Lewin was perhaps least interested of the four forefathers in the mass media; his chief concern was with communication in groups. Lazarsfeld was of the four perhaps most interested in *mass* communication and its effects. Hovland used film and broadcast as stimuli to study attitude change, of course, but he studied them by means of controlled experiments rather than by field surveys and in that respect was unlike Lazarsfeld. If they were different in the problems they chose and the way they went about their research, they were alike in the excitement and enthusiasm they brought to their students and the way in which they extracted theoretical insights from empirical studies. They brought to the study of communication a sense of urgency and challenge that had not been there before them.

In the next four chapters, we shall go beyond these generalities and convey some idea of what kind of individuals these forefathers were.

Notes

1. Editors' Note: Hovland's name was pronounced "HUHV-land." Lewin's name in Germany was pronounced "Luh-VEEN" but in America most people said "LEW-un" instead. According to Schramm, Lewin said he had no preference between the two pronunciations.

2. Editors' Note: Robert Park is here describing what today is called the agenda-setting process, through which a news issue rises and falls on the media agenda.

3. Editors' Note: Park may have influenced Wilbur Schramm to write, in 1949, "The Nature of News," *Journalism Quarterly,* 26, 259-269.

4. Editors' Note: Both Sapir and Hovland were in the Institute of Human Relations at Yale, so they undoubtedly knew each other (Rogers, 1994).

5. Editors' Note: The original text has a different order of sentences: "Linguistics is essentially the quest of MEANING. . . . (its real concern is) to light up the thick darkness of the language."

6. The original source of this statement is Whorf (1941).

7. Editors' Note: Lazarsfeld did not literally sign a contract with Iowa State for this audience survey. It was funded by the Rockefeller Foundation through Lazarsfeld's Office of Radio Research (later to become the Bureau of Applied Social Research) at Columbia University.

8. Editors' Note: Schramm's unit was the Institute of Communications Research at the University of Illinois, and the year was 1947.

9. See Chapter 8.

Harold Lasswell

Politics, Power, and the Significant Symbol

One of the best pen portraits of Harold Lasswell was written by Leo Rosten, whom you might remember as author of the Hyman Kaplan books.[1] Rosten studied under Harold at the University of Chicago from 1927 to 1930. In 1967, Rosten published a reminiscent note on his old teacher in the *Saturday Review* (reprinted in Rogow, 1969, pp. 1-3). Here are parts of it:

> I met him [said Rosten] at the University of Chicago, where I was a suffering sophomore, he a callow instructor. I thought him a bit of a freak: Pedantic, verbose, and ill at ease. He wore his hair in a short, stiff, Prussian cut, and his knowledge in a high, stiff, abrasive manner. He lectured us desperately, with a glazed stare into outer space, conspicuously unaware of whether we understood him and visibly unconcerned with what we might be thinking.

Harold Lasswell

He talked so fast, so frantically, tumbling idea upon idea in a torrent of excitation, that his nonstop monologues became a polysyllabic blur from which only startling words and phrases erupted to penetrate my dumbfoundedness: Context . . . frame of reference. Thanks to . . . anxiety . . . systematic . . . manipulate . . . symbols . . . insecurity . . . objectify . . . superego . . .

rigorous . . . anxiety . . . quantify . . . dialectical . . . explicit . . . insecurity . . . participant-observer . . . world revolution of our time. He baffled—nay, he flabbergasted me. He did not lecture so much as smother. He seemed unable to leave a moment of time unoccupied by language. I was not helped, of course, by his scrambling together of technical terms from a dozen unhomogenized disciplines: Philosophy, sociology, economics, anthropology, politics theory, psychiatry, statistics, pediatrics, linguistics, psychoanalysis, law, physiology, quantum physics (oh, yes).

The play of his nostril as he monologized intrigued me. His globular cheeks puffed out like those of a chipmunk with a nut in each pouch, and from those two round protuberances sailed forth a surprisingly thin nose—with mobile and expressive nostrils: They flared and narrowed and quivered in tune with his meaning, signaling disdain here, esteem there. He was in the grip, then as now, of a compulsion to be entirely objective. The goal was inhuman, to say nothing of inhumane.

Considerably miffed by this antiseptic pastor, and by [a] crushing chore he [had] assigned us, I mobilized my courage and my indignation and marched to Lasswell's office, where I gulped out my heartfelt complaints. He listened steely-eyed and silent. Thrown by his clinical stare, which made me feel like an incipient case-study, I even quavered that I sometimes did not understand what he was *talking* about. To this, at last, Harold Lasswell sniffed icily: "Communication is but the fortuitous parallelism of bio-psychic variables." I staggered out.

It took me years to discover why this phenomenally intelligent, prodigiously articulate man resorts to such lingo: He is entirely at home with it. It is his metier. Most men use language clumsily, to express their banal ideas and conceal their complex feelings; Lasswell uses words brilliantly—to conceal simple feelings and express complex ideas. I think he has a passion to be comprehended, and marmoreal defenses against being understood.

In those days, he always said, "We"—never, never, "I." He shunned the conventional exchange of pleasantries. He abhorred all small talk, even "hello." His totem was ideas. I once heard a harmless hostess ask him, "Isn't it wonderful weather we're having?" [There was a pause.] Only after [Harold Lasswell] had recovered sufficiently to analyze her motivations (and decide that it was not the right time to discuss meteorology), did he answer, "Yes." [I was surprised that he did not diagnose the meteorological determinants of the weather we were having.]

Do not misinterpret Rosten's feelings toward his teacher from this memoir that I have unkindly quoted only in part. His later verdict on Lasswell, as he said in a part of the memoir that I did not quote above, was that, "I learned, or was encouraged and jolted and inspired to learn, more from him than from anyone I ever met" (Rosten, 1967, p. 67). Later in these pages we shall explain why Lasswell's impact, despite his eccentricities, was so great.

I first met Harold Lasswell in about 1954. I was being invited to the Center for Advanced Study,[2] and had come to look at the place. Harold was there, and they apparently thought one social scientist deserved another (or some comparable punishment), so I was invited to his study. My experience was somewhat different from Leo's. There was a lot of talk to be sure, and later we had dinner and resumed the next morning. I noticed some of the same qualities than Rosten reported. For one, the ballet of his hands as he spoke. Rosten (1967) wrote,

> They are library hands, very pale, very soft, and when he talks, over drinks or food, they make small gyrations in the same ritual: The left hand is motionless, its thumb and forefinger forming an "O"; the right hand hovers over and dances around that "O." If, say, he is trying to illustrate Planck's Constant, or the dynamics of introjection, the right hand pulls an invisible thread within an invisible needle on a path horizontal to and away form the inner circle of the left-hand "O." It is astounding how the man can hemstitch theoretical points into imaginary petitpoint. (p. 66)

He spoke softly. He put aside a paper he was writing and about 200 bibliography cards, and gave me his full attention. He was genuinely interested in what I was doing, what I thought of some of the people working in communication, what I understood communication to be and how I defined it. When we got around to the significant symbol, predictably, George Herbert Mead began to appear in our talk.[3] But he really fired up when he found that I had Alfred North Whitehead in my academic background. He went off on a long soliloquy on Whitehead and his view of the emergence of an "ordered society." He spoke for a very long time without giving me much chance to talk, but still I didn't feel I was being "snowed" or overwhelmed. It was just a pleasant and intelligent talk and I was aware that I had met a learned and disciplined mind.

I came away with the conclusion that Rosten expressed at one point in his memorandum: that Lasswell was essentially a shy man. "He gives unstintingly of his time, his encouragement, his expertise," Rosten (1967) said,

> Yet in the almost four decades I have known him, I have not once seen the knob on the door of any apartment he occupied. He is embarrassed by intimacy ... parsimonious about the revelation of personal or familial data. Ask him a personal question, a truly personal question, and he will hem and haw while his face swarms with hues of red. (p. 66)

I would add that Harold never seemed to me to be parading his great erudition to show it off. More often, he was trying to think things out for himself, or to cover up, to avoid an uneasy pause or a possible embarrassing moment. He was completely relaxed with me, probably because I was a young scholar in a field that interested him, rather than a student whom he had some obligation to "teach." Also by that time, his reputation was made and he looked on me as a pilgrim to some of the shrines where he too had worshipped.

Even today I recall some of the things Harold said that day at the Center for Advanced Study in the Behavioral Sciences, although I hesitate to try to quote them because it has been so long. But recently I came upon a statement in one of his articles that is so close to a sentence I seem to remember him saying 30 years ago, and so typical of the way he talked and wrote, that I am going to repeat it for you: Thinking is comparable in its episodic, flitting, discontinuous character to the eccentric peregrinations of a grasshopper trying to escape from a faintly illuminated molehill.

You can see how that kind of style, maintained through 50 minutes, would baffle students in an undergraduate lecture course such as Leo's at Chicago or a roomful of would-be lawyers at Yale. Yet it is a rich and vivid style. It fits the subject he is talking about: the dangers of depending too much on the logical qualities in thinking. He even permits himself to include a homely image, although, to be sure, he dresses it up in quite a large number of syllables. But that is the way he was.

Lasswell's Career Takes Shape

What can we say about Lasswell's career? All the great pioneers in communication study had somewhat similar careers. All of them had very rich early backgrounds, went to excellent universities, and came into contact with great minds. They were broadly interdisciplinary in their interests. They were trained in a discipline that could not very easily be called "communication," but they turned to communication study through the experience of confronting "real world" problems. All of them had deep influence on young scholars at an important university. And all except one of them founded a research institute or program that attracted bright young people and able colleagues. The only one of these four who did not form such an institute was Lasswell, and his odd academic career helps to explain why.

Until he went to the University of Chicago, Lasswell lived mostly in small Illinois towns.[4] His father was a preacher, his mother a teacher. Therefore, they were part of the intellectual aristocracy of those small towns, and Harold grew up in a home where books were valued. Harold's father gave him Windelband's *History of Philosophy* (1898) to read and his mother introduced him to Karl Marx, which today we might not expect a school teacher mother to do.[5] In the public library he read Havelock Ellis. At a summer Chautauqua he heard William Jennings Bryan and Robert LaFollette. Through family friends he had a chance to meet John Dewey and have a conversation with the great man.

In 1918 at the age of 16, Lasswell entered the University of Chicago. These were Chicago's great years in the social sciences. He could study with Anton Carlson, the biologist; John Maurice Clark, the economist; and Jacob Viner, the authority on international relations and trade. As a graduate student he shared an office with Robert Redfield, the sociologist-anthropologist who made the first studies of the Mexican village of Tepotzlan.[6] His thesis director was Charles Merriam, the political scientist leading the movement toward "a new science of politics" (e.g., Merriam, 1925). He took classes with the sociologist Ernest Burgess, the specialist in minority problems Robert E. Park, and the philosopher George Herbert Mead. At Mead's house he again met John Dewey and was surprised to find that Dewey remembered their earlier meeting. Later, Mead introduced him to Whitehead, who had come to the United States to teach at Harvard. Whitehead's ideas were later to help the birth of systems theory, and Lasswell made them part of his thinking too. From Whitehead he also adopted the idea that people respond selectively to parts of their environment, rather than to the full context in which they live, and what turns them toward one part of the context rather than to others. This apparently was the origin of Lasswell's lifelong concern with focus of attention.[7]

As a graduate student and again as a young instructor at Chicago,[8] Lasswell spent some time in Europe (1923-1924). There he sat in seminars by John Maynard Keynes, Leonard Woolf, Graham Wallas, and G. Lowes Dickinson, among others (Marvick, 1977, p. 24). He volunteered his services to Bertrand Russell when Russell was running for Parliament from Chelsea and canvassed house to house for him. In the interest of full disclosure, although not without regret, I must report that Russell got so few votes that he lost his deposit. In Europe, also, Lasswell became deeply interested in psychoanalysis. For 6 months he went to Theodore Reick (author of *Listening With the Third Ear*, published in 1949)[9] for psychoanalysis and for instruction in how to conduct and interpret psychoanaly-

sis.[10] Back in the United States, Lasswell experimented with psychoanalysis on volunteers (e.g., Lasswell, 1930/1960). Some of his first lectures that
attracted wide attention were attempts to interpret Marx from a Freudian
point of view.[11]

Chicago was a great place for a young social scientist in the 1920s and
1930s. Social science as we know it today was taking shape there. People
began to take it for granted, as Dwaine Marvick (1977) said in his long
introduction to a book of selections from Lasswell, that it was necessary
to "formulate hypotheses," "gather data," "experiment," "quantify," and
"test a proposition." [and establish the "empirical warrant" for proposi-
tions] (p. 26). The social science disciplines became at one and the same
time more distinct and more encompassing. Even as subjects such as
sociology developed their own patterns, researchers reached out for everything in their environment that might help them understand society. Lasswell,
the young scholar, was a political scientist by diploma and departmental
affiliation, but his students would have said he was a political sociologist,
a political philosopher, a political psychologist, a political psychiatrist (if
one can image such a thing), and, needless to say, a specialist in political
communication.

Empirical research and interdisciplinary interests may be old stuff today
but they were not always so. Lasswell himself described the situation in
the 1920s, in a passage that shows he *could* write clearly and entertainingly
when he wanted to:

When I first became acquainted with the field of public opinion and communication research, there was no Roper, no Gallup, no Cantril, no Stouffer, no
Hovland. Lazarsfeld was neither a person nor a measuring unit, or even a
category. There was no survey research, content analysis, or quantified depth
analysis; no computerized systems of storage, retrieval, and utilization; no
inter-university networks of cooperation; no training institutes, research bureaus, professional bibliographies, or associations. So far as that goes, there
was practically no radio or television broadcasting, no instant photography,
either in black or in color, and no sonar [radar], infrared, or laser.

Lest you [should] think we were living in a wholly undeveloped country, I
ought to acknowledge that the horseless carriage had been invented. The cable,
telegraph, and telephone were fully operational. Mr. Griffith was already
midwife to a spectacular rebirth of a nation. The gas balloon was as well known
at country fairs as it had always been in politics. Heavier-than-air craft weren't
worth hijacking. You could take a long breath in Central Park without inhaling
lethal chemicals, swallow a clam with no fear of hepatitis, and smoke mari-
juana in a jazz joint without alarming the FBI. Highways were unpolluted.

They were, on the contrary, enriched by the nostalgic smell of horse manure, and twittering English sparrows. Men and women smoked cancerettes with peace of mind, with no apprehension that every body growth or sore throat signified a malignant growth. Beards and mustaches were on the way out as unhygienic and offensive to women and children.

Modern public opinion and communication research developed in response to a remarkable convergence of favoring conditions. The social sciences were in a spasm of inferiority when they compared themselves with their brothers, sisters, and cousins in the physical and biological sciences. Many of the leading figures were convinced that, unless the specialists on society were able to 'quantify' their propositions, they were doomed to the permanent status of second-class citizens in the universe of secular knowledge. (Lasswell, 1972, pp. 301-302)

On that fast track, a young man in social science would either drop out of the race or run faster. There was no question which of these Harold Lasswell would do. He published his first two graduate seminar papers as articles in learned journals (Lasswell, 1923a, 1923b). More than one professor has mentioned that example to his students. The year after Lasswell got his doctorate, he published his dissertation as a book (Lasswell, 1927/1971). It was an analysis of World War I propaganda. In addition to his classes at Chicago, he taught political sociology in night school for labor leaders. He wrote on subjects such as "Ethics" for the *Encyclopedia of the Social Sciences*.[12] His lectures on Freud and Marx were starting points for a book he published in 1935 titled *World Politics and Personal Insecurity,* which many readers considered his most profound (and perhaps most difficult) work. In 1936 he wrote another book and this one has been read by probably every graduate student of political science in America. The title was *Politics: Who Gets What, When, How* (1936b). If you notice any similarities to his well-known formulation of the communication process—*Who* says *what* to *whom* through *what channel* with *what effect* (Lasswell, 1948)—the resemblance is not accidental. This shorthand is one way that Lasswell simplified his ideas.

It was in the years between 1926, when Lasswell became a young instructor, and 1938, when he left Chicago, that he had his only direct effect on graduate students. Not all of them were political scientists. One came from another field: Herbert Simon, who received the Nobel Prize for economics. Others were V. O. Key, of Cornell; David Truman, of Columbia; Ithiel de Sola Pool, of MIT; Morris Janowitz, of Chicago; Heinz Eulau and Gabriel Almond, of Stanford; Barrington Moore; and Abraham Kaplan. It was an extraordinarily high quality list. All of these graduate students during Lasswell's Chicago years testify to his great influence on their intellectual growth.

In 1938, he left Chicago. His chief reason for leaving was that the distinguished humanist who was then president of the university, Robert Maynard Hutchins, "despised political science," or at least Lasswell's kind of political science, and would not give him a permanent appointment (Marvick, 1977, p. 32).[13] Out of that developed an extraordinary situation. Fewer than 10 years after Hutchins declined to promote Lasswell to full professor at Chicago, Hutchins became chairman of the influential Commission on Freedom of the Press and invited Lasswell to serve on the commission. And as for Lasswell, by an ironic twist in his career, after he became a full professor he never had another doctoral candidate in his department. His professorship, which came to him in 1947, the same year in which the Commission on Freedom of the Press filed its report (Commission on Freedom of the Press, 1947a, 1947b), was at the Yale Law School, where there were many bright young lawyers, but, in the School of Law at least, no political science doctoral students.

Turning Points in a Career

In another respect, 1938 was one of the great turning points in Lasswell's life. Not only was he moved from the rich intellectual subsoil of the University of Chicago, but when he was leaving, a moving van caught fire and destroyed all of his reading cards and research notes. Consequently, his academic life changed and his writing changed. Dwaine Marvick tried to categorize the change in Lasswell's scholarly writing by analyzing the content of his books into three periods (see Table 2.1).

Frankly, I do not see quite such sharp demarcations in Lasswell's career as Table 2.1 makes them appear. A great deal of his own empirical work on symbols was done before the symbol period—that is, when he was studying the propaganda symbols of World War I for his dissertation at Chicago, rather than during the middle period when he worked with that remarkable quartet of research assistants—Ithiel de Sola Pool, Daniel Lerner, Nathan Leites, and Heinz Eulau—analyzing World War II propaganda symbols at the U.S. Library of Congress and at Stanford University. Some of his most profound projections of the future came 30 years before he was classified as emphasizing "future options." In his later years, he was still deeply concerned with contemporary problems and with the special insights to be gained from the clinical view of personality, both topics that

Table 2.1   Summary of Lasswell's Word Production (in percentages)

Focus of Attention	Early Period (1923-38)	Middle Period (1939-54)	Late Period (1955-72)	Totals
1. Contemporary problems	48	14	5	18
2. Human psyche	18	13	17	15
3. Symbol appeals	19	51	11	27
4. Methods of inquiry	13	18	39	26
5. Options for the future	2	4	28	14
Totals	100	100	100	100
6. Wordage (in thousands)	900	1,300	1,700	3,900

SOURCE: From *Harold D. Lasswell: On Political Sociology* (p. 11), edited by D. Marvick, 1977, Chicago: University of Chicago Press. Copyright 1977 by University of Chicago Press.

are supposed to belong in his first period. Even a thumbnail content analysis of his titles shows the same words recurring: world, politics, power, revolution, propaganda, public opinion, content analysis, decision, future—in every period.

Marvick's threefold division of Lasswell's writings is interesting and useful. But I should have readers learn from it the consistency of Lasswell's themes rather than their division into time periods.[14] Another lesson is the enormous amount of writing that this small table represents. Figuring 350 words to the page, that is, if anything, an underestimate, Marvick arrived in 1972 at an estimate of 4 million words (Marvick, 1977, p. 10). Since 1972, we must add 1 or 2 million words. As a matter of fact, three volumes edited by Lasswell, Lerner, and Speier (1980a, 1980b, 1980c) were going through the East-West Center Press when Harold died in 1978, and they add at least half a million words to his total. Therefore, Lasswell must be credited with between 5 and 6 million published words.

Half of these may have been jointly written or jointly edited. The number of times that Lasswell's name has appeared as editor or coauthor of a book, often jointly with one or more of his former students or assistants, is astonishing. Yet most scholars think he was not an especially good editor. Rosten (1967) says he is

> a phenomenal generator of ideas, but an ineffective editor—of either his writing or the work of others. The trouble is, I suspect, his fear of confessing that something may not be relevant. Since *he* is always learning, rearranging,

recording, sorting, storing, what possible facts, however "trivial," what specu-
lations, however aberrant, *might* not—someday, somewhere, somehow—be
decisive? Think of what Sigmund Freud discovered from apparently incidental
information! (p. 67)

Suppose we estimate that 3 million of Lasswell's published words
represent joint writing and editing. That means that during his career
Harold Lasswell produced another 3 million words of erudite, incisive,
insightful, original published copy. It was this output and his personal
contacts and discussions that maintained his influence on scholars even
after he had left a social science department and no longer taught graduate
students in the social sciences. There was a strange period from 1937, when
he left Chicago, to 1950, when no article of his appeared in a political science
journal.[15] In its obituary of Lasswell, the *New York Times* said this was due to
"resistance to his ideas," and that "younger political scientists eventually
forced his recognition within the discipline" (Ennis, 1978). He always had
a great following among bright young political scientists whom he taught
or worked with, and it may have been that their influence had something
to do with rebuilding his reputation in the field. In any case, in 1955 he was
elected president of the American Political Science Association.

After 1938 he lectured, wrote, served briefly on the faculty of the New
School for Social Research, and then, like so many other academics, when
World War II started he answered the Government's call for expert help.
During the war years he directed a research project at the U.S. Library of
Congress[16] studying "world revolutionary propaganda" not for a book but
for real-world policy guidance (Lasswell & Jones, 1939). At the end of the
war, he accepted the directorship of a related project at the Hoover Institute
at Stanford,[17] analyzing world propaganda symbols and the opinions of
world elites. A study of the "prestige press" throughout the world was one
part of the latter project. In both activities, as we have mentioned, he had
talented young helpers who did the content analysis. Their presence was
itself a tribute to his leadership and his ability to attract some of the best
in the field. At the U.S. Library of Congress, he had Nathan Leites and
Heinz Eulau; at Stanford, Ithiel de Sola Pool and Daniel Lerner.

Lasswell got his professorship 10 years after he had expected it, indeed,
10 years after he had deserved it. It was at the Yale Law School in 1947, a
prestigious appointment. He interested himself, as always, in the problems
of the students around him. He wrote about international law and its
political ramifications (for a summary see McDougall, 1984). His students,
in this new incarnation of his, were certainly challenged by him, and

doubtless sometimes mystified. But his chief audience was the social scientists who were concerned with politics, power, and political communication. His rate of published output grew, although a higher proportion of it came from joint writing or editing.[18] He served on important committees and commissions, headed some of the chief academic societies in his field, and spent frequent leaves from Yale on research projects or at other academic centers. He retired from Yale in 1973, taught for a time at the City University of New York, Temple University, and Columbia, and then left teaching entirely in 1976. He devoted the 2 years before his death to the Policy Sciences Center in New York. This was another example of how his developing interests did not change sharply from period to period, but rather kept repeating themselves, recalling what he had learned and written about in earlier periods. He was always concerned with the relationship of science to policy, but his chief interest with policy science grew out of his wartime service, and a book, written jointly with Daniel Lerner at Stanford, on *The Policy Sciences* (1951).[19]

Lasswell's Contributions to Communication Study

How did he get into communication study? Lasswell had always been in communication. He wrote his doctoral dissertation, as we noted, on propaganda and that became his first book (Lasswell, 1927/1971). Almost all of the empirical work that he did or was responsible for concerned the study of symbols. His most extended public service was to help the U.S. government analyze the opinions expressed by elites in foreign countries. Other parts of his active service to communication have tended to be forgotten with the passing of time, for example, that he helped found *Public Opinion Quarterly*[20] and that he was a member of the Commission on Freedom of the Press that made a much discussed report in 1947, as mentioned earlier. Lasswell, along with Bruce Smith and Ralph Casey, also made the first substantial annotated bibliography on international communication in 1946, titled *Propaganda, Communication, and Public Opinion.* After he left Chicago, Lasswell wrote some pieces that would have astounded persons who knew him only for his scholarly prose: a series of remarkably clear and interesting radio plays on world leaders such as Caesar and Mohammed.[21]

Lasswell's major contributions to communication study were on the thinking rather than the doing side. As we reflect on his years with us, we tend to see his great intellectual contributions as threefold.

One contribution was that he greatly enriched the only research method that can be said to have originated in communication research. Neither the Hovland experiments on persuasion, the careful Lewinian observation of group process, nor Lazarsfeld-type surveys on mass media uses and effects were congenial to him. But he recognized the need to study the significant symbols of political life, and therefore, from the very beginning of his scholarly career[22] he found himself doing, or getting others to do, content analysis.[23]

Heinz Eulau, who was a member of the U.S. Library of Congress wartime research project, described what it was like to do content analysis for Harold Lasswell:

> What we did was apply the Lasswellian "value categories" to content analyses of international communications in the world press. . . . Doing Lasswell's work by day and reading his stuff at night for about six months had a profound effect on my thinking and doing. The thinking had to do with understanding Lasswell's extraordinary subtle and complex formulation of the political process; the doing involved a commitment to empirical research from which I never recovered. (Eulau, 1968, p. 9)

Thus Lasswell, who never did a great amount of empirical data analysis himself, could and did stimulate others to do it. His contribution was to the conceptualizing and broadening of content analysis rather than to the method, which he described as "simple" or "obvious"—and then usually recommended a method that was anything but simple or obvious. He could show people how to choose categories so as to be working in the heartland, rather than on the periphery, of a subject. He could show them how to interpret the figures that resulted from the counting so as to make them broadly meaningful in terms of social function and structure.

His central message to content analysts, and his example, were antisimplistic. Do not restrict too narrowly the focus of observation, he advised. And do not be satisfied with too simple a method of selecting and counting. He wrote,

> It is important to recognize that we obtain insight into the world of the other person only when we are fully acquainted with what comes to his attention. The full plan often appears only when the entire stream of communication is interpreted as a whole. (Lasswell, 1949, p. 51)

It must have been worrisome to Lasswell to leave out *anything* from the stream of message content, and yet when he was forced to come to grips with reality—to specify only as much counting as ordinary human beings could do—he did so. Ithiel de Sola Pool recalled how weary he became on the Stanford Project, counting and recounting symbols and statements. He tried to forget the boredom of detail-mining by generalizing in advance, that is, by trying to decide where the study was going and why the data that came from certain spokesmen or one certain subject turned out as they did. Not until some years later, he said, did he begin to see the wisdom of the broad focus and then he became more comfortable with Lasswell's methods.[24]

Similarly, Lasswell's teaching of content analysts was not to depend too much on empirical results, regardless of the number available: "As the history of quantification shows, there is never-ending fruitful interplay between theory, hunch, impression, and precision" (Lasswell, 1949, p. 51).

For example, voting, he said, has different meanings in different settings. "Mere inventories of events are misleading. Quantitative methods can be either rigorous or impressionistic" (Lasswell, 1949), and in some cases the latter "better suits the needs of both students of culture (who must not make too much of isolated external facts) and students of psychopathology (who must consider unconscious meanings as well as conscious ones)" (Lasswell, 1949). Perhaps more than any other political scientist of his time, Lasswell appreciated the complexity of social data and social life. Consequently, he was never quite satisfied with any one finding or with any one approach to a conclusion. This may have been a result of his early study of psycho-analysis, which taught him how complex the human personality and human relations are. In any case, he sought always to "get behind the data." Seeing Marvick's Table 2.1 (categorizing Lasswell's writings into three eras), he would certainly have rubbed his hands and started to analyze what reality lay behind the percentages. This is what he taught—and did.

As he enriched the study of content, so also he enriched the concept of propaganda, the content of which he spent so much time studying. Propa-ganda seemed to him so important not only because it was one of the few means through which to look at the distribution and exercise of power—and political science, as he saw it, was the study of power in society—but also because it is one of society's few alternatives to coercion and vio-lence.[25] Thus the image of propaganda in his writings is more favorable than it has usually been in America. Propaganda, he said, is "the control of opinions by significant symbols . . . stories, rumors, [reports,] pictures, and other forms of social communication" (Lasswell, 1927/1971, p. 9). It works by suggestion and illusion, rather than by force. Propaganda "depends upon the adroit use of means under favorable conditions" (Lasswell, 1927/1971, p. 185). In wartime, he said, society fights in symbolic ways as well as in violent ways. "All the voluble men of a country lend themselves to propaganda goals."[26] But he saw propaganda in modern life playing a role much beyond that of a nonviolent equivalent of warfare. Modern scientists, he argued, "lack the social solidarity of primitive tribal life; propaganda is the new instrument for welding millions into one amalgamated instrument."[27] We must understand propaganda, he said, because "to illuminate the mechanism of propaganda is to reveal the secret springs of social action. . . . Propaganda is an inescapable fact of life; democracies must adjust to it, not rail against it" (Lasswell, 1927/1971, pp. 222-223).

One reviewer of the book where these statements appeared was horrified. He wrote indignantly that Lasswell's study is a "Machiavellian textbook which should promptly be destroyed!" (Dulles in Marvick, 1977, p. 49). The reviewer was Foster Dulles, President Eisenhower's Secretary of State in 1952-1960.[28] We can imagine Harold, when he read that review, rubbing his hands in pleasure and starting to analyze the context in the reviewer's own background that led him to write what he did.

A third great contribution of Lasswell to communication study was to conceptualize the political role of communication in a way that included functions much beyond persuasion and election campaigns. In his essay on the "Structure and Function of Communication in Society," Lasswell (1948) said there were three social functions of communication: (a) *surveillance*—collecting the information that society should know about and the needs, threats, and opportunities to which a society must respond; (b) *correlation*—implementing society's response to relevant information, making policy, organizing itself, distributing powers and responsibilities, changing the pattern when necessary; and (c) *socialization*—by which Lasswell meant passing on the knowledge and values of society to its prospective members and its uninformed members, so that children will grow up to be responsible and useful citizens, and adults will coalesce around a nexus of knowledge and belief.[29] These three functions of communication sound simple and direct, but I assure you that in Harold's mind they were anything but that.

I had a taste of how he thought about it one evening when someone remarked in a discussion that, of course, Lasswell must have had in mind the functions of the news media, the government, and the school. Harold was silent about that, but then someone else asked whether the functions were different in other times, for example, when a watchman on a hill was responsible for surveillance for a primitive tribe, a chief for tribal correlation, and parents for socialization. Harold nodded his appreciation of the question and took off for an hour or more on a wonderfully imaginative and erudite discourse on how the watchman became the mass media, how his functions changed, and how the functions themselves were different in different places, times, and societies. As I remember, he concluded by analyzing how just one of the functions—surveillance—would be different in a tribe of nomads from what it is in an urban ghetto, the different kinds of information that must be collected, and how they were collected. That took care of only one of the three functions; a full treatment would have taken 3 hours rather than 1 hour. But the central point came through crystal clear: Although the functions are basically unchanged over time and place, the small differences are many and subtle and essential if one hopes to understand human communication and human society.

Lasswell and Social Science in General

Perhaps we are doing Lasswell an injustice by focusing on his special impacts on communication study exclusively. His intellectual impact was much broader than that, and what he said about the social sciences and about social scientists in general applies also to students of communication.

I think of his central influence as being basically nonsubstantive. Rather, it may have been his example of erudition, of breadth of knowledge and interest, his care in seeking and handling facts, his insatiable appetite for knowing everything in order to understand anything, and the mind-boggling breadth of his interests. This perspective emerges from his writing but it emerged even more from knowing him. It is something that we admire and marvel at, and wish we could go and do likewise, but we realize also that the standard is very, very high.

There was also Lasswell's insistence on approaching both theory and research in a nonsimplistic way. When I came away from our first meeting at the Center for Advanced Study in the Behavioral Sciences and reflected on it, I had the feeling that all the time he had been making hypotheses. His long elliptical disquisitions seemed always to lead up to a point to be tested or at least to be given serious thought and consideration. Clearly, he was on the hypothesis-making, rather than hypothesis-testing, side of science. And on the whole, I think his example is a good one for us. I am reminded of what an excellent psychologist, William McGuire (1973), wrote in the *Journal of Personality and Social Psychology* a few years ago:

> One drastic change that is called for in our teaching of research methodology is that we should emphasize the creative, hypothesis-formation stage relative

to the critical hypothesis-testing stage of research. It is my guess that at least 90% of the time in our current courses is devoted to presenting ways of testing hypotheses and that little time is spent on the prior and more important process of how one creates these hypotheses in the first place. (p. 450)

This is where Lasswell's breadth of knowledge and his acquaintance with the scholarship of many fields and scholars paid off. Perhaps he knew too much; it was difficult for him to settle on only one line of approach or one hypothesis. But I think the keynote is rather Lasswell's sense of the difference between social and natural science. There may not be a "key experiment" in most social science investigations. There may not be Newton's Laws to be discovered. These are not reasons for abandoning the scientific approach; rather, they demand that the hypotheses be chosen and the results be interpreted in the broadest possible understanding of the real world around them so that we do not waste research time (of which all of us have only a limited amount) and so that we do not draw unwarranted conclusions from a finding that may be fragmentary or incomplete. A false simplicity in social science, Harold might have said (if he remembered Emerson), is the hobgoblin of little minds!

When we turn to Lasswell's substantive impacts, we find more difficulty in identifying them sharply because, as others have pointed out, the formulations that Lasswell made half a century ago, many of which were received at first with doubt and shock, and sometimes with indignation, are now generally accepted. Marvick (1977) listed some of these,

Today it is generally agreed that people everywhere strive for conditions of welfare (health, knowledge, skill, wealth) and of deference (being respected, having affection, getting a voice in decisions and thus exercising power, possessing an acknowledged sense of rectitude); that politics is a question of the power aspects of any situation; that people act out their private problems in the name of public causes; that social upheavals stem basically from technological change and from the difficulties people have in adjusting to the changed conditions of deference and welfare brought about by the divisions of labor; that insecure people grow disenchanted with the established order of life and are receptive to revolutionary propaganda; that world revolution in our time is inevitably guided by professional specialists in violence and symbol manipulation; that modern intellectuals can best serve the cause of human dignity by becoming competent and imaginative policy scientists worth consulting by decision-makers. These ideas may be generally agreed to now, but they were by no means fully accepted in the 1920s when Lasswell began to write about them. (pp. 5-6)

Among his later formulations, however, one that has had, and continues to have, a wide influence is the study of elites. Not that the opinions of the average person are not worth studying; Lasswell believed strongly in the power of public opinion. But his style was to study the power centers of political systems, and to this end it was more efficient to study elites. Furthermore, his view of the future told him that elite behaviors and policies were likely to be a key to events. He thought he saw in recent Western history a tendency for emerging regimes to be controlled by skill elites: engineers, bureaucrats, party leaders, propagandists (Lasswell, 1937, 1977b). The "commonwealth of skill," is becoming more common, he said (Lasswell, 1937, p. 305). It will be achieved in many ways, including an attempt to share and spread out the skills and rewards of elites. Therefore, the task of society is to discover how to rid itself of these dislocations. Class consciousness would result in "grave dislocation" of skills and skill groups (Lasswell, 1937, p. 310). Therefore, the task of society is to discover how to rid itself of these dislocations. Consequently, one can and should study elites both as an index to power today and as an indicator of power distributions to come.

This topic brought Lasswell, and inevitably brings a reader of Lasswell, to consider the political future. One of the great influences that Lasswell exerted, and one of the ways he most excited and stimulated his student following, was by holding up a lamp to the future—challenging them to understand trends, to predict, and to prepare. One of his most famous maps of the future was the "garrison state," (Marvick, 1977, p. 46) that he suggested in 1941 when Europe was at war, but has by no means passed out of possibility since then (see Lasswell, 1941a). A garrison state is not inevitable, he said, but it is a "picture of the probable" (Lasswell, 1977a, p. 166). In such a state, specialists in violence will be the most powerful group. Experts in modern technology and management will be essential to the specialists in violence. So too will experts in symbol manipulation, because people must be persuaded both to fight and to produce in the garrison state.

What can be done about such a possible future, he asked his students. Lasswell said that the chief need will be to understand the possibilities. Understand them and then look for ways to avoid the least desirable ones. He raised a series of provocative questions: Can the military mind be recast into a more civilized pattern? How much can ordinary citizens take over from power elites the task of ruling themselves? Can elites be mobilized against an elite-ruled state? Thus, in Harold Lasswell's classes and in his

"All the voluble men of the day . . . are drawn onto the service of propaganda to amplify r voice" (Lasswell, 1927/1971, p. 221).
Lasswell (1927/1971) said,

aganda is one of the most powerful instrumentalities in the modern world. It has n to its present eminence in response to a complex of changed circumstances which altered the nature of society. Small, primitive tribes can weld their heterogeneous bers into a fighting whole by the beat of the tom-tom and the tempestuous rhythm e dance.
n the Great Society it is no longer possible to fuse the waywardness of viduals in the furnace of the war dance; a new and subtler instrument must d thousands and even millions of human beings into one amalgamated mass ate and will and hope. . . . The name of this new hammer and anvil of social darity is propaganda. (pp. 220-221)

Editors' Note: The author, Foster R. Dulles, was actually the brother of U.S. Secretary e John Foster Dulles (1888-1959) who was also often called Foster Dulles.
Editors' Note: In the essay Schramm describes here, Lasswell's term for the socialization n was "transmission."

books, despite their prolixity and their overcast of erudition, political science and communication were never seen as theoretical exercises but rather as intensely practical studies that involve the well-being of society and the shape of the future and challenge the power of political science and communication. Theory belongs in social science, of course, but the ultimate goal of this science is policy.

Quite properly, we come thus, in conclusion, to Harold Lasswell's championing of the policy sciences as one of his great influences. This is part of his concept of responsibility. A knowledge elite such as social scientists is responsible for making its knowledge useful to society. In wartime he saw many of the best scientists in the United States going to work for the federal government. He made the point that the same degree of responsibility holds in peace as in war. It holds for political scientists, economists, psychologists of learning, and many other kinds of scholars who are professionalizing their work around the problems of communication. He had a special message for communication specialists, and it may be appropriate to close with a little paragraph of vintage Lasswell:

The important thing about a profession is not conveyed by the traditional assertion that it has a distinctive literature. Today, practically every craft or trade meets this criterion. More relevant is a distinction between the [exercising] of a skill, and the coupling of a skill with knowledge of the aggregated process to which the skill is intimately related. Consider the difference between the businessman and the economist. . . . Economists are properly considered professionals because they have a verifiable image of the production, distribution, investment, and consumption of wealth. Physicians belong to the professional category because they are supposedly guided by a cognitive map of the individual and a collective process of health and disease. (p. 306)

It is not enough for communication specialists to acquire skill in surveying, content analysis, or other technical operations. A genuine profession can be said to complement skill with enlightenment. In the case of communication, this implies a common map of the trends, conditions, and projections of the entire process. It also implies the capacity to invent and evaluate policies for the accomplishment of postulated goals. (Lasswell, 1972, p. 306).

Notes

1. Under the *nom de plume* Leonard Q. Ross, Rosten wrote short stories for *The New Yorker* and other magazines about a comical eastern European Jewish immigrant named

Hyman Kaplan. These stories were collected in several books, and some appear in anthologies of American humor as well (see Ross, 1937; Rosten, 1938).

2. The Center for Advanced Study in the Behavioral Sciences, Stanford, California.

3. Mead taught at the University of Chicago from 1900 to 1930. According to Smith (1969), Lasswell took Mead's course "Advanced Social Psychology," and had "both course work and numerous conversations with Dewey and Mead" (p. 52).

4. The description here of Lasswell's early days owes much to Dwaine Marvick (1977).

5. Editors' Note: This episode is described by Smith (1969, p. 48), where the person who introduced Lasswell to Havelock Ellis and Karl Marx was identified as not his mother but his high school English teacher (a Mrs. Nelson). It was also thanks to her that "it was possible for Lasswell to have a rather extended conversation with John Dewey." See also Marvick (1977, p. 17).

6. Through Redfield and his other office mates, who were all in sociology, "he enlarged his social circle of acquaintances, meeting Robert E. Park, Ernest Burgess, and Albion Small" (Marvick, 1977, p. 21).

7. Regarding Whitehead's influence on Lasswell, see Heinz Eulau (1969), "The Maddening Methods of Harold D. Lasswell," in Arnold A. Rogow (ed.), *Politics, Personality and Social Science in the Twentieth Century: Essays in Honor of Harold D. Lasswell,* University of Chicago Press, especially Section II.

8. "While still an undergraduate, Lasswell had begun to offer courses for trade union groups (the ILGWU) and at the May Business College" (Marvick, 1977, p. 19). In 1922, after he received his bachelor's degree, "Merriam immediately employed him as a teaching assistant" (Smith, 1969, p. 56). Lasswell was just 20 years old.

9. Reick was a "well-known writer on psychoanalytic theory and a first generation disciple of Freud" (Smith, 1969, p. 57).

10. Editors' Note: Lasswell visited Reick to undergo psychotherapy during his third trip (not his first) to Europe, which was in 1928-1929. This trip was made possible by a fellowship to Lasswell from the Social Science Research Council. At that time, he was an assistant professor in the Department of Political Science at Chicago.

11. These lectures were the basis for Lasswell (1935). Smith (1969) makes minute notes on the influence of Marx and Freud on Lasswell (see especially pp. 57-69).

12. Editors' Note: Lasswell reviewed the *Encyclopedia* for a journal on ethics (see Lasswell, 1936a). His entries in the *Encyclopedia* dealt with related subjects. He contributed the following items to the *Encyclopedia of the Social Sciences*: "Adams, Brooks," Vol. 1, pp. 429-430; "Agitation," Vol. 1, pp. 487-488; "Bribery," Vol. 2, pp. 690-692; "Censorship," Vol. 3, pp. 290-294; "Chauvinism," Vol. 3, p. 361; "Compromise," Vol. 4, pp. 147-149; "Conflict, Social," Vol. 4, pp. 147-149; "Faction," Vol. 4, pp. 194-196; "Feuds," Vol. 6, pp. 220-221; "Fraternizing," Vol. 6, pp. 425-427; "Morale," Vol. 10, pp. 640-642; "Propaganda," Vol. 12, pp. 521-527.

13. Editors' Note: On the basis of Lasswell's 1938 personnel file now archived in the Regenstein Library at the University of Chicago, Lasswell's decision to leave Chicago was different from what is recounted by Marvick and by Schramm here. Lasswell had been granted tenure; he apparently resigned because his university career was not advancing at the rate that he thought it should, and he had attractive alternatives.

14. Referring to *World Politics and Personal Insecurity,* Smith (1969) makes a similar comment: "In a sense, almost all of his multifarious activities for the ensuing thirty-odd years might be thought of as elaborations, revisions, clarifications, and testings of many of the main ideas in this one volume" (p. 69).

15. "From 1937 to 1950, Lasswell did not publish a single article in th[e] *Science Review* or any other political science journal, although his writing[s] frequency in the *American Journal of Sociology, Public Opinion Qua[rterly]* psychiatric journals" (Rogow, 1969, p. 137).

16. During World War II, Lasswell worked in the U.S. Library of C[ongress] the War-Time Communications Research Division (Smith, 1969, p. [?]. Congress effort was what Lasswell called a 'World Attention Survey'" [(p.] p. 207). (See also Lasswell, 1941b; Lasswell & Leites, 1949).

17. The institute is now called the Hoover Institution on War, Revolut[ion] (1969) notes that the project was "in the Hoover Institution Symbol S[eries] World War II when Lasswell was codirector of the Hoover Institute at [?]. (Smith, 1969, p. 76). Reports, all published by Stanford University Press, (1951); Lasswell, Lerner, and Rothwell (1952); Lasswell, Lerner, and [?] and de Sola Pool et al. (1951).

> The RADIR (Revolution and the Development of International Rel[ations]) at the Hoover Institution from 1948 to 1953 was also a world attenti[on] time for a sixty-year period, 1890-1950. The purpose was to documen[t] construct labeled "The World Revolution of Our Time." Newspap[er] prestige papers in five countries were examined to ascertain the ris[e] political concepts. (de Sola Pool, 1969, p. 208)

18. Smith (1969, p. 47) provides a partial list of coauthors.

19. According to de Sola Pool (1969), *The Policy Sciences* is "one [of] the RADIR project" (p. 209).

20. *Public Opinion Quarterly* was launched in 1937, and "Lassw[ell at its] start and for some years" (Smith, 1969, p. 75).

21. "Unable to get a university post, Harold proceeded to write a [for] radio, dramatizing traumatic moments in the life of Caesar, Mohammed, [?] (Rosten, 1967, p. 67).

22. The earliest examples of content analysis are said by Smith [to be in] Lasswell (1925).

23. Janowitz and de Sola Pool each contributed a chapter on Lassw[ell's] work to Rogow's book (see Janowitz, 1969; de Sola Pool, 1969).

24. de Sola Pool (1969) wrote, "As one of those chiefly involved i[n] think I may fairly say that however much we were committed to policy at that time, understand what that would demand of the research" (p. 2[?]).

> In his forties, Lasswell had development concepts very much in mi[nd] design of both the Library of Congress Project and the RADIR Proj[ect] associated peripherally with the one and centrally with the other, I f[?] only in the scientific generalizing aspects of these studies and bent m[?] in that direction. . . . Now a decade and a half later, Lasswell's stra[?] more understandable and congenial to me. (de Sola Pool, 1969, pp[?]

25. As to the importance of propaganda, Lasswell (1927/1971) sai[d?] fought on three fronts: The military front, the economic front, and [?] (p. 214).

Paul Lazarsfeld

From Market Research to Media Effects
to Social Reinforcement

What sort of person was Paul Lazarsfeld? Hearty, humorous, warm, energetic, vital. Full of ideas for study, suggestions for how to do it and how to interpret the results. Not essentially a theorist, but always with an eye on the deeper theoretical meaning of a study or a result. Not a great writer, but an exciting speaker when he spoke about research. Seldom great on the lecture platform, but very effective with a group of young researchers. By common consent, a great entrepreneur. Not especially good at handling the details of administration, but remarkably capable at getting money to support an ongoing institute or department and even more remarkable at stimulating its members. Basically a humble man, despite his great accomplishments, I remember that he sent me a copy of his new

Paul Lazarsfeld

book on communication research, jointly edited with Frank Stanton (published in 1949), and inscribed it in his impossible script, "To Wilbur Schramm, who greatly overrates his friends." The reference was to something I had written about a previous book of his.

No disrespect is intended by the title of this chapter. Quite the opposite, in fact. True, it is not usual to write of a great scholar and theorist in terms of market research—even if he were the "inventor" of market research, as Paul may very well have been. But think of it from another perspective. How often does a young scholar rise from research institutes that he had to support during the depths of a depression on no income other than market research—rise from that to become head of the best-known communication research institute in the world, director of the Bureau of Applied Social Research, Quetelet Professor and Chairman of Sociology at Columbia University, and the only American sociologist on whom the University of Paris has ever conferred an honorary degree? Furthermore, in Paul's case it is almost impossible to understand his accomplishment without knowing his career and almost impossible to understand his career without knowing his relationship to market research. That is the reason for the chapter title.

The Vienna Years

The story begins in Vienna. It is rather extraordinary to think of market research, which seems such a typically American activity, as beginning in Austria, and of an activity that seems such a natural outgrowth of capitalism beginning among fervent young socialists. Yet that is indeed the case. To see how it came about, we look back at the early years of Paul Lazarsfeld's career.[1]

Paul was born in Vienna in 1901. His father was a lawyer, although not a very prosperous one; his mother a psychologist without formal training. The family were fervent socialists. The leaders of the Social Democratic Party, such as Victor and Friedrich Adler, and Paul Renner, who became in 1945 president of the second Austrian Republic, came often to the Lazarsfeld home. Paul followed the usual educational route of the upper-middle-class student in Europe—grammar school, gymnasium,[2] and university. He was active in political affairs and helped organize a League of Socialist Gymnasium Students. Because he was talented in many fields, he had difficulty in deciding in what university subject to specialize. Finally, a letter from Friedrich Adler himself, who was First Secretary of the Socialist International but at the time in jail on a political murder charge, decided the question. Adler, who was himself a mathematician and physicist, advised Paul to keep up his study of mathematics because it would give him an advantage in many fields. That settled the matter. Paul graduated in mathematics, writing his doctoral dissertation on a mathematical aspect of Einstein's gravitational theory (Lazarsfeld, 1925). He then opted for the relative security of a civil service position teaching mathematics and physics in a gymnasium. From teaching in an Austrian secondary school to the directorship of the Columbia University department of sociology is a long step in a career.

How did this change come about? Remember that when Lazarsfeld was a student and a young school teacher in Vienna, Austria was an intensely political nation. Paul Neurath, who we know for his studies of the radio rural forums in Poona, India, and of school television in Delhi, went through this period with Paul and describes Lazarsfeld's early years as well as anyone (Neurath, 1960). He noted in a memorial lecture at Columbia University that young socialist intellectuals in Vienna at that time were deeply interested in psychology and psychoanalysis because they wanted to participate in the creation of the "new man" for the new socialist society. "They read large quantities of Freud," Neurath (1983) said, "went to public lectures of Alfred Adler and flocked into any university lectures that were different from the very conservative traditional psychology" (p. 15).

Paul was one of those bright young socialist students. He became acquainted with a psychologist, Charlotte Bühler, who had recently been called (with her husband Karl) from Wurzburg to establish an Institute of Psychology at the University of Vienna. Paul attended her seminar. One day he presented at the seminar an analysis of questionnaires that a leader of the young socialists had collected from workers. It was a typical Lazarsfeld event. When he asked the man who gathered the questionnaires, "Why don't you *count* [the answers]?" the documents were promptly handed over to Paul to do the counting.[3] At that time, social statistics were far less familiar than they are now, and Paul's treatment of the data was striking and original. His mathematical training stood him in good stead. Indeed, Dr. Bühler made him her assistant (Lazarsfeld, 1969, p. 284; Neurath, 1983, p. 16).

It was a remarkable opportunity: to work with ambitious students, most of them young socialists who wanted to work in social psychology. The one problem was money. Young Dr. Lazarsfeld could not afford to give up his job teaching in the gymnasium for the small salary that Dr. Bühler could pay him, and if he continued to teach he would have little time for research. So he persuaded Dr. Bühler and her psychologist husband to let him found an institute for market and consumer research,[4] related to the Bühler department of psychology but not a part of the University of Vienna.[5] Because it was not a branch of the university, Lazarsfeld's research institute could accept what we today call "contract research." There was no such term then. The hope was that this outside research would support Paul Lazarsfeld and his coworkers, keep the institute going, and leave enough to pay for more theoretical social and psychological research (Lazarsfeld, 1969).

Neurath (1983) said,

> It must be difficult for the younger ones among us to envisage, and not easy even for the older ones to remember, what the world was like 50 years ago when there were as yet no university institutes with staff trained to do this kind of work; nor any money with which to finance it; no university, no government, no foundation money, not even commercial money to do straight commercial research. The very idea itself of doing commercial market research was still practically unknown.

There was less money than had been hoped to support the circle of friends and coworkers who made up Lazarsfeld's new institute. Hans Zeisel (1979), one member of the Lazarsfeld generation in Vienna, described what it was like:

> Instead of operating capital, that of course we didn't have, we co-workers had nothing to invest but our own labor . . . I am afraid that the only thing we paid punctually was the coffee for those of our co-workers who, sitting in some corner of a Vienna coffee house, worked on their reports. Whether we ever paid them more than that, I am no longer sure, because toward the end of the month those of us who had a job (I for one worked as a trainee in my father's law office) had to contribute part of their own income toward the running of the institute.[6]

Another member of the little circle was Marie Jahoda, who later became the first Mrs. Lazarsfeld. She had this to say about Paul's new research institute,[7]

> Many of us had no other income. . . . We had among our interviewers people with doctorates in Law and Economics . . . for whom this was their [only] income. That was in that time that was so horrible in Austria, especially for young people, so much of a justification that we did not have any time left for having a bad conscience.

Jahoda continues,

> Paul made this wonderful invention of market research; with that we made surveys for industry. But the money that we got for it, we used for sociopsychological studies . . . always with the one thought in the back of our minds:

How much money can we get towards that, which we really wanted to do? (in Neurath, 1983, p. 17)

She described the institute as a social organization in these beautifully chosen words: "It was less a research institute than a style of life. . . . The *Forschungsstelle* [the research institute] derived its existence from the fact that a large number of young intellectuals were unemployed. *It was a circle of friends, not a commercial enterprise.*"[8]

What kind of research did they do? Anything with a sociopsychological slant that they could get paid for. Neurath (1983) indicated a variety of market research topics that they studied: "Coffee, tea, chocolate, beer, shirts, shoes, flowers, perfume" (p. 17). Whenever possible they tried to revise a commercial question so as to give it deeper meaning. For instance, when a laundry wanted to know why more housewives did not make use of its services, they set out to discover on what occasions housewives sent the laundry to be done outside the house. As a result, the firm learned to watch for occasions such as births, deaths, weddings, and the like. Studying the purchase of different kinds of foods, they made a profile of the "proletarian" consumer as compared to the middle class consumer.[9] When Radio Vienna wanted to know what radio programs people preferred, they made a social class profile of tastes for light versus heavy music. Many years later, Lazarsfeld recalled this study as a progenitor of his American audience research (Lazarsfeld, 1969).

They were able to make another interesting use of their commercial research. Students at the University of Vienna and in the Bühlers' department came to the Lazarsfeld research institute and learned to do research by participating in it. Paul taught a class or two (without pay) in the formal academic structure of the university. In this way, his institute gained research assistants, and the students in the academic department got research training. Theoretical propositions raised in university classes could be checked against the institute's data from field research, and the research could in return suggest new theory.

I have discussed this early chapter in Paul Lazarsfeld's career in such detail because many of the ways of working and the patterns of organization that he developed in Vienna came with him to America. More than one of the members of the later Bureau of Applied Social Research, hearing Neurath, or Zeisel, or Jahoda talk about the early Lazarsfeld years in Vienna, remarked that it all sounded quite familiar. The Vienna experience was in the spirit of what the later scholars had learned to do in Newark or New York, in Paul's more opulent and better-financed U.S. operations.

Lazarsfeld in America

How did Paul transfer his activities to the United States? In the early 1930s, Lazarsfeld, Jahoda, and Zeisel made a study of the little Austrian town of Marienthal where, in the early years of the Great Depression, not only was there unemployment, but *almost everyone* was unemployed (Lazarsfeld, Jahoda, & Zeisel, 1933, 1960, 1971). It was a moving study at the time, and still moving when we read it today because it looked both at the effect of unemployment on individuals and on society. One of the questions Lazarsfeld and his colleagues wanted most to answer was whether widespread unemployment of this kind would make people revolutionary or apathetic. The answer, they regretted to report, was that unemployment seemed to make them more apathetic. The book was published in German in 1933 at precisely the time that Hitler came to power, and it was at once suppressed and not republished in German until 1960, and not in English until 1971. But copies of the book and its data circulated, and Dr. Charlotte Bühler, among others, was greatly impressed. She sent Paul to report his findings at the International Congress of Psychology in Hamburg, where some of the world's best-known psychologists were in attendance.[10] They too were impressed. The European representative of the Rockefeller Foundation saw some of the Marienthal study material and offered Paul a one year traveling fellowship to America. In October 1933, he arrived in New York.

Lazarsfeld went to see many of the scholars that he had met at the International Congress of Psychology. One of his first calls was on Robert Lynd, the coauthor of *Middletown* (Lynd & Lynd, 1929). Lynd was a professor of sociology at Columbia University and was studying the effects of unemployment in Montclair, New Jersey. That was a very familiar topic to Paul and he offered to help as a volunteer with the field work. Lynd, ever kindly and thoughtful, felt it would be exploiting Paul to accept that offer but asked Paul to assist him in a graduate-level class that he was teaching at Columbia. This relationship was one of the most fortunate that Paul developed, for again and again Lynd came to Lazarsfeld's aid when he was building an American career and in need of help. Paul traveled to meet many of the pioneers in empirical social research—Luther Fry, who wrote the first book on the subject,[11] Stuart Chapin at Minnesota, George A. Lundberg, who was at that time studying problems of unemployment for their New Deal administration, and others. Lazarsfeld worked as a volunteer for the Federal Emergency Relief Administration on a study in the Chicago area and also on a study for the Psychological Corporation in New

York, thereby acquiring a great deal of knowledge in the process about how field research in America differed from that in Europe.[12] Austria, meanwhile, was looking less and less attractive. A fascist coup had taken place. Paul's parents were imprisoned for having hidden a well-known socialist from the police. Paul asked the Rockefeller Foundation for a second year of fellowship support. He got it.

Before his fellowship ended, Lazarsfeld decided to transfer his career to America. He returned to Europe to close his business affairs and replace his student visa with an immigration visa. The latter became somewhat more of a problem when his U.S. job offer evaporated—a position in Pittsburgh that he had been offered and on the strength of which he intended to immigrate as an "employed person."[13] But he already had his travel papers and decided to go to Austria anyway. He returned to New York— like a typical immigrant, penniless and jobless.[14]

His angel, Lynd, came to the rescue again and got him a job at the University of Newark in New Jersey. The job was to be supervisor of student relief for a New Deal organization, the National Youth Administration, in New Jersey. What did that title mean? Chiefly, it meant that he was to invent or create work for otherwise unemployed young people who were to be supported by the NYA. That was a very familiar sort of problem for Paul. He found 10,000 questionnaires that had been collected from unemployed youth.[15] Hand-tabulating was then the fashion; computers and punch cards were still in the future. Therefore, the 10,000 questionnaires would keep his young people busy for months.[16]

But this was not enough for Paul. Later he recalled, "I told the president [of the University of Newark], Frank Kingdon, that if he wanted to make his organization into a big university,[17] he had to have a research center" (Lazarsfeld, 1969, p. 288). A few months after he arrived, Lazarsfeld established a research center.[18]

The Research Center was much like his *Forschungsstelle* in Vienna— organized outside the university so that it could legally accept "contract" research. Paul was made a part-time instructor so that the University of Newark could pay half of his salary. The university housed the center in an abandoned brewery and assigned to it the students supported by the NYA to earn their little money as research assistants. The situation looked more and more like the Vienna institute as Paul began to attract a group of bright young colleagues, who had to be supported, if at all, by contract research. Rose Goldsen, later a professor of sociology at Cornell University, described the Newark Center at the 20th anniversary of the Columbia Bureau of Applied Social Research, in 1957, as such:

How were we supported? Hans Zeisel, on the occasion of Paul's fiftieth
birthday (in 1951) [celebration] mentioned . . . that the financial structure of
social research, as we know it, had been laid down in the early days of the
Vienna Institute. I am now going to give a name to this Vienna fiscal
principle—the cliffhanging principle of finance. We were all cliffhangers in
those days. Those were the days of the Depression . . . as a result, Paul
Lazarsfeld spent his days peddling to potential "marks" the idea of hiring us
to do research for them. Research on anything.[19] (Neurath, 1983, p. 20)

But there was a special quality about those "cliffhanging" years, as
Professor Goldsen saw them:

There was, then, the exhilaration that came from watching a creative thinker
think, from rising to the occasion, from using yourself to your greatest
capacity—even beyond your own limitations. But it was more than that. It was
doing [these] things in an atmosphere of intense emotional involvement, at a
time when we were all young, full of energy, full of confidence, full of
optimism, and—if I may say so—full of love. (Neurath, 1983, pp. 22-23)

The Radio Research Project

So the Newark Center was very much like the Vienna research institute
and, to no small degree, like the Columbia bureau when it was founded a
little later. But there was another step between Newark and Columbia.
Hadley Cantril, a professor at Princeton, had proposed to the Rockefeller
Foundation a study on the effects of radio (then only a little more than a
decade old) on its listeners. But he had trouble finding a director for the
study, someone who had the requisite stature and also the confidence to
leave a permanent job for two years in the middle of the Depression to
manage someone else's research project. Robert Lynd—who else?—suggested Lazarsfeld, and it was at once apparent that he could do the task.
Paul was interested, but he had two obstacles: For one thing, he did not feel
that he could leave his newly founded institute at Newark to move to
Princeton; second, although not much was said about this, he did not work
very comfortably with Cantril. Therefore, when Lazarsfeld was hired, the
radio project was nominally headed up at Princeton, but the work was
actually done at Lazarsfeld's research center at the University of Newark.[20]

One fortunate coincidence of the new project was the appointment of
Frank Stanton (then research director and later president of CBS) as
Associate Director of the Radio Research Project, under Cantril. Some

years later, Paul described the organization with his typical whimsy: "Cantril was there to see that Paul didn't run away with the money," he said, "and Stanton to see that he knew what he was doing" (Lazarsfeld, 1969). If Lynd was Paul's first and most helpful friend in New York, Stanton was his second.

Stanton brought the Austrian research director into contact with the mass media offices, researchers, and funders in New York. He played an essential role when Paul decided that the Radio Project should be moved to New York. But relationships with Cantril were not good: The University of Newark was not long for this world, and the media were, for the most part, in New York. With Stanton's support, Princeton University was persuaded to let the remainder of the Radio Research Project be transferred elsewhere, and with Lynd's help, Columbia University was persuaded to take it over. Therefore, the Newark Research Center and the Princeton Radio Project, renamed the Columbia Office of Radio Research (later to become the Bureau of Applied Social Research), set up housekeeping in New York, at first in rented space in Union Square and then in an abandoned building of the Columbia Medical School.[21] Paul was given a faculty appointment and taught a couple of classes without pay.[22] The Rockefeller Foundation continued the grant for the Radio Research Project for several more years, and Paul went about his now familiar pattern of raising research funds and managing an amazingly informal organization of young researchers. Paul and Columbia together attracted the young researchers. Radio was as potentially threatening and promising in the 1930s as television was to become after 1950. The widespread concern over the impacts of media (illustrated by the Payne Fund studies of film's effects in the early 1930s[23]), and the practical concern among radio networks and advertisers about audience size and reaction, meant that there was funding for studying media audiences. A keen observer who had already learned the difficulty of financing a high-quality research organization could hardly miss the practical importance of that situation.

The Columbia Bureau

The formation of the Bureau of Applied Social Research was a chapter heading not only in the career of Paul Lazarsfeld but also in the history of American social research. The 1930s and 1940s were a period when social research institutes were being born in the United States. We are fortunate in having a discussion of this development by the founding director of the bureau himself. Lazarsfeld was called on by the University of Colorado in the 1960s to advise on a new social research institute that the university was planning to establish in Boulder. As part of his consulting duties, he wrote a background paper that the university later published (Lazarsfeld, Klein, & Tyler, 1964).

"The twentieth century seems to be the age of the social sciences in higher education. The sixteenth century was the time when humanistic studies were integrated into the universities, and the most characteristic institutional event was probably the founding of the College de France. In the seventeenth century the natural sciences emerged in the curriculum; the Royal Society in London was both leader and symbol. The nineteenth century brought into being the modern integrated university, for which the German universities, chiefly the University of Berlin, set the pattern.

"In the twentieth century," he said, "we are seeing a rapid expansion of empirical work in the social sciences, and this is being done by a great many centers, institutes, bureaus, and so on, linked to their universities in a variety of ways, without sound financial foundations, and engaged in a mixture of research and consulting which has not been clarified, let alone planned."

These have come into being, he said, because a number of scientists:

> "Want to do large-scale empirical studies and need staff, technical facilities, and money to carry out their plans.
>
> "Become intrigued by the new challenge of the empirical social sciences and . . . want to try out the new tools.
>
> "Feel confined by the narrowness of their special disciplines and look for interdisciplinary contacts.
>
> "Want to bridge the gap between the academic world and the world of action . . . remain scholars and still participate in . . . the making of public decisions.
>
> "Want to add an increment to a meager university salary by doing consulting work without 'going into business on their own.' "

Concomitantly, university administrators noted the value of such institutes in building public image and in attracting superior students. Also, various philanthropic groups and government agencies were looking for data of a kind not usually provided by conventional sources of social bookkeeping.

Paul thought that he could identify four historical phases in the growth of organized social research in the United States (Lazarsfeld, 1964). The phases began, before World War I, with community studies, largely done by social workers to learn more about the problems of communities. In the early 1930s a second trend appeared, originating, he said, "in data rather than problems." Commercial consumer studies, public opinion polling, radio audience surveys, were all seen as useful and became popular both with field researchers and users. These data, he said, "became the raw material for the new field of communication and opinion research." At that time, he noted, a few institutes were created to conduct social research for its own sake, "most typically the Bureau of Applied Social Research at Columbia University." After World War II, from 1939 to 1945, a third wave of institutes was created. These grew largely out of the government's use of empirical social research. Examples of these new organizations were Carl I. Hovland's program at Yale for the study of communication and attitude change and Samuel A. Stouffer's Harvard Laboratory of Social Relations, both of which grew out of the wartime research in the U.S. Department of Defense, and the Michigan Survey Research Center, the roots of which were in the U.S. Department of Agriculture and the Office of War Information. In the late 1940s and the 1950s, there was yet another wave of institutes created when some universities felt the need to have organized social research but wanted to build it within or close to their existing departments rather than setting up something entirely new and separate. These universities, he felt, were looking for a director, not for a whole staff. This impetus led to such organizations in our field as the communication research institutes at Illinois and Stanford and the research programs at Wisconsin and MIT. The Annenberg Schools for Communication at the University of Pennsylvania and at the University of Southern California may represent a fifth cycle or they may be a continuation of the fourth phase. In any case, these communication research institutes came too late for Paul to classify in his historical paper at the University of Colorado.

So Paul Lazarsfeld came to America at a fortunate time, when organizations were ready to found social research institutes. It should be remembered, though, that each of these new creations required a certain degree of imagination and foresight, strong leadership, and the necessary salesmanship to finance a not inexpensive venture. All of these qualities Paul had.

Great years! When he moved to New York in the late 1930s, Paul Lazarsfeld was chiefly interested in the kind of radio study for which support was easiest to obtain: audience research. He was never much interested in *how many* people were listening, but rather in *who* listened, what programs they listened to and why, and what use they made of what they heard. Gradually, his interest and that of his bureau turned to understanding the effects of radio, and this broadened to include the uses and effects of film, television, printed media, and interpersonal communication.

Paul was always fascinated, said Frank Stanton, with the study of what people liked and what they didn't like. Some of the first work of the new bureau was done with a program analyzer, built especially for Stanton and Lazarsfeld, and known affectionately at the CBS network as "Little Annie." Little Annie could record and tabulate the responses of a studio full of persons who were listening to a radio program or viewing a film. At regular intervals, signaled by a light, listeners pushed one of two buttons—one red, one green—to indicate whether they liked or did not like the program at that moment. Thus the machine provided a profile of changing audience reactions to a message. The machine could be used for formative research on new programs, or on any program, new or old, to establish general principles of what audiences liked and why.

The first two books published by the bureau, however, indicate better than did Little Annie the kind of research that was going on in the abandoned (and rent-free) building that Paul's people occupied in New York. *Radio Research, 1942-43,* edited by Lazarsfeld and Stanton, contained almost 600 pages of studies by staff members of the bureau.[24] The first 30 pages were an impressive article by Herta Herzog on "What Do We Really Know About Daytime Serial Listeners?" Herzog was Lazarsfeld's second wife. The first had been Marie Jahoda, who worked with Paul in Vienna; the third was Patricia Kendall, a student and then a staff member at the bureau. All three were skilled communication researchers; all did important work on the mass media. The 1942-43 study by Herzog was based on very large audience surveys, plus 100 intensive interviews. This combination of large surveys and a smaller number of intensive interviews was a typical bureau methodology. Herzog analyzed the intensive interviews to understand individuals' motivations for listening to the radio serials and to obtain the resulting gratifications. This motivations-gratifications approach was being talked about, and experimented with, in the bureau 25 years before Elihu Katz and others wrote books on it. Herzog found three main reasons why women in 1940 tuned in to daytime serials: emotional release, wishful thinking, and advice seeking. The fact that these radio serials were actually used as a source of advice for listeners' personal and family problems had been, for the most part, unsuspected and made a considerable stir both among radio broadcasters and social critics.

The Herzog chapter was followed by Rudolf Arnheim's detailed analysis of the content of daytime serials for different kinds of women. These three papers by talented members of the bureau looked at one of the most popular of radio forms from three related viewpoints—content, audience, and use. There followed 150 pages analyzing the use of radio in wartime (the book was published in 1944). America's use of radio was analyzed by Charles Siepman, Britain's radio audience by Robert Silvey, who later became director of audience research for BBC, and Germany's use of radio by Hans Speier and Ernst Kris, among others. Experiences with Little Annie were described at length, with a summary of findings. John Gray Peatman wrote on radio's use of popular music, the audiences for this kind of entertainment, and the medium's power to make popular music popular. Among other studies in the volume was an examination of *nonlisteners* to radio—who were they and why didn't they listen. There was also a paper by Ernst Dichter, in typical Dichterian style, on what advertisers should do to make radio advertising effective. The last paper in the book was on a medium other than radio—biographies in popular magazines by Leo Lowenthal, who was later at the University of California at Berkeley; it is still today his best-known publication.

The Lazarsfeld and Stanton book set a new standard for media audience study as a part of social research and told a wider audience what insiders had known for some time: What an exciting place the bureau was, and the high quality of work going on there.

Lazarsfeld and Merton

About the same time as the compendium we have been describing was published, another book came out of the bureau and the Department of Sociology at Columbia. This was *Mass Persuasion: The Social Psychology of a War Bond Drive* by Robert K. Merton, the leading theorist among Columbia's sociologists, but not averse to doing field research (Merton, Fiske, & Curtis, 1946). How Merton happened to be associated with the bureau is a story worth telling. Until the end of the 1930s Lazarsfeld was an unpaid teacher in sociology at Columbia; his income came from the research funds of the bureau. But a vacancy came about on the professorial staff at Columbia because of the death of a professor who taught statistics and demography. Lynd wanted the replacement to be another empiricist, and his candidate—hardly to our surprise—was Lazarsfeld. Robert Mac-Iver, chairman of the Columbia sociology department, on the other hand, wanted to fill the vacancy with a theorist, Robert K. Merton, a Harvard PhD who was then chairman of the Department of Sociology at Tulane. As often happens in the politics of university appointments, the department decided to find a way to get both of these men. Lazarsfeld, the older and more experienced of the two, was appointed an associate professor; Merton, an assistant professor. The stage was now set for an awkward bit of jealousy and competition in the department. But nothing like that happened.

Merton and Lazarsfeld became good friends. Merton became very much interested in the bureau and the kind of research that it did and soon became its associate director. His theoretical background was valuable to the other members of the bureau, particularly when the bureau grew into the principal research training ground for the department's graduate students. In turn, the bureau's lively empirical approach was useful to Merton. So the publication of *Mass Persuasion* was an event of greater importance than a mere addition to the bibliography of communication research.

Merton's book was a study of Kate Smith's radio telethon that resulted in the sale to the listening audience of millions of dollars worth of government War Bonds. The sum might not seem so large today, but it was considered phenomenal in 1939. Using survey data and intensive interviews, Merton went about finding why Smith's performance was so remarkably effective. The explanation was the chemistry of Smith's personality, the appeals that she used, and the situation in which the radio program was heard. The striking aspect of Merton's analysis was the skill with which the individual pieces of data were generalized into broad patterns of interwoven cognitions, values, affects, and behaviors. The book must have opened the eyes of many scholars to the close relationship between social psychological theory and field research. To me, one of the most remarkable features of *Mass Persuasion* is that a theorist such as Merton could be sufficiently interested in media research to carry it out. That fact itself may be a testimony to the effectiveness of Lazarsfeld as a research catalyst.

The second volume of collected investigations from the bureau showed how much the research program had broadened beyond radio studies. Television was not studied yet because the war had postponed the coming of television, but Lazarsfeld and his people studied a variety of other media. This book was *Communication Research, 1948-1949,* again edited jointly by Lazarsfeld and Stanton (who had in the meantime become President of CBS).[25] The previous collection had begun with an analysis of women's reactions to their favorite radio programs; this book started with an article on children's media use by Katherine Wolf and Marjorie Fiske. Kenneth Baker contributed an analysis of commercial radio programming. Lazarsfeld, with the aid of Helen Dinerman, wrote a long paper on "Research for Action" that was almost a textbook case of how to use sophisticated social research for improving the effectiveness of commercial media. Lazarsfeld and Dinerman began by presenting evidence that radio's potential morning audience is divided almost equally into three audience categories—one that listens to the daytime serials, one that does not listen at all in the morning, and a third that listens, but not to the serials. The latter two categories did not feel well served by radio. Lazarsfeld and Dinerman analyzed, as well as they could from the existing data, what the broadcasters could do about it. Their theoretical suggestions were both penetrating and practical.

The next paper in the book is one that you may know well: "What Missing the Newspaper Means" by Bernard Berelson. Like Merton's study of Kate Smith, this chapter represented a target of opportunity; it had to be done at once or not at all. A general newspaper strike occurred in New York. Paul saw the possibilities. "Why don't we find out what they miss in the newspapers?" he asked. Berelson seized on the idea. Many of the bureau's studies came about like this one: Paul suggested the idea; someone picked it up. Money was needed for a field survey; Paul could make that available. A design had to be formed quickly, before the newspaper strike ended; skilled people were there, ready to cooperate on the design. Field interviewers were available. Berelson, with others looking over his shoulder, analyzed the results. Data analysis was one of the bureau's strong points as the Merton book and the Herzog article demonstrated. Berelson surprised a number of journalists and journalism scholars by what he learned about why people read a newspaper. Not only did his readers very much miss several types of content that the newspapers had seldom regarded as their most important services—for instance, funeral announcements and movie schedules—but also they missed the paper for various nonspecific reasons. For example, because they felt "out of it," as though a curtain had gone down and they couldn't see what was happening in the world (although they might not have looked out the window anyway). People were accustomed to starting out the day with a newspaper and they felt a vague sense of unease when they were no longer able to maintain this familiar pattern.

Another article in the Lazarsfeld-Stanton book was "The Analysis of Deviant Cases in Communication Research," by Patricia Kendall (the third Mrs. Paul Lazarsfeld) and Katherine Wolf. The study of deviant cases in order to understand audience behavior was an innovative approach that Lazarsfeld and his colleagues had developed. It made many other researchers say, "Why didn't I think of that?" Kendall's deviant cases came from the "Mr. Biggott" study, a campaign that used cartoons to make fun of antisemitism. It had been a monumental failure. Lazarsfeld was unwilling to let either a great success, such as the Kate Smith radio telethon, or a great failure, such as Mr. Biggott, pass by without trying to understand *why*. In this case, Kendall interviewed a sample of audience members in depth and then looked at the deviant cases. Formerly, deviant cases had been considered little more than an embarrassment to the researcher, but the people at the bureau felt that they might throw some light on what happened. Indeed they did. It was an excellent example of how an innovative social research organization operates when its goal is to understand rather than merely to describe.

The book also contained Merton's first report on the "Rovere" study. This investigation attempted to identify the "influentials" in a suburb in New Jersey. The study came about because a news magazine was trying to ascertain the types of persons that it should reach with its advertising. That is what the magazine wanted out of the study. Merton and the bureau wanted the study to answer questions of greater generality: Who in a society has influence, over whom and for what, and how is such influence exerted? Both parties got what they wanted, a typical example of how a Lazarsfeld-led research organization worked. The organization satisfied practical needs in order to obtain financing, and the same interviews contributed to communication theory.

The last paper in the Lazarsfeld-Stanton book was a long report by Alex Inkeles on domestic broadcasting in the U.S.S.R. This chapter was a part of his distinguished study of Soviet communication, later published in book form.

The Era of Minimal Media Effects

Studies of interpersonal influence and media effects were beginning to take up a larger and larger part of the bureau's attention. Notable were two studies of U.S. Presidential elections. They were large panel studies of opinions and media behavior aimed at finding out why people changed their opinions (and their votes) during a Presidential election campaign and how this change related to what they heard or read in the media. The first of these studies was of the 1940 presidential election in Erie County, Ohio; the second, of the 1948 election in Elmira, New York.

Both studies were highly praised and skillfully conducted. But they were many years before publication. The book on the 1940 election, *The People's Choice*, by Lazarsfeld, Berelson, and Gaudet, appeared in 1944. The second volume, *Voting*, by Berelson, Lazarsfeld, and McPhee, did not appear until 1954, 10 years later. Data analysis required lengthy gestation time at the bureau. Design was relatively fast, and field work was carried out with the punctual smoothness that comes with experience. But the data from a large study tended to sit around, to be picked up again and again, looked at by different people, talked about and debated, until someone finally devoted a considerable stretch of time to it, developed the theoretical implications, and—with collaborators—produced a book manuscript.

This deliberate process also happened with the book *Personal Influence,* which was published in 1955, but reported data that were more than 10 years old (Katz & Lazarsfeld, 1955).[26] Elihu Katz made the book his doctoral dissertation, and it made his reputation. I have been told by several members of the bureau that Katz was much admired for his success in interpreting such old data in a relevant theoretical framework. Perhaps it was because of the difficulty of making theoretical interpretations of field data. Lazarsfeld favored secondary analysis of his data and was concerned with creating data banks in which the results of important investigations could be stored until researchers could work on them. There was no shortage of talent or sophistication at the bureau; its books typically had as authors one or two top-notch senior scholars, with the aid of a talented and technically skilled younger person. People at the bureau were busy. One study came on the heels of another. The studies were not neat laboratory experiments, such as Hovland's or many of Lewin's, but rather large, complex field studies. It was not until Berelson got some free time from the Ford Foundation, or until Katz could take a year off to work on his dissertation, that important book manuscripts were produced.

A second point about the studies we have been discussing is that the general bureau perspective in the 1940s and early 1950s was to doubt that the mass media were important in changing individuals' opinions or behavior. The Erie County study (Lazarsfeld et al., 1944) found only a small percentage of all voters changed their opinions during the presidential election campaign in any way related to their media exposure. Rather, they were influenced, if at all, by their friends, families, and neighbors. The authors of this book hypothesized that influentials among the public most likely absorbed political opinions from, or were otherwise influenced by, the mass media, and they, in turn, passed on these ideas to other persons. This "two-step flow" hypothesis argues that the influence of the media is likely to move in a two-step pattern rather than directly; the media influence a few individuals who in turn contact a larger audience. This idea was advanced by the Lazarsfeld, Berelson, and Gaudet book on the 1944 election, and was not disconfirmed by any of the bureau studies until after the Katz and Lazarsfeld book of 1955. The two-step flow hypothesis was widely quoted and used through the 1950s and 1960s, although now it has been revised and is generally felt to be too simple to describe reality.

The general concept basic to bureau media effects studies for a considerable time was that the chief effect of the mass media on individuals' opinions and resulting behavior was social reinforcement—that is, to reinforce behavior that already existed. Most people, the bureau researchers came to believe, used the media to shore up, rather than to revise, what they believe. They select media messages that promise to reinforce what they have already accepted. This general conclusion was stated in Klapper's *The Effects of Mass Communication*, published in 1960. The Klapper book serves to sum up what the bureau had decided about media effects in its first 20 years. Klapper was then director of social research for CBS, of which Stanton was president in 1960, and that therefore had a rather special relationship to Lazarsfeld's bureau. Klapper wrote an excellent, careful, thoughtful book that leads one to regret that he spent so much of his career running a commercial research operation. His conclusions in the book were that mass communication *ordinarily* does not serve as a necessary and sufficient cause of audience effects. Rather, the media work through a "nexus" of mediating factors and influences. These are such that they usually render mass communication "a contributory agent, but not the sole cause, in a process of reinforcing the existing conditions" (Klapper, 1960, p. 8). There are certain conditions, Klapper concedes, in which the media may directly cause change. Some of these conditions we understand and some we don't. Two that are known are the possibility that the mediating factors may be inoperative in a certain situation or that the mediating factors may themselves work toward change. The latter case must have been operative when Kate Smith's telethon had such strong impact (see Merton et al., 1946); the former, when the Orson Welles "Man from Mars" radio program presented listeners with such an unfamiliar experience that they had no adequate cognitive structure with which to mediate it (see Cantril, Gaudet, & Herzog, 1940).

In general the trend has been away from this minimal effects point of view. More and more cases, more and more situations, have been discovered in which the media *do* seem to have important social effects. But the Lazarsfeld conclusions were of great value in moving us away from an unreasonable fear of mass media propaganda that was common in the 1920s and 1930s. More recent developments have been helpful in striking a balance, and in evolving a new synthesis, not completely like either the early viewpoint or the later one represented by Klapper and the bureau voting studies.

Contributions to Communication Study

The contribution of Lazarsfeld and his bureau to communication research and theory can hardly be overestimated. When Lazarsfeld retired from communication research in 1956, saying he would not take any more communication research PhDs (Katz was the last one) and was going to study mathematical sociology, he took out of the field one of its most stimulating and innovative forces. The bureau did not come to an end until after Paul's death in 1976, and Paul would never completely retire from anything that had so deeply interested him. Why did he leave the field of communication research? The challenge of maintaining the bureau was no longer so attractive to him as it had been. In 1936, everything his research center did was new. It was the only organization of its kind. It was cutting a trail through unknown territory. As the only organization of its kind, it was essential to the U.S. mass media as well as to the academic development of communication study. By 1956 the Bureau of Applied Social Research was surrounded by other research organizations, many of which had less serious financial problems. The bureau was no longer as necessary to the mass media. The problems it was taking up were no longer so new. This situation happens in a scholarly career, especially when one has been as successful as Lazarsfeld. One tires; one no longer feels the excitement of newness; one finds oneself doing the same thing over and over again. This feeling is especially strong when one has founded an organization, nursed it through its early illnesses, and let it become an important part of one's life.

Some scholars, in that case, have been able to retire from administrative leadership but continue their own research and their theoretical leadership. Paul, however, produced nothing in communication research during his last 20 years to equal the level of excitement of his middle years. He administered the Columbia Department of Sociology, but that was neither his great joy nor his great talent. As an elder statesman, he continued to give wise advice and to encourage interesting projects and good people, spoke occasionally and effectively, sat on important committees, and was honored by people and institutions who appreciated him. After he retired at Columbia University, he taught sociology at the University of Pittsburgh until the final years of his life. Like many other scholars, he wasn't a man to retire quietly.[27]

How shall we sum up Paul Lazarsfeld's enormous contribution to communication research? As we conceded at the beginning of this chapter, he was not a great theoretical force. Rather, Paul was a force *toward* theory.

He was a *creative* force. His monument is what the bureau did, and what his best students did, there and elsewhere. The people who worked in the bureau, and those among them who studied with Paul, include a remarkable group: Robert K. Merton, Bernard Berelson, James S. Coleman, Elihu Katz, Joseph Klapper, David Sills, Charles Glock, Leo Lowenthal, Rudolf Arnheim, Herta Herzog. Paul influenced them in different ways—some, such as Katz, as teacher and research supervisor; others, such as Merton, by helping to provide money and a staff for field research, and a stimulating atmosphere in which to work; still others, such as Coleman and Klapper and Herzog, by providing a place to work where they could exercise their creativity and interact with others as creative as they were. For all of them, Paul provided a challenge and an example.

"He used numbers in a humanistic way," said Merton, after Paul died of cancer in 1976. "He was not a technician. He used numbers to arrive at ideas" (Merton, 1979, pp. 19-20). "It was not so much that he was an American sociologist," said Coleman in summing up Lazarsfeld's career, "as it was that he determined what American sociology *would be.* . . . What made Paul unique was not his involvement with ideas or his involvement with people, but his ability to stir the two together." For the scholars we have mentioned, and many others, he was responsible for creating—again in Coleman's words—"the excitement of working together with ideas or problems planted by Paul." [28]

Notes

1. Most of this description of Lazarsfeld's young days appears in Paul F. Lazarfeld (1969). It is also recounted in Paul Neurath (1983).

2. The European gymnasium corresponds approximately to the American high school in the educational sequence.

3. The result was presented in a paper at the Bühler seminar (Lazarsfeld, 1969, p. 284). According to Neurath (1983), these were published in Lazarsfeld, Bühler, Biegeleisen, Hetzer, and Reininger (1931).

4. *Wirtschaftspsychologische Forschungsstelle.* According to Lazarsfeld (1969), this title is "a term connoting broadly the application of psychology to social and economic problems" (p. 274).

5. Editors' Note: The German word *Institut* is roughly equivalent to "department" in an American university, so Karl and Charlotte Bühler were professors in the Psychology Institute (that is, the Department of Psychology) of the University of Vienna.

6. Much of this quotation appears in Hans Zeisel (1979). However, Schramm is probably quoting from a longer essay presented at the memorial service for Lazarsfeld held at Columbia University, on which Zeisel's chapter is based.

7. Marie Jahoda's statements are from Greffrath (1979). Jahoda had been interviewed by West German Radio in 1978.

8. Editors' Note: This comment appears in Neurath (1983) as follows: "The *Forschungsstelle* could only exist on the basis that a great number of young intellectuals were unemployed. It was a circle of friends, not a commercial enterprise" (p. 18).

9. According to Lazarsfeld's memoir, his "proletarian" concern developed while he was working on the data collected from unemployed youth. "For my *Jugend und Beruf,* I coordinated a large amount of data from various sources into a rather coherent system of concepts. She [Mrs. Bühler] was pleased, and also accepted my position on the need to distinguish between middle-class and working-class adolescents" (Lazarsfeld, 1969, p. 285).

10. The International Psychological Congress was held in 1932. Among those attending were Gordon Allport, Otto Klineberg, and Goodwin Watson (Lazarsfeld, 1969, p. 293). Lazarsfeld's paper presented at the Congress was published in an English translation a year later as Lazarsfeld (1933).

11. In his memoir Lazarsfeld (1969) wrote: "During this early period I spent some time at a few places in which empirical social research was taught. I went to the University of Rochester to become acquainted with Luther Fry, who had written the first book on techniques of social research" (p. 294).

12. The Psychological Corporation was a nonprofit organization created by "a group of prominent American psychologists, including E. L. Thorndike and J. M. Cattell" (Lazarsfeld, 1969, pp. 295-296).

13. According to Lazarsfeld's memoir, David Craig, who was then director of the Retail Research Institute of the University of Pittsburgh, "arranged for me to get a temporary appointment at this Institute" (Lazarsfeld, 1969, p. 299).

It will be remembered that I went to Vienna to apply for an immigration visa based on the promise of an appointment at the Retail Research Institute at the University of Pittsburgh. The day after I got my visa, I received a cable from Craig telling me that he was leaving Pittsburgh because he had taken the job of research director of the Retail Foundation; my appointment would have to be delayed until a successor could confirm it. (Lazarsfeld, 1969, p. 303)

14. The word *penniless* appears in Lazarsfeld's memoir (1969): "I thus arrived in New York as the classic immigrant, penniless" (p. 304).

15. Editors' Note: This description is somewhat different from that of Lazarsfeld (1969, p. 288). According to his memoir, it was the New Jersey Relief Administration that had collected these questionnaires as a project of the National Youth Administration and then turned to Frank Kingdon, president of the University of Newark, for help with the data analysis.

16. The research results were presented in an unpublished report in 1937, *Coming of Age in Essex County: An Analysis of 10,000 Interviews with Persons 16-24 Years Old,* Office of the Essex County Superintendent and the University of Newark Research Center.

17. When Lazarsfeld accepted the position, Kingdon "had just been made president of the University of Newark, a small institution that he was expected to develop into a place of higher learning for underprivileged students of Essex County, Newark" (Lazarsfeld, 1969, p. 288). However, the university collapsed not long after.

18. The Research Center of the University of Newark. In 1937, Lazarsfeld took responsibility for the Princeton Office of Radio Research while he was also the director of the Newark Center. This "symbiosis between Princeton and Newark University" (Lazarsfeld, 1969, p. 308) ceased when the Office of Radio Research increased its "functional autonomy" at the same time that

the University of Newark declined. When the Center was asked to move from Princeton, a new location was found at Union Square in New York City in the fall of 1938.

19. Goldsen was Lazarsfeld's secretary at the Newark Center and during his early New York years.

20. Formally, Lazarsfeld was appointed as a research associate at Princeton University (Lazarsfeld, 1969, p. 308).

21. The Office of Radio Research at Princeton University was established in 1937 and transferred to Columbia University in 1938. According to Lazarsfeld's memoir, this transfer was partly due to "internal difficulties" between himself and Cantril. The Rockefeller Foundation consulted Stanton about how to resolve the situation, and Lynd persuaded the president of Princeton University to release the Radio Research Project (Lazarsfeld, 1969, p. 329).

22. At that time, Lazarsfeld was appointed a lecturer. In 1941, he was made a permanent member of the department of sociology. "This made finally effective my classificatory change from psychologist to sociologist" (Lazarsfeld, 1969, p. 329).

23. The Payne Fund studies include Blumer (1933); Blumer and Hauser (1933); Charters (1933); Dale (1935a, 1935b, 1937); Dysinger and Ruckmick (1935); Holaday and Stoddard (1933); Peterson and Thurstone (1933); Renshaw, Miller, and Marquis (1933); Shuttleworth and May (1933).

24. This book was published in 1944. Chapters appearing in this book are Herta Herzog, " What Do We Really Know about Daytime Serial Listeners?" Rudolf Arnheim, "The World of the Day-Time Serial." Helen J. Kaufman, "The Appeal of Specific Day-Time Serials." Charles A. Siepman, "American Radio in Wartime: An Interim Survey of the OWI's Radio Bureau." Robert J. Silvey, "Radio Audience Research in Great Britain." Ernst Kris and Howard White, "The German Radio Home News in Wartime." Hans Speier and Margaret Otis, "German Radio Propaganda to France During the Battle of France." Hans Herma, "Some Principles of German Propaganda and Their Application to Radio." Tore Hollonquist and Edward A. Suchman, "Listening to the Listener: Experiences with the Lazarsfeld-Stanton Program Analyzer." John G. Peatman, "Radio and Popular Music." Disney Fishman and Sydney Roslow, "The Study of Adjacent Listening." Boyd R. McCandless, "A Study of Non-Listeners." Charles H. Smith, "The CBS Forecast Panels." Alfred Udow and Rena Ross, " The Interviewer Bias." Ernest Dichter, "On the Psychology of Radio Commercials." Adolf Sturmthal and Alberta Curtis, "Program Analyzer Tests of Two Educational Films." Leo Lowenthal, "Biographies in Popular Magazines."

25. This book contains the following chapters: Katherine M. Wolf and Marjorie Fiske, "The Children Talk About Comics"; Kenneth Baker, "An Analysis of Radio's Programming"; Paul F. Lazarsfeld and Helen Dinerman, "Research for Action"; Bernard Berelson, "What 'Missing the Newspaper' Means"; Babette Kass, "Overlapping Magazine Reading"; Patricia L. Kendall and Katherine M. Wolf, "The Analysis of Deviant Cases in Communication Research"; Robert K. Merton, "Patterns of Influence: A Study of Interpersonal Influence of Communication Behavior in a Local Community"; and Alex Inkeles, "Domestic Broadcasting in the U.S.S.R."

26. Interviewing was conducted in two waves in the summer of 1945. "The whole organization of field work for the study was in the hands of C. Wright Mills" (Katz & Lazarsfeld, 1955).

27. Neurath (1983) recalled, "When I once remarked to a colleague about his strenuous kind of retirement, I got the answer that encompassed it all: 'Paul needs students.' " (p. 24).

28. Editor's Note: We have been unable to locate any documentary record of these quotations. Coleman (1980) expressed similar views on Lazarsfeld's career at a 1978 meeting of the Eastern Sociological Society.

Kurt Lewin

The Field, the Group, and Communication[1]

The psychologist finds himself in the midst of a rich and vast land full of strange happenings. There are men killing themselves; a child playing; a child forming his lips to say his first word; a person who, having fallen in love and being caught in an unhappy situation, is not willing or not able to find a way out; there is the mystical state called hypnosis, where the will of one person seems to govern another person; there is the reaching out for higher and more difficult goals; loyalty to a group; dreaming, planning; exploring the world; and so on without end. It is an endless continent full of fascination and power and full of stretches of land where no one has ever set foot. Psychology is out to conquer this continent, to find out where its treasures are hidden, to investigate its danger spots, to master its vast forces, and to utilize its energies.

(Lewin, quoted in Marrow, 1969, p. 3)[2]

That is how Kurt Lewin viewed the world of his profession—with an excitement and wonder that never dimmed. He was interested in every bit and kind of human behavior around him. He was the Columbus, the Francis Drake, the Captain Cook of social psychology. I have never seen him when the excitement of exploration did not come through in everything he did and said. He was always in the process of "conquering the endless continent."

This is the picture of Lewin that I remember most clearly: his thin, intelligent face flushed with excitement, eyes shining behind glasses, arms flailing, pacing back and forth in front of his chalkboard, asking, constantly

Kurt Lewin

challenging us: "Vot haf ve vergotten?" Sometimes he said "vergotten," sometimes "vergassen." His language was never completely English or completely German. It didn't matter, his enthusiasm carried us along with him.

"Vot haf ve vergotten?" I heard him ask that question perhaps a hundred times. He was always thinking about the lifespace that enters into human behavior, the field of knowledge and motivation one has to know about in order to understand why a person does what he does. He was asking how completely we had filled out that lifespace for some individual that we were studying, what essential elements we might have neglected to include.

In this urge to see the whole picture, Lewin was somewhat like Lasswell, but in other respects very different. Like Lasswell he was a great talker, though not a particularly great lecturer. He would be talking with a student, oblivious to time although alert to every idea—half-baked or one-third baked—that the student might advance. Then he would look at his watch and remark apologetically that it was 3 hours past dinner time; or keep the conversation going with an out-of-town visitor until Mrs. Lewin glided in and mildly reproved him for keeping someone, just off the train, up until 2 a.m. But unlike Lasswell, he never seemed to feel he was on stage when he talked. His conversation was never one-way. Lasswell took over the conversation, directed it, often monopolized it, made a virtuoso performance of it. Lewin was completely unselfconscious as he talked, caught up in the idea he was trying to X-ray, or the problem he was trying to solve. At Stanford they tell a story about a late afternoon seminar when Lewin stretched out on a table at the front of the classroom and kept the class going from there.[3] It was a very un-German, very un-Stanford thing to do, and the people who knew him best say it never happened. But it was not wholly out of character for Lewin. He was probably tired. He was not self-conscious. The class and the discussion were important to Lewin, so they went on.

If Lasswell was shy, Lewin was humble. Clearly one of the great psychologists of the world, he was nevertheless deeply modest about what he knew. He encouraged even us young fellows to speak our ideas fully and to work through an idea. His classes and his office meetings were places for wonderful exchanges of ideas and plans. Exchanges. Not monologues. His side of the talk might be in broken English or fractured German; that didn't bother him or us. Most of the chalkboard was for us to sketch out our own foggy ideas, but he always kept one corner of the board so that at the proper time he could recast our ideas, turn them upside down, sharpen them, develop them, show something about them that had never occurred to us. Lasswell overwhelmed some of his students, sometimes discouraged them by his sheer brilliance. Overall, Lewin excited them. One could hardly come out of one of his sessions without wanting to rush away and do an experiment!

But what one remembers most clearly from meetings and classes with Kurt Lewin, beyond the power of his field theory (which we shall talk about a little later), is the breadth of his interest and the intensity of his drive—qualities that come through in the Lewinian quotation at the beginning of this chapter. Lewin felt that a psychologist is challenged to understand everything about human behavior and human motivation, and nothing in the world is more exciting than that challenge.

Lewin's Career

How did Kurt Lewin get that way? I was not really as close to him in his later years (or in his early years in Europe) as I was to some of the other pioneers we talk about in this book. I was on his campus for several years before being called away for wartime service, and then lost contact with him after the war, especially in his last years at MIT. Look at his life dates: Born 1890, died 1947. Born 11 years before Lasswell, 12 years before Lazarsfeld, 22 years before Hovland. He was in the breaking wave of modern psychology, and his career ended relatively early in the history of communication research.

He was born in Posen, which was then a small town in Prussia, now a part of Poland. His father ran the general store. The family was Jewish, which was even then a handicap to a young man's career in Germany. But this young man committed himself rather early to an academic or professional career. After trying the Universities of Freiburg and Munich, he went to the University of Berlin, where he found the place he really wanted to be, and studied right through to the doctorate.

At the time, German universities were still organized in the four medieval faculties—theology, jurisprudence, medicine, and philosophy. Anything that could not be called one of the first three was assigned to philosophy—including all the natural sciences, the social sciences, and the humanities. Lewin studied philosophy, but the part of it that excited him most was the theory of science; and later a new field that did social and laboratory research in the spirit of the natural sciences—psychology.

At Berlin, as elsewhere at that time, most of the professors lectured and the students filled notebooks with paraphrases of what they heard. But this was changing somewhat with the emergence of research laboratories and

institutes separate from the departments. The chief psychological laboratory in Germany (at Leipzig) was in the charge of the famous Wilhelm
Wundt; his psychology was psychophysics. Lewin was attracted by a new
laboratory at Berlin under Wilhelm Stumpf, where a new approach to
human behavior called Gestalt psychology was beginning to emerge. Kurt
Koffka, Wolfgang Köhler, and Max Wertheimer were there, and these men
had the courage to study what they called "questions of the soul" (Marrow,
1969, p. 8). This was the intellectual home that Lewin had been looking
for. Even more than Koffka or Köhler, Lewin criticized conventional
approaches to human behavior, and it was to the credit of the psychology
laboratory that he was permitted freely to do so. He chose Stumpf as his
"thesis-father," (see Marrow, 1969, p. 7) and conducted research in what
we would now call social psychology, meaning that he wanted to study
questions of human behavior and human relations that had previously been
considered beneath "hard" scientists and too empirical for philosophers.

In 1914, Lewin completed requirements for the PhD degree and then
promptly entered the German army, from which he retired in 1918 with an
Iron Cross for bravery—although to us who knew him in the 1930s, he
seemed a most unlikely soldier (Marrow, 1969, p. 10). He returned to
teaching in the Psychological Institute at the University of Berlin. By that
time, Gestalt Psychology was flourishing, and he found the holism perspective congenial—the idea that one could think of perceptions as organized
wholes, different from the sum of their parts (Marrow, 1969, p. 13). One
year he would lecture in philosophy and have a seminar in psychology; the
next year he reversed the combination (Marrow, 1969, p. 17). But Horace
Kallen, who knew him in 1923, said that whereas Köhler, Koffka, and
Wertheimer were philosophers first and psychologists second, Lewin was
"psychologist first and coincidentally a philosopher of the mind" (Marrow,
1969, p. 17). He was centrally interested in motivation rather than perception—in experiments that would apply psychological theory to behavior.
Unlike most of the Gestaltists around him, he was basically concerned with
practical applications.

The untold story of this period in his life was his struggle to make an
academic career despite his Jewish background, and to make that career in
Germany where psychology was of the highest quality, but where life for
Jewish psychologists was becoming less and less tolerable. He had to leave
Germany, in fact, to flee from it in 1933. Lewin, despite his brilliance,
never moved higher on the academic ladder than Associate Professor
without Civil Service Rank,[4] which was not a permanent appointment but
was the highest level that a Jewish person could hope for. He sublimated

his personal problems with prejudice and concentrated on his scholarly growth.

Some of his students recalled what he was like as a teacher at that time, and because their experience was so much like the later experience of his American students, I am going to quote some of their recollections. He was an "apple-cheeked young man," they said (Marrow, 1969, p. 23). Initially, they were not greatly impressed by his lectures, which they compared unfavorably with the brilliant and polished talks of Köhler and others. But they quickly forgot his word skills in the brilliance of his ideas. "We would sit . . . completely absorbed, as Lewin began to develop his train of thought," Vera Mahler said. "I shouldn't say he lectured—he really didn't do it in a conventional, well-organized manner. He was creating as he was speaking. He would sometimes pause in mid-sentence and seem to forget his audience. Then he would pour forth new ideas that were coming into his mind" (in Marrow, 1969, p. 23).

The *Quasselstrippe*

He and his students soon held regular meetings every Saturday. They started in the morning and sometimes went on until late evening. The same custom appeared later at Iowa and at MIT when he went there to teach. Norman Maier, who was later at Michigan, recalled those meetings. "The interaction between Lewin and this group of students was so free, and the disagreement so intense, that I remember them as one of the most stimulating experiences I have ever had," he said.

> Historical approaches to psychological questions were swept aside. It seemed as if all questions were being approached from scratch. . . . These were creative discussions during which ideas and theories were generated, explored, and controverted. I'm sure that Lewin owes much to his students in working through the theories he himself finally reached. (quoted in Marrow, 1969, p. 24)

Move the time up 15 years, and change the location to the American Midwest where Kurt was on faculty of the University of Iowa. He still created as he lectured. His most important contacts still occurred at informal meetings outside of the classroom. In Berlin, the group was called the "*Quasselstrippe.*" "*Quassel*" means to ramble on; "*strippe*" is a string (Marrow, 1969, p. 26). Even without perfect translation the idea comes through. In Iowa City, it was called the "Hot Air Club"[5] and met in the top-floor room of a restaurant where a kind proprietor in those Depression years let students bring their own lunches if they would just buy coffee or tea. The talk went on as long as it had in Berlin, which was usually until Lewin would look at his watch—after 8 hours or so—and express mock regret for keeping everyone so late. The picture that his students remember of the Hot Air Club is people sitting on the floor with pencils in four colors to sketch out topological diagrams. Every line was likely to be challenged; every interpretation had to be defended.

"Kurt was right in imputing creativity to the collective," Donald Adams said. "[But] there was no doubt [in anyone's mind that] he [Lewin] was the indispensable member. He neither dominated nor overwhelmed, but his willingness to grant an enthusiastic hearing to even the most adventurous speculation supplied the ferment that made each participant rise above himself" (quoted in Marrow, 1969, pp. 26-27). Donald MacKinnon said that the group around Lewin was as loyal as the group around Freud, but there was an important difference. Freud required loyalty and conformity to his views.

> As a result, the inevitable apostasies against Freud were very messy, whereas people could move out of Lewin's immediate circle . . . and still maintain ties with him and others in his circle. If you drifted away, you wouldn't feel guilty about it, and you weren't accused of disloyalty." (quoted in Marrow, 1969, p. 89)

The Berlin Research

The *Quasselstrippe,* and later the Hot Air Club at Iowa, centered on the field theory that Lewin was developing as a framework for much of his scholarship. Lewin's admirer, Alfred Marrow, cites an account by Don MacKinnon as to how the well-known experiment on the Zeigarnik effect was designated. At this time, Lewin was still in Berlin.

> As is the custom in European cafes, you have a cup of coffee and talk and chat, and then you order a piece of cake, more time goes by, some more cake, another cup of coffee, a process that may go on for two or three hours. On one such occasion, somebody called for the bill and the waiter knew just what everyone had ordered. Although he hadn't kept a written reckoning, he presented an exact tally to everyone when the bill was called for. About a half hour later Lewin called the waiter over and asked him to write the check again. The waiter was indignant. "I don't know any longer what you people ordered," he said. "You paid your bill." (MacKinnon, quoted in Marrow, 1969, p. 27)

Lewin saw this behavior instantly as an effect of tension systems, organized by goal-directed activities, on the memory process. Lewin's group began to discuss the significance of what they had observed and how it could be studied through experiments. The result was a doctoral dissertation by Bluma Zeigarnik, under Lewin's direction, on what came to be called the "Zeigarnik effect"—the greater likelihood of being able to recall uncompleted tasks than completed ones (Zeigarnik, 1927). It was only one of many topics studied by the *Quasselstrippe*. Another famous study, for example, dealt with the conditions for arousing anger (Dembo, 1931). These experiments helped make the career of Lewin in Europe, and they illustrate how a Lewinian study group worked.

Zeigarnik's experiment, like most of the others that came out of Lewin's group, was designed against the background of what came to be called "field theory." Lewin wrote a thoughtful book on his theoretical approach (Lewin, 1951), and this is hardly the place to try to do in brief what took Kurt Lewin a book to explain.

Migration to America

Lewin's career in Germany was perilously near an end before any of his writing on field theory got into print. He was becoming well-known in Europe, both as a researcher and a teacher, he was able to attract bright students, encourage interesting research, and to produce well-trained doctoral students. But even as he became better known outside of Germany, he became less welcome inside Germany. It is not a pretty story. He was invited to read a paper at the International Congress of Psychology held at Yale in 1929 (Lewin, 1929). Even though the paper was read in German, it still made a strong impression on American psychologists. Articles began to appear about him in English language journals (e.g., Brown, 1929). In 1932 he was invited to teach for a term at Stanford University. His title was Visiting Professor, and he noted ironically that it was the first real academic appointment that he had been able to get. At Stanford, as later at Iowa, his fractured English made some hilarious moments for his students. Once when one of his ideas had been challenged by a new student, he listened carefully, and then replied quietly, "Can be. But I sink absolute ozzer" (Marrow, 1969, p. 66). His students picked up the phrase and thereafter whenever we heard a discussion or an argument at a learned society meeting punctuated by "Can be. But I sink absolute ozzer," we knew that one or more Lewinians were in the group. His students took somewhat unfair advantage of him by teaching him what they explained was "better English." One thing they told him was that the preferred way to say in English that someone had "said a lot," was "slobbered a bibful." Soon afterward, a visiting scholar came to the campus, and after the lecture Lewin rose from the audience to compliment the speaker. "Professor So-and-So has slobbered a bibful," he said appreciatively. The meeting broke up.[6]

Developments occurring in Germany made it more and more difficult for Lewin to return.[7] "*Juden heraus!*"—"Jews, get out!"—resounded in the streets. The University of Berlin was closed three times because of rioting. But Lewin *had* to go back because his wife was about to have a baby. He had a difficult time getting their medical doctor to attend to her—non-Jewish doctors were not supposed to treat Jewish patients—but Lewin managed it, and as soon as possible thereafter brought his family to America. Then, and for some years afterward, he made every effort to bring his mother out of Germany. These efforts were in vain, and in the early 1940s he learned that she had died in, or near, one of the concentration camps.

The early 1930s was less than an ideal time to immigrate. The Depression froze jobs in America. A foundation financed two years for Lewin at Cornell, where, as quietly as before, he designed interesting new research and made a deep impression on students.[8] One of the students who remembered him after 50 years was Allen Funt, the originator of the "Candid Camera" television show. Funt was in the early 1930s a $15-a-month research assistant at Cornell, and his only contact with the new German visiting researcher was to observe through a one-way glass some of the techniques used to get foundlings to eat different kinds of food. He made notes on his observations for the visiting professor. Fifty years later when Funt was interviewed for *Psychology Today* by Professor Philip Zimbardo of Stanford University, he remembered that experience and even recalled the German professor's first name. "Kurt Lewin is probably the most influential figure in all of social psychology," Zimbardo told the unaware Funt (Zimbardo, 1985, p. 44).

In 1935, Lewin got an appointment at the Iowa Child Welfare Research Station at the University of Iowa. That was not as incongruous as it may sound. Good research was under way at the Station, and George Stoddard, a competent psychologist who later became president of three different universities, was head of the unit. Lewin was deeply interested in the psychology of childhood. So he settled in at Iowa for 10 years, attracting wonderfully able students as always, leading an exciting research program, and rapidly becoming a national figure in the United States. This eminence gradually drew him away from Iowa. He started two research institutes. One was the Research Center on Group Dynamics, which he established at MIT (although only 2 years of his life were left to develop it) and which moved to the University of Michigan after his death. The other was the Commission on Community Relationships in cooperation with the American Jewish Conference. Whereas Paul Lazarsfeld fled Hitler's Germany and made a completely new career in America, Lewin continued doing what he had been doing in Berlin.[9] Of course, Lewin was 10 years older than Lazarsfeld when he came to the United States, but he maintained the same type of relationships with his students, the same attitudes and interests in research, the same humility as in Europe. When he moved to MIT, the old Berlin-Iowa pattern of Saturday discussions was reestablished, and some of the brightest young psychologists in the country flocked to them. Before the new institute could realize its full potential, however, Lewin died—in 1947.

Lifespace and Field Theory

Let us turn from Lewin's career to his ideas. This is not so very far, however, because his ideas and the students who absorbed them *were* his career, and it was through his ideas and his students, rather than through direct participation in communication activities or by association with communication leaders, that he had his considerable influence on communication study.

People who remember the practical bent of Lewin's experiments on changing food habits in wartime (Lewin, 1942; see also Marrow, 1969) may have to be reminded that he thought of himself primarily as a theorist and that his experiments grew out of new hypotheses and led back to new theory and new applications. It was *new* theory, new insights, that he constantly emphasized. Probably every student who ever studied with Lewin heard him say at some time that theory has two functions—to account for what we know and to point our way to new knowledge (Marrow, 1969, p. 30). "The basic character of science," most of his students remember him saying, "is that eternal attempt to go beyond what is regarded as scientifically accessible at any specific time" (Marrow, 1969, p. 30).[10]

Lewin came from Europe bringing field theory with him. Physicists had begun to think in terms of fields of energy, in which forces operate as a matrix. The Gestalt psychologists had been impressed by this physical approach, but Lewin went much further than they did with it. He was never completely at home with S-R psychology. He was interested more in genotypes than phenotypes (Lewin, 1931). He seldom used large samples, preferring to "look harder at less." He used very little laboratory equipment, preferring to talk with people and observe their interactions. He was very skillful at this. His friends said he had "more critical insight, more depth than most psychoanalysts. You couldn't discuss any psychological problem without his immediately seeing it in a new light" (Marrow, 1969, pp. 40-41).

The concept that Lewin used to humanize field theory was "lifespace." This meant to him the total psychological environment—"all the facts, relationships, forces that have existence for the person at a given time" (Marrow, 1969, p. 35). These include, Marrow said, "needs, goals, unconscious influences, memories, beliefs, events of a political, economic, and social nature, and anything else that might have a direct effect on behavior" (p. 35). Lewin was suspicious of any explanation simpler than that. He was always asking, in the act of trying to interpret a bit of behavior, "Vot haf ve vergotten?"

Lifespace was for him the theater in which the drama of behavior is acted out. He used Einstein's definition of *field*—"a totality of existing facts" that are conceived of as mutually dependent (Marrow, 1969, p. 34). Therefore, relationships within lifespace constitute a system. To explain what happens in this system, he used terms borrowed from physics and mathematics, such as energy, tension, need, valence, and vector.

Needs arise from a lack of equilibrium among forces in the field. Needs give rise to tensions. In Lewin's language, these are not to be avoided but rather are necessary because they release energy and bring about action. Different behaviors have negative or positive valence; that is, they are attractive or unattractive to us. We often find barriers in the path of high-valence behavior. We are torn between positive and negative valences of approximately equal strength, or have to choose between two valences of approximately the same strength but with the same sign—two goods or two evils, so to speak. Not until such conflict is resolved can movement toward the goal be made and equilibrium reestablished.

Because Lewin was determined to find a way to approach *social* science as adequately as physicists had been able to approach natural science, he insisted on considering a large number of variables in order to understand how any individual behaves. He made this relatively complex approach more palatable by example and illustration. He was a sort of genius with pictorial materials, although he was neither professional artist nor photographer. Lewin was especially skillful at following children around with a movie camera and recording bits of action that would illustrate his insights into their behavior. When he first came to the United States in 1929 to give a lecture at the International Congress of Psychology held at Yale, he brought a short film of an 18-month-old girl, Hanna, still walking rather shakily, who wanted to sit down on a large stone. Positive valence. On the other hand, she had learned by experience that it was dangerous to sit down on something that one could not see. Negative valence. So she went around the stone, trying to reduce the temporary conflict in her lifespace. Finally, she solved the problem. Bending down, she looked between her legs at the stone, backed carefully up to it, and sat down safely.

Given this pictorial interest, it is not surprising that Lewin turned to topology to illustrate lifespace. He was trained in mathematics and often thought—so his colleagues said—in a mathematical way. But he was really not much interested in numbers or in using them to statistically analyze data. Leon Festinger, one of his best pupils, said he never saw Lewin doing any statistics.[11] In topology, however, Lewin found a nonquantitative geometry that had a high valence for him, and he used topology diagrams to fill a number of two-dimensional "eggs" with compartments and lines dividing the lifespace. Once when he was giving a lecture at Harvard, Henry Murray asked him how he represented *qualitative* differences in the forces he was representing within the little egg pictures—cognitive, affective, physical, social, and so forth. "In that event," said Lewin in his charming way, "we simply use different colors of chalk" (Marrow, 1969, pp. 137-138).[12] That is why his Iowa students sat on the floor drawing topological diagrams with boxes of colored crayons.

So he found field theory to be a good basis for his concept of lifespace and topology a good way to express his psycho-logic. Still, he would never claim to anyone that he had a theoretical system. He never conceptualized a theoretical relationship and then looked for data to confirm it. Tamara Dembo, who had been his student in Germany and later was his colleague in the United States, said that if you asked Lewin, "How can one do this topologically?" he would invariably reply, "What's the problem? Let's first look at the problem and see whether any of this is possible" (in Marrow, 1969, p. 40).

He held up before his students not so much a theory as a challenge of finding methods to solve the kinds of problems that psychologists had not yet found ways to study: such complex problems as the meaning of success and failure, the nature of anger, the nature of different forms of motivation, the meaning of levels of aspiration, and the nature of substitute goals and substitute actions.

The Iowa Research

Because he had a close relationship with his students, they took up problems such as these and wrestled with them. The dissertations produced by his students at the University of Berlin in the late 1920s and early 1930s were some of the most remarkable student work in the history of psychology. The studies produced at Iowa in the next decade were just as distinguished, although they emphasized somewhat different topics. The Berlin students worked chiefly on problems suggested by the concept of lifespace, the Iowa students chiefly on topics built around group relationships.[13] His MIT experience was so brief that what it might have produced is but a tantalizing speculation.

The first important Iowa study that he directed concerned the effect of frustration on child development (remember that he was working in the Iowa *Child Welfare* Research Station). Roger Barker, Tamara Dembo, and Lewin observed children at various ages between 2 and 6 years under conditions when each child was or was not frustrated (Barker, Dembo, & Lewin, 1941; Lewin, Barker, & Dembo, 1937). The frustration was usually achieved by putting up a wire fence in front of toys that the children wanted to play with. Every effort was made, as Lewin had so long advocated, to understand the behavior of these children in terms of their total psychological environment at the moment. The results were a historic step forward in child study. Frustration was found to result in "an average regression in the level of intellectual functioning, in increased unhappiness, restlessness, and destructiveness, in increased ultra-group unity, and increased out-group aggression . . . all related to the strength of frustration" (p. 15).

If these conclusions sound familiar in psychological reports, the second important Iowa study sounds far more familiar: The Lippitt-White study of autocratic versus democratic leadership in children's groups (Lippitt & White, 1940; see also Lippitt, 1940; Lewin, Lippitt, & White, 1939). Two groups of students met 11 times, after school, with Ron Lippitt as leader. In one group he played the part of an autocratic, authoritarian leader; in the other, of a democratic leader who permitted an open atmosphere within the group. The differences were striking. The experiment was repeated with more groups and tighter controls. The conclusions were confirmed: The autocratic mode resulted in less initiative, greater discontent, more aggression, and less group unity. When children were transferred from the autocratic to the democratic situation, they greatly preferred the new group, but some of them became vaguely uneasy because they missed central direction and because fewer tasks were specified for them. When children were transferred from the democratic to the autocratic group, however, said Lewin,

> The group that had formerly been friendly, open, cooperative, and full of life, became within a short half-hour a rather apathetic-looking gathering without initiative. The change from autocracy to democracy seemed to take somewhat more time than that from democracy to autocracy. Autocracy is imposed on the individual. Democracy he has to learn! (Marrow, 1969, p. 127)

Group Dynamics

As a result of these experiments, the new element that was emphasized in the Iowa studies was the *group*. The basic concepts of lifespace and field of forces were unchanged. But now the group became central in a series of Lewin's important investigations. With this importance of the group, Lewin influenced the development of communication research and practice.

As a matter of fact, the more that Lewin's experiments came to focus on group activity, the more he was compelled to think about communication. In particular, when he came to his series of food studies at the beginning of the World War II years, he had to face squarely the need to understand communication as a part of group structure and function.

The food experiments were practical as well as theoretical (Lewin, 1942, 1943). They were vital to conservation during the time of wartime food shortages. The anthropologist Margaret Mead was one of the persons instrumental in turning Lewin to this kind of research. She was serving as secretary of the Committee on Food Habits of the National Research Council. The committee was trying to help the federal government teach people to conserve food—in particular to eat unusual cuts of meat that Americans had usually not deigned to eat. Margaret knew of Lewin's work. So she flew out to Iowa City from Washington on a C-47 that arrived just as the sun set on the prairie. She loved the atmosphere of the Hot Air Club and would often stay at Iowa for several days to work with Lewin and his students on hypotheses that she saw as important, and they saw as feasible, to study. The result of this planning was a series of classic experiments. The central finding from these food studies, reflected in a variety of practical programs throughout the world, was the importance of group decision as a means of individual social change. "Motivation alone does not suffice to lead to change," Lewin said later, summing it up.

This link is provided by decisions. A process such as decision-making, which takes only a few minutes, is able to affect conduct for many months to come. The decision seems to have a "freezing" effect which is partly due to the individual's tendency to "stick to his decision," and partly to the "commitment to a group.' "[14]

In other words, the Iowa experiments showed that a discussion group has far less change effect than a decision group, and public commitment to change within the group has the most effect of all.

In Canada, in India, and in Ghana during the last 20 years, I have heard these findings repeated to me as guides for the radio farm forums that were designed to help modernize agriculture in those countries. "A man named Lewin found this out," P. V. Krishnamoorthy told me in Poona, India.[15]

As World War II went on, the research of the Iowa group took a new turn: from studies of how to get people to eat less popular but more plentiful cuts of meat to studies of how to improve the human aspects of industry. Alex Bavelas had been one of the leaders in the food studies because of his great skill in leading groups, and he was also one of the innovators in the organization studies. He, John French, and others were soon able to confirm the group-decision hypothesis in factories (French, 1950; French & Coch, 1948; French & Marrow, 1945). They found that workers who were allowed to "pace themselves" as long as they were above a certain production quota were both happier and more productive. One of the problems raised by this and similar innovations in the management of workers was how to change the stereotypes held by supervisors: If more of the decision-making power were to be shifted to workers, then the supervisors had to revise their concepts of their own jobs. The researchers soon discovered, however, that it did very little good to *tell* the supervisors this: They had to be put into a situation where they would see for themselves what was needed. So the supervisors were encouraged to undertake a "research project" of their own. This project led to an impressive amount of behavior change; most of the supervisors did adopt a new management role for themselves.

A related problem was leadership training (e.g., Lewin & Bavelas, 1942). From the earlier experiments, Lewin and his group expected that lectures and rhetoric would not be very effective in change. Role-playing, problem solving, and group decisions would be far more useful. That is what they found. Self-examination, feedback, confidence building, group problem solving were the techniques that proved superior in achieving change. These were precisely the techniques introduced by French at the beginning of the National Training Laboratories (NTL) held at Bethel, Maine, in 1947. The basic principle of NTL came out of the long effort by Lewin and his colleagues to understand the problems of overcoming resistance to change. If a person were allowed to *participate* in the process of decision making, the individual's morale would be higher, the level of aggression would be lower, and change would be more likely to occur (French & Coch, 1948).

This kind of research and training activity came to be called "group dynamics." The name carried forward when Lewin succeeded in financing a research center at MIT in 1945 called the Research Center for Group Dynamics. Lewin took some of his best assistants with him to the new post at MIT—Bavelas, Festinger, Lippitt, among others. As usual, he attracted talented doctoral student recruits: Harold H. Kelley, Morton Deutsch, John Thibaut, to name a few. By group decision—as we might expect—Lewin and his people decided on six problem areas that were investigated at the Research Center for Group Dynamics.[16] One area was communication, with Leon Festinger, Stanley Schachter, and Kurt Back taking chief responsibility for it (Festinger, Schachter, & Back, 1950).

The MIT venture was promising, and it was a pity that Lewin had so little time left to give it. But he had too many responsibilities. He was busy trying to organize a new activity, parallel to the MIT venture, but concerned with community and ethnic prejudice. On the east coast, he observed the growing number of "incidents" involving Jewish and non-Jewish young people. He threw himself with his usual energy into starting the Commission on Community Interrelations to conduct studies of gang behavior, group loyalty, how to handle bigots, how to develop a community self-survey instrument, and ultimately to develop and apply sensitivity training to overcome prejudice.

But he was overburdened and overcommitted. During the last years at Iowa, preoccupied with the problems of giving advice to action programs and with his desire to fund and organize the two new research institutes, he repeatedly made the 24-hour trip by train to Washington, D.C., or New York. His absences from the Iowa City campus, of course, neither endeared him to faculty colleagues nor conserved his energy. His friends noted signs of increasing tension and exhaustion at MIT. On February 11, 1947, he put his head down on his arms to rest. Friends, coming by the office, thought he might have collapsed. But he said he was all right and went home. That evening he died.

The Research Center for Group Dynamics moved to Michigan without him. When Lewin was no longer present, people realized what they had lost. At his memorial service,[17] Edward Tolman, the theorist of learning, spoke of the excitement he felt at "Lewin's originality and courage in carrying out experiments under precisely controlled conditions on such problems as the effects of different types of leadership, of war morale, of eating habits, of worker productivity, and of intergroup conflict and community tensions." Gordon Allport, the psychologist of attitudes, listed concepts that psychologists had widely adopted from Lewin: the dynamic power of unfinished tasks (the Zeigarnik effect), escape from the field, level of aspiration, differentiation, detour, time perspective, cognitive structures, levels of reality, barrier, rigidity, satiation, lifespace, marginal affiliation, group decision, change experiment.[18] Margaret Mead later said, "Lewin and his group represented something wholly alive and significant for the whole country" (quoted in Marrow, 1969, p. 223).

But if the excitement of the research program had come from Lewin's ideas, the glory of it was the quality of the young scholars who came into it and continued to work on the growing edges of social psychology that Lewin had pointed out to them. These people talked about him in a way that any teacher would love to hear from students. They recalled that he always worked *with* them but seldom put his name on their papers, as senior professors sometimes do; that he was usually a jump ahead of them, but always genuinely delighted when one of *them* had an insight new to *him*. "95 percent of today's social psychology is Kurt Lewin's and the interest he inspired in group dynamics," said Festinger (in Marrow, 1969, p. 232). French wrote, "Somehow he seemed to be able to transmit to others a little of his own enormous creativity" (in Marrow, 1969, p. 235).

Contributions to Communication Study

How can we sum up Lewin's relationship to communication study? Lasswell was *always* in that field, but Lewin was *never* in it. Neither statement is accurate. It is true that Lewin did not talk much about communication and never set it up formally as part of his thinking until he and his followers made it one of the six research topics at the MIT Research Center for Group Dynamics. Rather, he *assumed* communication. It was part of all the human relationships that he dealt with. In the experiments on social change at Iowa, he had to deal directly with communication— information and persuasion, lecture versus discussion, discussion versus commitment, and the like. He usually dealt with these in a macro way. Given enough years, he might have felt it necessary to analyze the kind of communication that takes place in a group, such as in a gang encounter or in a decision situation. Certainly many of his students went in that direction. Bavelas, for example, examined the networks of communication in small groups and gathered fascinating data on the effect of different patterns of communication within a group on the group's morale and its ability to carry out tasks (Bavelas, 1949). Festinger studied the flow of rumor through a community, and the reaction of "true believers" when the mass media failed to confirm a cult's prediction that the world would end on a certain day (Festinger et al., 1948; Festinger, Reicken, & Schachter, 1956). Festinger's *A Theory of Cognitive Dissonance* (1957) draws on Lewin and belongs in the current of thought represented by Heider's balance theory, Newcomb's A-B-X model, Osgood and Tannenbaum's congruity theory, McGuire and others' consistency theory, and even Hovland's 1960 volume on persuasion (Rosenberg & Hovland, 1960; Zajonc, 1960). Lewin's former students and colleagues are among the most prolific and most highly respected of modern social scientists contributing to the deeper understanding of human communication.

If we want a short-form definition of Lewin's contribution to communication study, I think we can say that he did more than anyone else to put the group into communication theory and research, and more than anyone else to show us who to study and to use communication for bringing about targeted social change. Beyond that, we have reason to be grateful for the many concepts that we borrowed from Lewin and that became accepted parts of communication theory and research. One of these, for example, is the idea of communication *gatekeepers* (see, for example, White, 1950).[19]

It may be just an accident, or it may tell us something about the man, that a high proportion of the remembered stories about Lewin are communication stories. Previously, I told you about "slobber a bibful" and "sink absolute ozzer." In conclusion, let me tell you one more such story. Lewin was visiting Harvard to give some lectures and became ill. Gordon Allport came to take him to the campus infirmary for treatment. They went out to the elevator. Lewin was bundled up and walking unsteadily. The elevator came, and a man, hair flying, dashed frantically out of it. "How do you get out of this damn trap?" he demanded, "I've been going up and down and can't make it behave!" Allport recognized the man as Bertrand Russell, also a visitor at Harvard that week. Allport thought over the situation. Here were two persons he should certainly introduce to each other. On the other hand, they were also two of the world's greatest and most voluminous talkers. If he introduced them, would Lewin ever get to the doctor and would Russell ever get to the right floor? Would they even get in the elevator door? He put them into the elevator without telling either who the other was (Marrow, 1969, p. 137).

That is why Lewin got treated for his influenza on that cold night in Cambridge. Whether he ever had a talk with Bertrand Russell, I do not know.

Notes

1. Most of the anecdotes about Kurt Lewin are quoted from the biography by Marrow (1969).

2. Some portion of the text here is different from Marrow's version. The original source is Kurt Lewin (1940).

3. This episode is quoted from an interview with Roger Barker in Marrow (1969, p. 66).

4. He was given the title of *Ausserordentlicher nicht beamteter Professor* in 1927 (Marrow, 1969, p. 54).

5. This is the translation of *Quasselstrippe* by the Iowa students (Marrow, 1969, p. 88).

6. This anecdote was recalled by Ronald Lippitt (in Marrow, 1969, p. 88). According to Lippitt, the two graduate students who told Lewin this phrase were Alex Bavelas and Harold Sheels.

7. The harsh situation in Germany is described in Chapter 7 of Marrow (1969).

8. The foundation was the Emergency Committee on Displaced Scholars, funded by the Rockefeller Foundation.

9. Editors' Note: Lewin's research in the United States was more social psychological than his investigations in Berlin, which centered on individual psychology (Rogers, 1994).

10. Marrow (1969) wrote that Lewin "ascribed this attitude toward science to Ernest Cassirer" (p. 30).

11. Marrow (1969) said, "Lewin had little use for statistics, according to Festinger, who 'never saw him do mathematics' and never knew if he was 'much of a mathematician.' 'But,' says Festinger, 'we started very early to argue about statistics' " (p. 106).

12. Lewin visited Harvard in 1936. This episode was described by Gardner Murphy in Marrow (1969).

13. A list of Berlin and Iowa dissertations is provided by Marrow (1969) in Appendices B and D of Lewin's biography.

14. Editors' Note: Lewin's comment seems to have been made about a series of experiments at the Harwood Manufacturing Corporation by Alex Bavelas and others, rather than about the food studies (Marrow, 1969, p. 144).

15. Editors' Note: The link from Lewin's Iowa studies on changing food habits to the radio farm forums in India was Dr. Paul Neurath, a colleague of Lazarsfeld's in Vienna and New York, who led the study of radio farm forums in Poona, sponsored by the United Nations Educational, Scientific and Cultural Organization (UNESCO).

16. According to Marrow (1969) these areas were (a) group productivity, (b) communication, (c) social perception, (d) intergroup relations, (e) group membership and individual adjustment, and (f) the training of leaders and the improvement of group functioning.

17. Held for Lewin by the Society for the Psychological Study of Social Issues during the 1947 convention of the American Psychological Association.

18. Tolman's and Allport's speeches are quoted in Marrow (1969, pp. 228-230). The third speaker was Marrow.

19. Lewin is also cited as the source of the gatekeeping concept in Donohue, Tichenor, and Olien (1972). The reference is Kurt Lewin (1951).

5

Carl Hovland

Experiments, Attitudes, and Communication

When one of my Stanford classes asked a longtime colleague of Carl Hovland's, Nathan Maccoby, what he remembered best about Carl, the answer came without hesitation: "He was unquestionably the world's most non-authoritarian leader." My students looked a bit disappointed. They probably expected a remembered incident, or the kind of reminiscence that Rosten reproduced so amusingly about Lasswell, or perhaps the kind of word-picture that I gave you in the preceding chapter about Lewin and the Hot Air Club. But what they heard may have been the fairest and most accurate picture of Carl that could possibly have been drawn. For there was nothing really odd or spectacular or side-splittingly funny about Carl Hovland. He was a leader and he was not flamboyant. He was not "a character." He did not convulse his students with language mistakes, as Lewin sometimes did. He did not talk for 6 hours nonstop, as Rosten reports

Carl Hovland

Lasswell doing. Actually, Hovland's talk was economical and to the point
with few words wasted. He did not forget the time and dinner hours, as
great (and absent-minded) scholars are supposed to do. I have gone perhaps
a half dozen times to Morey's, the famous drinking and talking place in
New Haven. (Are you too young to remember Rudy Vallee singing the
"Whiffenpoof Song"—"At the tables down at Morey's, the place we love

so well"?) In all of these visits I didn't hear one hilarious story about Carl Hovland. From all the hours that I spent with him, I can't remember one funny anecdote worth telling. He was simply one of the nicest and brightest men, and one of the best researchers whom I have ever known. He was the kind of leader whom everyone except the newest newcomer to the laboratory called "Carl," but always with the greatest respect.

If you were to put in front of me one of Charles Osgood's semantic differential scales and ask me to fill it out to best describe Hovland, I suppose *quiet* would get the maximum score, as would *calm*—his intensity was all inside. *Friendly, kind, helpful, whimsical* all described Hovland's behavior. There would be high ratings for adjectives such as *sharp, bright, systematic,* and *careful.* On the other hand, another list of adjectives—*spectacular, funny, eloquent, fiery, committed, effervescent, dramatic,* and *electrifying*—would get low ratings. I would have a hard time scoring terms such as *exciting* or *excited.* Excited Hovland certainly was when he was designing or interpreting an experiment, and yet he kept the excitement bottled up. Working with Carl was one of the exciting experiences in communication research; yet he had no grand scheme to present, as Lewin did, and he had few of the entrepreneurial qualities of Lazarsfeld. *Entrepreneur? Salesman?* I supposed he would get a low rating on these dimensions, yet he never had trouble raising money when it was needed to finance the large communication research program at Yale.[1]

Perhaps we should note that the first descriptive term that Carl's old friend, Nathan Maccoby, settled on when he met with my Stanford class and was asked about Carl was *leader.* Carl was clearly and unquestionably a leader. For 15 years at Yale, he led one of the best communication research groups in the world. He introduced a phenomenal number of very bright students to research on communication. He coauthored half a dozen of the top communication research books in the field. And he did all this quietly—speaking quietly, moving quietly, persuading quietly, leading by example and intellectual challenge rather than by executive order or vested authority.

Hovland's Early Career

He was unlike Lazarsfeld in many ways, not the least of which being the fact that when they moved into the field of communication study, Hovland continued to think and work like an experimental psychologist, whereas Lazarsfeld continued to feel and act like a survey sociologist. Hovland and

Lazarsfeld were alike in the respect that each made a significant midstream change of career.

In 1933, at the age of 32, when he came to America and moved into communication research, Lazarsfeld had a doctorate in mathematics and a close relationship to some of the best psychologists in Vienna. In 1942, at the age of 30 when Hovland went to Washington, D.C., and moved into communication research, he was one of the leading young experimental psychologists of learning in America. He had reached that pinnacle quietly, without fanfare, as he did everything else. He was born in Chicago (in 1912), went to Northwestern for his first two degrees, then to Yale for doctoral training. As both Lazarsfeld and Lewin, he had a strong back-ground in mathematics, physics, and biology, although he did not have Lazarsfeld's doctorate in mathematics or Lewin's deep acquaintance with philosophy. Of the four pioneers we talk about in this book, he was the only one on whom Freud did not have much effect.[2]

Rather, the chief scholarly influence on Hovland came from Clark Hull's rigorous program of research at Yale. Hull at that time was dean of American scholars of learning and motivation. Hovland was Hull's re-search assistant, and as soon as he took his PhD in 1936 (Hovland, 1936), became Hull's coinvestigator in the notable series of studies of human learning that led to the book *Mathematico-Deductive Theory of Rote Learning* (Hull, Hovland, Ross, Hall, Donald, & Fitch, 1940). Hovland's name appears first among the other authors of that volume, and inasmuch as the names are not in alphabetical order, that placement is significant. Irving Janis said that Hovland contributed to the work not as much by suggesting comprehensive theoretical insights—à la Lewin or Hull him-self—but rather through "discovering new functional relationships by working closely with the available findings, noting inconsistencies and reversals that others might be inclined to overlook, and then proceeding to unravel the puzzles by ingeniously testing a series of alternate explanations with a new set of data."

This sounds very much like the kind of work that Hovland was doing 10 years later, working with data on human communication. The break in Carl's career in 1942 was not so much a change in the way he *did* research as in what he did research *on.*

When Hovland was learning to be an experimental psychologist at Yale in the 1930s, he had the example not only of senior scholars such as Hull but also of younger scholars such as Donald Marquis, Kenneth Spence, Ernest Hilgard, John Dollard, Neil E. Miller, and O. H. Mowrer, who were on the New Haven campus during the same years and making important contributions to learning theory. Leonard Doob, George Murdock, Robert Sears, and John Whiting were other contemporaries of Hovland's at Yale. Another source of intellectual influence was the distinguished parade of visitors who spent a year or more at the Yale Institute of Human Relations—that created the Human Relations Area Files (Ember, 1988; Levinson, 1988). One of this institute's purposes was to encourage interdisciplinary development, and so Hovland had the opportunity to become well-acquainted with the ideas of Edward Sapir, the anthropologist and language scholar who came from Chicago (see Chapter 1); Robert Yerkes, who left (for a time) his studies of primates in Florida; Walter Miles; Dusser de Barenne from France; and others. These contacts in the Institute of Human Relations may have been less of an interdisciplinary experience for Hovland than Lasswell, Lazarsfeld, and Lewin had, but it was a significant influence on a Chicago boy who had completed all of his education in the United States.

When Hovland left Yale to go into wartime communication research in 1942, his chief journal publications had not been on communication or attitudes but were rather a series of articles on the generalization of conditioned response. In addition to his role on the important 1940 volume on learning, Hovland collaborated in a 1939 volume on *Frustration and Aggression,* of which John Dollard was chief author (Dollard, Miller, Doob, Mowrer, & Sears, 1939).[3] Hovland taught young psychologists at Yale and played an active part in a number of laboratory studies. It was from this background that he made a significant career change brought on by World War II.

The Wartime Research

Hovland was just 30 when he went to Washington in 1942. Lazarsfeld had been 33 when he came to the United States, a refugee from Hitler, and became head of the Rockefeller Foundation-funded Office of Radio Research. Heading a new research institute amidst the New York media, Lazarsfeld saw the opportunity to begin to systematize the new field of communication and attitude research under equally remarkable research conditions.

The fact that a 30-year-old experimental psychologist should be offered the job of studying the effects of persuasive communication for the Army says something both about Hovland's reputation and about the ability of Samuel Stouffer, the Harvard sociologist, to see beyond a rat learning laboratory to the requirements for directing a massive study of human attitudes. In any case, how could a scholar refuse such an invitation during wartime when told his country needs him? So Hovland took leave from Yale, moved to Washington, and found himself in a research situation that most of us could only dream about.

Carl Hovland was assigned to study a field that never before had been systematically examined. It was not that the U.S. Army wanted to build a systematic theory of human communication but, rather, that it needed practical guidance concerning its persuasive instructional messages. Researchers such as Hovland, however, could see the theoretical implications. As Chief Psychologist and Director of Experimental Studies for the Research Branch of the Information and Education Division of the U.S. War Department (fortunately, he did not have to use this title very often!), Hovland was in charge of a research program that could get as much research money (within reason) as it needed. Furthermore, he could move out of the laboratory into the field when necessary and still retain a high degree of control over experimental conditions. He could use very large samples of human subjects on whom large amounts of data were already available, and he didn't have to pay them or persuade them to participate. They could be *commanded* to be there and they would be.

Hovland recruited able young scholars to work in his military laboratory: Irving Janis, Arthur A. Lumsdaine, Nathan Maccoby, Fred D. Sheffield, and M. Brewster Smith. That was quite a group. Janis later headed the research program at Yale, and Sheffield was with him. Lumsdaine has been head of psychology at Washington. Maccoby succeeded me for a time at Stanford. Smith is at the University of California at Santa Cruz and has served as president of the American Psychological Association.[4] Most of these scholars came from Yale. Maccoby had been drafted, given three stripes, and assigned by request to the Army Research Branch under Hovland. Maccoby considered himself, he said, "The luckiest sergeant in the U.S. Army!"

The basic assignment of the Research Branch was to study the nature of morale in the army. Hovland therefore helped Samuel Stouffer and Leonard Cottrell plan a number of large-scale studies that provided data for the post-war volumes on *The American Soldier* and discussion of these research materials (see Hovland, Lumsdaine, & Sheffield, 1949; Merton & Lazarsfeld, 1950; Stouffer et al., 1950; Stouffer, Lumsdaine, Lumsdaine, Williams, Smith, Janis, Star, & Cottrell, 1949; Stouffer, Suchman, DeVinney, Star, & Williams, 1949). His specific assignment was to study the effectiveness of a series of army training films titled "Why We Fight." He went about his task with the same precision and care for detail that he had used in the psychology laboratory at Yale. The war years were not the time to publish theoretical results, but the military studies—reanalyzed, reinterpreted, supplemented—became the raw material of the noted volume *Experiments on Mass Communication,* published in 1949. It was, indeed, the starting point of the Yale Program in Communication and Attitude Change.

How He Did Research

How did Hovland work as a communication researcher? Very much as he did when he was a learning researcher. For example, take the case of the "sleeper effect" (Hovland et al., 1949, p. 71 & chap. 7). Early in their studies of the army training films, Hovland and his associates showed that the films *had* an effect—audiences learned attitudes and beliefs from them.[5] Learning was greater when the audience perceived the communicator to be trustworthy and credible.

How long did the effect persist? Was it long-term or short-term? Would effects of a trustworthy communicator persist longer than those of a less trustworthy source? There was some reason to think that trust in the communicator would contribute to the lasting quality of the attitudes learned as well as to initial learning. An experiment was designed with supposedly trustworthy and untrustworthy communicators (although in the ancient and honorable tradition of experiments, all communicators gave exactly the same message). The audience's learning was measured before, immediately after, and some weeks after exposure to the message.

The results were not what was expected. Persons who learned from the supposedly trustworthy communicators had indeed learned significantly more than the other respondents. That was immediately after seeing the training film. During the next few weeks, the effect on the respondents decreased, as one would expect from the familiar "curve of forgetting." Individuals who had been exposed to the communicator presented as "untrustworthy," however, demonstrated no such loss of effect with time. In fact, several weeks after exposure these individuals seemed to have gained in learning.

These results, as one might imagine, created an intellectual bomb in Hovland's laboratory. There was no good theory to explain them. Some observers doubted the data. Everyone looked for a new theory to explain the apparent discrepancy in long-term communication effects. For want of a better term, the finding was called the *sleeper effect* and was published in the first book from Hovland's post-war Yale laboratory (Hovland, Janis, & Kelley, 1953; Hovland & Weiss, 1951).

Hovland tackled this problem exactly as Janis had described his earlier tactic in the Yale learning laboratory: working closely with the available findings, noting what others might be inclined to overlook, then proceeding to unravel the puzzles by ingeniously testing alternative hypotheses with a new set of data. Hovland began to wonder whether the experimental subjects might have forgotten the communicator as well as the message. What effect would such forgetting have on retention of the desired attitude? So a new experiment was designed, with a large sample and tight controls, and with one important change in the procedures: the reintroduction of the "untrustworthy" communicator at the time of the later measurement. That is, subjects were reminded at that time who had told them what they had heard. When this was done, the results became clear. The previous difference between the effects of the "trustworthy" and the "untrustworthy" communicators was re-established. The "sleeper effect" had a simple explanation. The audience tended to forget not only the message but also from whom they had heard it. As they forgot the low-credibility communicator, they became less likely to reject the attitude change (Kelman & Hovland, 1953; see also Hovland et al., 1953, pp. 256-259).

While not losing sight of theory, Hovland gave the army reliable, detailed evidence on whether the training films were effective, what made them effective, and for what kinds of soldiers in what situations the films were most effective. For example, one of the influential findings that he communicated to the U.S. War Department was on the effect of a one-sided versus two-sided presentation (Hovland et al., 1949, chap. 8). The conclusion was exactly contrary to a basic doctrine of Nazi propaganda—that to be most successful, a persuasive communication should not mention any counterarguments but simply state its own arguments over and over again, buttressing them with emotional appeals. Hovland showed that a two-sided presentation was more persuasive for some people, for example persons initially hostile to the desired point of view, who would consequently suspect the communication message if the arguments *they* had learned were ignored. Persons likely to also be exposed to the other side of the argument, who could to some extent be inoculated against the counter-argument by hearing both sides in advance, and persons better educated than the average and therefore inclined to suspect any persuasion that gave only one side of the argument—in these cases also there is reason to introduce the counter-argument along with the persuasive argument that one desired to "sell" (Hovland et al., 1949, pp. 212-225). Findings such as these were of theoretical interest, but during World War II they were also of great practical usefulness.

At the end of the war, in 1945, Stouffer and Hovland went back to Harvard and Yale. Stouffer became director of the Harvard Laboratory for Social Relations; Hovland, chairman of the psychology department at Yale. In a few years, Hovland was given a prestigious Sterling Professorship, and founded the Yale Program of Research on Communication and Attitude Change. Stouffer told me, with many chuckles, over a long lunch in New York during one of the last weeks of his life, how he and Carl had loaded all of their research data in a large truck and dispatched it to Cambridge and New Haven on the last day of their army careers lest the IBM punch cards all disappear into government storerooms. "Ugly cards," he said, "from which, like the Phoenix, emerged beautiful volumes of research."

Building the Yale Program

Hovland took several of his army research assistants with him to Yale, including Janis, Lumsdaine, and Sheffield. Around this nucleus, as in the case of Lewin and Lazarsfeld, he gathered a remarkable group of bright doctoral students and junior staff whose names later appeared on important communication research. Among these were Herbert Kelman, Harold M. Kelley, William McGuire, Morris Rosenberg, Robert Abelson, Wallace Mandell, Brewster Smith, Walter Weiss, Arthur R. Cohen, Gerald Lesser,[6] and Lloyd Morrisett.[7] Almost without exception, these scholars became professors in leading departments of psychology, and their papers and books are read in classes studying human communication.

A researcher such as Hovland thinks of research design as a multidimensional matrix of interrelated variables. These can be tested against each other in different combinations and, in theory, should be so tested in order to comprehend the entire matrix, but no one has the time, the manpower, or the money to do this. Anyway, it would be wasteful to do so because some combinations of conceptual variables are much more promising than others. Furthermore, one set of interactions suggests other combinations to be tested and other variables to be added, so that "testing everything" turns out to be a task of almost infinite size. Here we see one way in which experimental research is essentially different from survey investigations. An experiment requires one to theorize about certain relationships within a possible matrix of manageable size. Conditioned to experimental studies, I shall not forget the shock when I first heard a well-known sociologist tell his research assistant on a sample survey to "run everything against everything."

When Carl began to design the army communication research program (that later merged into the Yale communication research program), he undoubtedly was asked quite specific questions: Are the army orientation films having any effect? Which films are having more effect than others? How can such effects be maximized? One way to go about answering such questions would be to test one film after another against a dependent variable such as attitude change, but that would be like adding more knots to the same string. It would provide only a limited base for understanding what the War Department really needed to know: What qualities of a training film really make for effectiveness? So to understand the effect of films on attitudes, it was necessary to make the design decisions against a theoretical framework. What variables are most valuable to test, in what order, and in what combinations?

The study of the military training films began by looking at the question of primary interest to the army: Were the films having any effect? They were. Soldiers were learning the desired attitudes from them. Furthermore, it was easy to see from analyzing content against learning that the greatest changes came from topics that were treated directly and specifically. Viewers were more likely to learn what they heard and saw, as opposed to what they could derive from implication. So the Army was given some practical guidance: If its filmmakers wanted to change attitudes, they would be well advised not to depend on indirection and implication but to deal directly and specifically with what they wanted learned (Hovland et al., 1949, pp. 20 & 114-117).

I am sure that when Hovland saw these results on direction versus indirection, he made a mental note to find out whether this relationship holds for all kinds of audiences, especially more versus less highly edu- cated soldiers, and whether it worked for all kinds of subject matter. But these questions were put aside for the moment. The independent variable that seemed most promising to Hovland was the communicator. Most of the films used a narrator; some introduced several commentators. The qualities of these communicators must have made a difference, in particular the degree to which they were trusted and respected by the audience. Therefore, it was promising to make several experimental versions of a film in which the same narrator said the same thing, but in one version of the film, the narrator was described as "trustworthy" and in another version as "not trustworthy." As expected, more attitude change took place when audiences trusted the communicator than when they did not. Furthermore, certain other elements could be teased out of the analysis to enrich the definition of "trustworthiness." Soldiers preferred narrators who were experienced—who had "been there." More important, it appeared that attitudes were more likely to be influenced by scenes of realistic action than by pictures of a narrator merely talking about the topic behind the action (the "talking head"). Closeups of the narrator explaining or persuading actually had little effect unless the speaker was himself especially prestigious or interesting. The viewers in general seemed to be saying, "Don't tell me; show me" (Hovland et al., 1949, chap. 5).

So the U.S. Army had a rich beginning from which to derive practical guidelines, and the researchers had a rich supply of questions to sharpen. It was easy to determine whether viewers considered a certain communicator as trustworthy, but what exactly is "trustworthy"? Is it expertise, experience, being well-meaning, or being well-known? Hovland must have made a mental note to clarify the finding about the effectiveness of action versus the ineffectiveness of implication: Doesn't a considerable amount of implication have to intervene between action pictures and opinion change (see Hovland et al., 1953, chaps. 1 & 8)?

Then there was the question of retention. Learning from the army films was not necessarily permanent learning. Only when retention was added to the communicator credibility experiment did the puzzling "sleeper effect" appear. Long-term effects for persons who heard a trusted communicator were apparently different from the effects for persons who heard a distrusted communicator. This finding had to be put aside and later sorted out when the opportunity arose to do so (Hovland et al., 1949, chap. 7).

We already described the early studies of the persuasive effects of one-sided versus two-sided arguments. Some characteristics of the audience were introduced as intervening variables, for example, their initial position on the question at issue, their level of education, and the likelihood of their being exposed to counter-arguments. These variables made some difference in whether one-sided or two-sided arguments were more effective (Hovland et al., 1949, chap. 8).

Another audience variable, intelligence, was tested against the ability of the audience to make valid interpretations of the persuasive messages. The amount of learning from the films was less than expected, regardless of individuals' intellectual capability. However, more intelligent viewers were more likely to see and learn *valid* interpretations than invalid ones. Less intelligent viewers, probably because they did not fully understand the persuasive argument, were more likely to accept *invalid* interpretations (Hovland et al., 1949, chap. 6).

One other audience variable was tested in Hovland's first Army experiments: audience participation (Hovland et al., 1949, chap. 9). Lewin, of course, had found that group commitment, and an individual's public commitment made in a group, made more difference in communication effects than did group discussion. All of these group variables were more effective than individual reading or viewing of a message. Hovland approached group participation as a learning phenomenon. How much difference does actual practice of an idea make? The army experiments showed that there is more learning when the response is actively practiced by the audience during a film's showing. If responses cannot actually be practiced during a film (for example, it would be difficult to practice auto driving or surfing in a classroom during the presentation of a film), then it helps to rehearse the symbolic responses mentally. One can learn at least *something* about how to dive or to fly an airplane or to shoot a basketball by rehearsing the process in one's imagination with the film as an expert guide.[8] Then, when the individual actually tries the newly learned skill, it will be easier.

These studies were reported in *Experiments on Mass Communication.* How far had Hovland's research program progressed by the time this book was published? Hovland had worked with four variations of the independent variable: one-sided versus two-sided messages, trustworthiness of the communicator, specific versus nonspecific treatment, and the "show versus tell" presentation. Three dependent variables had been examined: attitude learning, retention, and the validity of interpretation. Hovland's military research group had made a start in investigating intervening variables (five audience characteristics): intelligence, formal education, initial attitudes, likelihood of hearing counter-arguments, and participation.

These variables had by no means been tested in all possible combinations or even in all the combinations that promised to be especially meaningful. As a matter of fact, a large number of additional experiments were already called for, and some were on the drawing board. This situation again illustrates one of the differences between working with surveys and with experiments. Surveys are large, expensive, and time-consuming. Unless one is Roper or Gallup, or the Michigan Survey Research Center, one plans few surveys and tries to answer as many questions as possible with each study. Experiments can be programmed to answer a few questions at a time and to interlock with other experiments until the picture comes more completely into focus. Of course, surveys and experiments each have special advantages, but more about that later.

Hovland and his colleagues moved along some of the lines suggested by the first set of experiments and gradually added new questions and new variations. The Yale group's next series of experiments, reported in *Communication and Persuasion,* included, for example, a clarifying chapter on the "sleeper effect": People who had heard the "untrustworthy" communicator tended to forget the communicator and therefore tended to remember the message favorably (Hovland et al., 1953). One related finding was that a person always learns *some* of the argument even though it is originally rejected because the communicator was perceived as untrustworthy. This means that if an argument gets through to an audience, a trace of it will remain as a base for possible attitude change in the future.

In the second volume from their research, the Yale researchers also contributed to the understanding of credibility's effects (Hovland, 1957). What perceived qualities of a communicator make the source's credibility high or low? Is a source more likely to be thought untrustworthy or believed not to be expert on what he or she is talking about? Here Hovland and his group were unable to get a complete answer. So they put the problem aside for further study with additional variables (Hovland et al., 1953, chap. 2).

The Yale scholars returned to the effectiveness of drawing specific conclusions in persuasive messages. They tested specific versus nonspecific conclusions against some audience characteristics. Drawing specific conclusions in the presentation of a message makes the most difference with less intelligent, or less alert, audiences. More intelligent viewers or listeners can be counted on to draw the desired conclusions themselves (Hovland et al., 1953, chap. 4).

They also returned to the one-sided versus two-sided study and tested those treatments against a broader set of variables. They found that they were not studying a general effect. With certain audiences they found that it is better to give only one side of the case. With other audiences, it is better to let them know that you are taking both sides of the case into account, if for no other reason than to "inoculate" them against counter-arguments that they are likely to hear in the future (Hovland et al., 1953, chap. 4).

Hovland and his Yale investigators turned to new problems. One was a favorite tool of the propagandist: fear appeals (Hovland et al., 1953, chap. 3). Hovland's results, however, were not precisely what most propagandists would have predicted: Overall, fear appeals are likely to turn an audience off (Janis & Feshbach, 1953). This principle was applied in toothpaste advertising, which was once full of pictures and descriptions of the grisly results of gum disease and bad-smelling mouths. Better to advertise toothpaste with gleaming white teeth and lovely models' faces, the merchandisers decided. If a persuasive message *does* arouse fear, the Yale researchers concluded, it is important to relieve that fear by suggesting to the audience what to do next; otherwise, the audience is likely to ignore the threat and do nothing. Furthermore, any strong emotional appeal is more useful in eliciting a specific single response than in bringing about sustained attitude change behavior. Therefore, it is better to use fear appeals on special occasions rather than in general.

The Hovland group next added some variations to what they had learned about audience characteristics (Hovland et al., 1953, chap. 6). These studies relate to Lewin's studies of food habits during wartime and illustrate differences in how Hovland and Lewin did research. Hovland always thought about a research problem as a learning theorist would. Lewin saw a situation and sought to understand it holistically. Hovland tried to think of it in terms of variables and examined as many of them as could be efficiently handled in an experimental design. Both might decide on the same variables. Lewin was deeply concerned with the action effects of public commitment in a group; Hovland was thinking of the effects of practice. If an individual audience member verbalized a convincing argument, he hypothesized, that person would be likely to change his or her attitudes in that direction. Similarly, Harold Kelley's experiment with boy scouts concerned the effects of membership in a group and the effects of group loyalties (Kelley, 1952; Kelley & Volkart, 1952). Actually, the Lewin findings fit very well with Kelley's, who concluded that the more highly an individual values group membership, the more likely the individual is to change opinions and behavior so as to conform to the group consensus position and to resist arguments contrary to what the group believes. Therefore, if a communicator wants to present an argument contrary to group consensus, it is well to suggest other loyalties and interests and be rather quiet about the group membership. There was no essential contradiction between Lewin's and Hovland's research on this matter, but it is illuminating to see the different roads that they followed to reach the same conclusion.

These and other persuasion experiments appeared in the second Yale volume, *Communication and Persuasion* (1953). "I feel better about having this represent us," Carl said when he gave me a copy of this 1953 book. Well he might, for he had picked up many of the loose strings from the first volume and tied them in the second. More squares in the matrix were filled, and some important new variables were added.

Attitudes as Dependent Variables

It is impossible to look at a research program such as Hovland's, so logically organized, so intelligently interlocked, without feeling admiration for the minds behind it. Yet one wonders why Hovland was content with attitudes and opinion as dependent variables. He was basically interested in human behavior: Why didn't he insist on overt behavior as a dependent variable? There are a few hints in what he said on occasion. Opinion change could be measured more easily and sharply in the laboratory, and could be related more confidently to theory and practice. Perhaps his best-known comments on this point came in his paper comparing experiments with surveys (Hovland, 1959). Survey research (such as by Lazarsfeld) typically gave the impression in the 1950s that very few people are affected by mass media communication, whereas experimental research on opinion change showed that one-third to one-half of an audience is significantly affected by even a single exposure to a persuasive message. This apparent contradiction, Hovland said, can be accounted for by a number of factors that are too often overlooked. Laboratory experiments use captive audiences, utilize remote or unfamiliar issues in treatment messages, and exclude or control influences other than the primary variables being tested. Field surveys, on the other hand, involve an audience's self-selection from the various messages available and high ego-involvement in at least some of the messages. Audiences in the field are subject to a large number of counter and conflicting influences and inhibitions. That is why Albert Bandura could find striking effects of television violence in the laboratory (Bandura, 1977), but the U.S. Surgeon General's study had a difficult time finding them in society (National Institute of Mental Health, 1972).[9] Hovland's conclusion reminds us of Lewin's favorite question, "Vot haf ve vergotten?" Hovland (1959) said that the two research approaches needed to be used together to cover the field, "combining their virtues so that we may develop a social psychology of communication with the conceptual breadth provided by correlational study of process and the rigorous but more delimited methodology of the experiment" (p. 17).

Hovland was, as we quoted one of his former colleagues, "the world's most non-authoritarian leader." He encouraged his students and younger colleagues to study the scholarly question that most interested them, insisting on theoretical significance and rigor—himself making many incisive contributions to the planning and design. A result of this approach was that after the second volume, the Yale persuasion group began to fill in areas of special interest to some of its members rather than publishing general volumes such as the first two. A number of members became interested in trying to clarify the relation of primacy to recency in their effects on learning and opinion change. Experiments conducted before 1950, although not well controlled and most of them without using statistical tests of significance, had for the most part come out on the side of primacy: It is better to get in the first word. Later studies seemed to be on the other side. The Yale psychologists decided (as reported in *The Order of Presentation in Persuasion;* Hovland, 1957) that they could find no generalizable law of primacy versus recency in persuasion. Sometimes one strategy works better, sometimes the other. When a single communicator presents contradictory information, the items presented *first* tend to dominate audience learning. Similarly, when an authoritative communicator presents both pro and con arguments, the items presented first have a better chance of exerting an effect. When arguments highly acceptable to the recipient are presented first, more opinion change occurs than when less acceptable arguments are presented first. Group surroundings tend to have a considerable effect on primacy. For example, if a member of a group publicly indicates his position after hearing only one side of an argument, the effectiveness of later arguments on the other side is reduced. If a presentation can arouse audience needs first and then show how to satisfy them, that works better than to give the suggestions first, and then arouse the need. This states the general tenor of the findings on primacy and recency. But they were perhaps not as easy to obtain as they sound; they resulted from long hours of thinking and discussion, and some dozens of carefully designed and conducted experiments.

The nature of persuasibility was much debated in the Yale group. Is it an individual characteristic that can be isolated? Are some people more persuadable than others? A number of experiments were conducted along this line (Hovland et al., 1953, chap. 6; Hovland & Janis, 1962). Hovland and his research group concluded that there is a factor of general persuasibility: Some people are more persuadable than others. No relation was found between persuasibility and general intelligence. Two out three studies showed significant differences between the persuasibility of males and females; females seemed to be more easily persuaded (this may come as something of a shock to the readers of this book who are male and married).[10] There was not evidence in the Yale attitude studies that persons who were hostile and aggressive were harder to persuade, yet when some of these same individuals were observed in action, the expected result—more aggression, less persuasibility—was found. Perhaps the clearest relationship was between self-esteem and persuasibility. People who have high self-esteem are more difficult to persuade. If they show signs of feeling inadequate or of "social inhibition" (meaning that they are shy about taking a position and easy to "push around") they are more easily persuaded.

Toward the end of the 1950s a number of the young Yale scholars, William McGuire for one, were investigating the cognitive reorganization that takes place with attitude change (McGuire, 1985). This research was in the shadow of Lewin's work and was a topic of great interest to Fritz Heider and to Leon Festinger, who wrote his book *A Theory Cognitive Dissonance* (1957) on that theme. The research was also of interest to Osgood and Tannenbaum (1957), who had found one manifestation of cognitive reorganization when Tannenbaum was writing his dissertation using the semantic differential (Tannenbaum, 1953). The Yale experiments dealt with a theme that came to be called "cognitive consistency." When it is possible to alter the affective component of an individual's attitude, then a corresponding and consistent cognitive reorganization will occur toward the object of that affect. When people experience cognitive discrepancies as a result of persuasion attempts, they tend to seek (a) a solution that maximizes balance and consistency and (b) a solution that minimizes potential loss of consistency. When an individual is in a dilemma of belief, the least effortful way out is usually chosen. Consequently, people are more easily persuaded by messages that increase consistency than by those that reduce consistency. But when persons commit themselves to a great deal of discrepant behavior, they tend to resist communication messages that oppose such behavior because that challenges their inner consistency.

This impressive collection of findings shows how far the persuasion research program had moved in the direction of a general theory of communication from the first studies on the effects of training films on military recruits during World War II.

Computer Simulation

It is not well known that Hovland was doing important work in computer simulation during the 1950s. He wrote an influential paper on the subject that he called "A 'Communication Analysis' of Concept Learning" showing how mathematical theory could be applied to computer simulation of the way people form new concepts (Hovland, 1952). Another paper, "Computer Simulation of Thinking," also was widely influential among scholars on the growing edge of the field (Hovland, 1960). During the 1950s, as computers became widely available and easier to use, Carl designed a series of computer simulation experiments to help understand aspects of complex learning, notably the acquisition of concepts. If this work had not been so near the end of his career, Hovland might have contributed in the next decade to computer-communication studies with the same energy and insight that he had applied to communication and attitude change.

*   *   *   *

When Carl developed the first signs of cancer in the late 1950s, he did not change his work habits, although he was clearly less influential in the book he wrote with Sherif (Sherif & Hovland, 1960; the last volume that bears his name as a coauthor) than in the earlier volumes of the Yale series. He kept working quietly with his students and colleagues as long as the disease allowed him to do so. When he found it was no longer physically possible for him to work, he went home, sat down in his bathtub, filled it with water, and quietly as always, let himself drown.

Many of his students and former students gathered at the New England Psychological Association a year after his death to memorialize him. They spoke of his "uncanny ability to integrate and focus knowledge, to discern the central aspect of a problem" while carrying out his leadership role in a "gentle and supportive way." They remembered with gratitude his quiet guidance, lack of authoritarianism, and the atmosphere of freedom of inquiry that he maintained in his laboratory. The American Psychological Association (1958) gave him its award for Distinguished Scientific Contributions saying that, "His work has been of central importance in advancing attitude research from the early stage of merely demonstrating that changes can be produced, to the point of making predictions about when and where they will occur. His work has provided a convincing demonstration of the value of a sustained and integrated program of research" (p. 158).

He received many other honors and awards. In a 1962 program reviewing communication research that was broadcast over the Voice of America, I said that his program of experiments at Yale between 1945 and 1961 may be "the largest single contribution . . . to this field any man has made."

I still believe that.

Notes

1. The Yale Communication and Attitude Change Program, directed by Hovland, was originally funded by the Rockefeller Foundation.

2. Editors' Note: Freudian theory had some influence on Hovland through his colleagues in the Yale Institute of Human Relations, especially regarding frustration and aggression (Rogers, 1994).

3. Hovland worked as one of the collaborators in this research with Clellan S. Ford and R. S. Richard.

4. Editors' Note: At this writing in 1994, Janis, Lumsdaine, and Maccoby were deceased, and Sheffield and Smith were retired.

5. A summary of the descriptive analysis is reported in Chapters 1 and 2 of Hovland et al. (1949).

6. Gerald Lesser became the principal research adviser to the children's television series *Sesame Street.*

7. Lloyd Morrisett became president of the John and Mary R. Markle Foundation, a leading source of funding for mass communication research.

8. Editors' Note: This mental rehearsal is usually called "visualization."

9. After reviewing the survey evidence, the committee concluded that "there is a modest relationship between exposure to television violence and aggressive behavior or tendencies," and that there was no evidence to support the counter-hypothesis "that aggression leads to violence viewing." But they suggested that the relationship might conceivably be explained by "a third condition or set of conditions" that had not yet been identified (NIMH, 1972, pp. 8-9).

10. Editors' Note: The subjects in the experiments described here were high school students and college freshmen. A later review of some 50 experiments covering a wider age range concluded, "In the relatively impersonal situation that is involved in persuasive communications, neither sex is more suggestible than the other" (Maccoby & Jacklin, 1974).

The Heritage They Left Us[1]

Throughout this book we have been concerned with the formative years of communication study and therefore have concentrated on the earlier parts of this century. Now we shift our point of view away from history and add a brief epilogue on what kind of communication field emerged from the formative decades that we described in the previous chapters.

The Rise of Communication Study

It is a bit startling to realize how much has happened to communication study in such a short time. All of the developments we described in this book took place in less than a century. Even the generation of scholars that we spoke about as "forefathers of the forefathers" were not much heard of before the 1930s. Charles Horton Cooley, it is true, was already teaching in the last years before the turn of the century, as was John Dewey, but they were young instructors and not yet making great intellectual waves. Robert E. Park began to teach at the University of Chicago in 1914 and Edward Sapir in 1925, the same year that Harold D. Lasswell was appointed an instructor there. Walter Lippmann's pioneering book, *Public Opinion,* was published in 1922. Kurt Lewin was already building his great reputation in the 1920s, but that was in Germany, not the United States. The first school of journalism was founded at the University of Missouri, as we noted, in 1908. Thus the waves were building by 1930, but it was hard to find anything that we might call a "movement" in communication study before that time.

Even in the 1930s, developments in communication study did not speed up much. But gradually the field *did* speed up. By the 1930s, the four great pioneers were launched on their American careers. Lazarsfeld and Lewin came to the United States in 1933, leaving behind the shouts of "*Juden heraus!*"and facing the bleak prospects of the Great Depression. Lewin began his appointment at Iowa in 1935, and the Bureau of Applied Social Research at Columbia was to follow 9 years later. Carl I. Hovland finished his PhD degree in 1936, was promptly absorbed into Clark Hull's research program at Yale, and published his first book in 1939. Lasswell ended his teaching career at Chicago in the late 1930s and moved east. The field of communication study was growing up around these leaders. There had been only one school of journalism in the first decade of the century, but there were 400 by 1935. There had been no journal of communication study before the 1920s, but by the 1930s there were two and more were on the way.

During the 1940s, Lazarsfeld's Bureau of Applied Social Research became vigorous. At the beginning of the 1940s Hovland was Chief Psychologist and Director of Experimental Research for the U.S. War Department, concentrating on studies of persuasive communication. Lasswell was in charge of a major content analysis project in the U.S. Library of Congress that investigated Allied and Axis propaganda. Lewin was going ahead in his quiet but nevertheless exciting way at Iowa, attracting star students and conducting pioneering studies of group communication and group effects.

The years before the 1940s, then, were mostly preparation. The productive years for these forefathers were chiefly the 1940s and 1950s. These years were also, for some of them, the final years. By the beginning of the 1960s, Lewin and Hovland were dead, and Lazarsfeld had left communication study. Lasswell was still publishing, but he was away from the centers of communication research and teaching. It was a disappointing time for many of the followers and admirers of the four. Lewin had taken his new Research Center for Group Dynamics to MIT, but it never really got started at MIT because of the loss of its leader. Hovland left behind him 20 years of plans for his Yale Program on Communication and Attitude Change. Lazarsfeld, who had been so productive and stimulating, now was absorbed in other research, and one of his closest colleagues, Bernard Berelson, who had been head of the communication study program of the Ford Foundation, wrote a much-discussed article that was in effect a dirge for communication research (Berelson, 1959). Its time was over, he said.

Berelson was wrong, of course, as communication study continued to be challenged even after the end of its great 30 years and the loss of three of its four pioneers. Perhaps its continued growth is the highest compliment that we can pay the important events of the 1930s, 1940s, and 1950s.[2] The numbers of scholars now engaged in studying communication are far greater than before. Teaching and research in the field are now more firmly anchored than before in universities and in other institutions. Whereas it is very hard to say how well the ideas in the communication field and the present day publications compare with the very high standard set in midcentury, there are still important ideas in the field and heated arguments over them. Publications in communication study are certainly no fewer in number and perhaps no less in quality (although this is a comparison I hesitate to make). In any case, communication study has greatly expanded its field of interest and usefulness.

The Magnitude of Change

What kind of communication field of study have we inherited from the scholars of the mid-1950s? The sheer size and strength of the field today might well surprise the scholars who were setting its patterns in the 1930s, 1940s, and 1950s. Lasswell, who could not get a permanency at Chicago. Lewin, who had set up his sophisticated studies of adult social psychology in a child welfare research station. Lazarsfeld, who had to admit, as he did in his 1969 memoir, that he felt it necessary early in the history of the Bureau to decline an assignment from a colleague at Harvard to prepare a study of the relationship between the U.S. Congress, the Federal Communications Commission, and the broadcasting companies because "a budding research institute is dependent on the media and must try to avoid losing their support" (in Noelle-Neumann, 1983, p. 160). Elisabeth Noelle-Neumann reported Lazarsfeld as saying to her that the real reason he left communication research and turned to mathematical sociology was that he could no longer take the pressure that the media exerted on a communication researcher.

Paul would find today that communication research programs are more firmly entrenched in universities than the Bureau was ever able to establish itself and depend far more on the university for support than did the Bureau at Columbia. The fact that upward of 100 doctorates in communication study are being awarded this year,[3] that some thousands of graduate students are taking advanced courses in communication, might well please the four scholars who got all this started. Journalism and speech communication are now strong graduate, as well as undergraduate, departments.[4] And the paths cut by Lasswell, Lazarsfeld, Lewin, and Hovland in the other social sciences are still being followed. Political science, sociology, psychology, economics, anthropology, and history have scholars working on communication, a considerable list of publications on communication, and in some cases meetings about communication within their learned societies. Communication study has its own concentrations within these departments: public opinion, political campaigns, news flows, international communication, small groups, distance teaching, national development, and information theory, to name but a few. Analogies from social communication are being found helpful in biological and physical models.

In addition, it hardly needs saying that the study of communication has become an important element in dozens of everyday activities in the modern world: political campaigns, sales, advertising, teaching and learning, the presentation of news, industrial and business management, and many others. The training function for many of these activities has been turned over to universities (advertising and education are examples), and such training carries with it responsibility for research and publication.

This inventory is impressive because a century ago almost none of it existed. Education was a subject of importance then, of course, but there was very little bridge from it to communication study. Newspaper journalism was an extensive activity, to be sure, and the appearance of Walter Lippmann's *Public Opinion* in 1922 demonstrated that some journalists were thinking like scholars. But the brief history of journalism study that we provided earlier in this volume is represented by a plaintive guideline suggested by the American Association of Schools and Departments of Journalism in 1941: "Instructors should be encouraged to carry on research work and contribute to the literature of journalism."

One of the four communication leaders in midcentury, looking at communication study today, would probably perceive a considerable role reversal in the field. In the 1930s, 1940s, and 1950s, pioneering scholars in the social sciences examined the communication activities around them and interpreted these activities in terms of their own discipline. Now, in the last decades of the century, pioneering communication scholars examine the activities around them that have traditionally been the private turf of the other social sciences and contribute to the understanding of this turf from what has been learned about communication. Along with this role reversal has increasingly come a merger of intellectual resources. Just as Hovland, an experimental psychologist, Lewin, a social psychologist, Lazarsfeld, a sociologist, and Lasswell, a political scientist, had to learn a great deal about communication in order to work on it, so does the modern communication scholar find that it is necessary to learn a great deal about the psychology, sociology, politics, economics, or anthropology of the topic that he or she is studying. This relationship is healthy. It contributes to both sets of disciplinary fields and to the richness of the product.

What kind of communication field have we inherited from its 20th century founding? The changes are far deeper than mere size or extent. It is a rich, flourishing intellectual field. In many respects it is a *new* field. The ideas are different; communication researchers do different things than they used to. "Ferment in the Field" is more than a cute title for the *Journal of Communication* to put on its 1983 issue, for the field *is* in ferment. Questions are being asked that have all too seldom been asked before, questions about what communication study is, what communication research is, what a communication researcher should be doing. And if we hope to comprehend what we have inherited from our forefathers, we must look at some of these questions and the changes that they have brought about.

The Challenge to Simplicity

A growing discipline, as a growing child, goes through dramatic rites of passage from a simple environment to a complex one. In the case of communication study, that change happened in the years we described as the period of the "forefathers of the forefathers."

I have never known a serious scholar to endorse or make research use of the so-called "Bullet Theory" of communication effects (the Bullet Theory means that communicators can line up targets in the sights of their "media-guns," and shoot their audience members down one by one with the silver bullets of propaganda). This concept became popular about the time of World War I (1914-1918), but it was a part of popular, not scholarly, wisdom. If any scholar did make serious use of this concept, it signalled the childish side of the act of passage. For it was soon realized that the communication process is too complicated to be described as bullets.

From the Bullet Theory to the original linear conceptualization of the communication process—the transfer of a message from source to receiver—is not such a great leap out of simplicity. It is certainly a long way from the interactive theories, the cognitive, social, and cultural theories that are more commonly in use today. But it provided a framework on which theorists could work to complicate their picture of the communication process toward something more closely approaching reality.

Harold Lasswell's description of the communication process, familiar to every student of communication, is this:

Who
Says What
To Whom
Through What Channel
With What Effect?

This model is not, of course, meant to be a paradigm of the communication process but, rather, a convenient way to catalog some of its chief elements. Lasswell was issuing, at one and the same time, an invitation to review what Blumler (1983) later called "the contributions . . . of the various actors involved" (p. 172), and also to view the entire process in holistic terms, taking into account all of the parts and interrelationships. This led to the study of both parties in a communication relationship, and especially to the ideas of active rather than passive receivers, senders who are themselves products of influences and controls, content which is often best described in terms of the audience, channels that are interpersonal as well as mass media communication, mass communication that in many cases is less likely to communicate persuasion than a framework for thinking or talking about an idea, and the unique languages of the media, that, as Innis, McLuhan, and Salomon, among others have taught us, play a special part in changing the societies that receive these languages.[5] In other words, once one fills in Lasswell's five questions catalog, one can never again think of communication as a simple five-factor process.

Doubts About Some Old Models: Minimal Effects

This process of desimplification led to questioning patterns and conclusions that had drawn strength from the scholars of the 1940s and 1950s.

For instance, it became evident that conclusions advanced in the 1940s and 1950s to explain the effects of the mass media, despite the great skill of the researchers involved, might have been "peculiar to the political conditions and media systems of the 1940s" (as Steven Chaffee put it, referring to the voting studies in Rogers & Chaffee, 1983, p. 22), or determined in part by the short term of the study, which made it necessary to observe effects in a special situation. An example is the doctrine of "minimal effects" (through reinforcement of existing opinion by the media) that emerged from the midcentury studies of media effects on voting and other such behavior, and which has since received harsh criticism. "It is much easier to present theses or findings related to effects research today because the long reign of the hypothesis of media reinforcers of public opinion is over at last," Noelle-Neumann wrote in 1983 (p. 157). "The reinforcement or 'minimal effects' hypothesis of media began to break down in the mid-sixties under the weight of empirical research results. Today, most researchers assume that the mass media can have a decisive effect on people's conception of reality" (p. 157). The Klapper formulation also came under fire for its downgrading of media effects on opinions and behavior. Klapper (1960) was careful to say that "mass communication *ordinarily* does not serve as a necessary and sufficient cause of audience effects but, rather, functions among and through a nexus of mediating factors and influences" (p. 8). These "mediating factors" are nonmedia; the direct effects of the media, as found in the Bureau's voting studies, were likely to be "minimal."

"The minimal effects theorem was a boon for the media industry," said Kurt and Gladys Lang in reviewing Klapper's contribution,

> In its denigration of the importance of media messages and its emphasis on the quantitative predominance of "reinforcement," Klapper's summary [of the state of knowledge about media effects] seemed to support broadcasters' opposition to any regulation of content or even efforts at self-reform. The problem—to the extent that there was one—as well as its solution could be shown to lie not with the media but with the society as exemplified by the mediating factors. (Lang & Lang, 1983, p. 135)

As a result, the blame was taken off the media.

The Langs' own work, for example their remarkable study of the pseudo-reality created by the television broadcasters to ornament the parade staged in Chicago to welcome General Douglas MacArthur on his return from Korea, could offend the broadcasters (Lang & Lang, 1953). So too could most of the studies of television violence and children. The trend of media

after the 1950s was to concentrate on social rather than
ns of effects and to examine carefully such evidence as
gathered on media effects, good or bad. In 1948, I published a
paper on media effects by Bernard Berelson, chief author of the Bureau's
second election study, which certainly showed no sign of underplaying the
effects of television (Berelson, 1948).[6]
So we are left with the question of whether the "minimal effects"
hypothesis was a bow to the broadcasters who helped support the Bureau's
studies or merely an early step in the development of communication
research. The move away from the "minimal effects" position was change
indeed, and an example of the kind of change that came to communication
study after midcentury.

Doubts About Some Old Methods

Chaffee observed, quite correctly, that there is "not so much agreement
today on the unique promise of behavioral research" (Rogers & Chaffee,
1983, p. 22). In the 1940s the behavioral approach was a means to make
communication study more "scientific." But today, Chaffee says,

> Scholars who specialize in historical, legal, critical, and other methods of
> inquiry are challenging the behavioral approach, and some of us who used to
> think of ourselves as mainly concerned with individual behavior are now
> attempting to study structural factors and historical contexts of communication
> systems more carefully. (Rogers & Chaffee, 1983, p. 22)

The recent history of mass media research, said Stuart Hall a few years ago,
is a movement from essentially a behavioral to an ideological perspective. A
similarly negative reaction to behaviorism comes from the speech communication side of the field, in which leading scholars such as Gerald R. Miller
emphasize the importance of human volition rather than the "law-governed,
deterministic paradigm of communication behavior" (i.e., rules, rather than
laws) (Miller, 1983, p. 31). Miller, along with others among the ablest scholars
of interpersonal communication, resents both the rationalist approach represented by Plato's philosopher kings, with their allegedly superior insights, and
positivist epistemology, represented by empiricist scholars with their allegedly
superior research techniques. The latter's dictum was, "Knowing is knowing
how to verify" (Miller, 1983, p. 31). Miller quotes with approval John Bowers'

joking reference to Noam Chomsky's rationalism: "It appears that only God and Chomsky can make a tree" (p. 31).

So movements from a behavioral toward an ideological approach, from an empirical toward an analytical one, and, more recently, from an individual toward a societal framework have helped to change communication study from what it was in midcentury to what it is today.

Communication as a Study of Culture

One change in communication study is a greater emphasis on the study of culture as a component of communication effects. Particularly in England in the late 1960s and 1970s, the study of "lived cultures" was emphasized: religion, education, colloquial conversation, sports and other recreation, and so forth.[7] The text of communication has therefore been interpreted as a series of "lived meanings," and the media have been seen by "critical" researchers as the chief instrument by which ruling elites try to maintain ideological control of the cultural framework.

In America, James Carey (1977) has proposed a "shared culture" model in which culture is created, shared, modified, and transformed by communication. The effect of this emphasis, as Elihu Katz (1983) says, has been to reunite "the social sciences and the humanities as in days of yore, and extend the circle to include anthropology, linguistics, folklore, and the study of popular culture" (p. 52).

The changes that we are noting here are changes in emphasis rather than in basic substance. There have always been approaches to communication study that are analytical rather than behavioral, societal rather than individual, cultural rather than scientific. The interesting aspect in the past several decades is how many of these alternatives to the mainstream of midcentury research have appeared.

Communication as "Sociology"

James Halloran, past president of the International Association for Mass Communication Research, closely allied to UNESCO, noted the increasing adoption of what he calls a "sociological perspective" of communication (Halloran, 1983). This shift, he says, "has led to a more holistic approach in which media are studied not in isolation but in relation to other institutions and the social system generally, and in which communication is regarded as a social process" (p. 275).

Halloran (1983) says,

> No longer are the media [always] placed at the center of the stage; no longer do we ask simple questions such as "What do the media do to people?" The audiences, the publics, are located in their appropriate historical and sociological environments, and their use of the media and the implications of that use are examined from these positions. This perspective applies both to studies of the implications of the media's current operations and to studies dealing with the possible use of the media to achieve given objectives, say in health education, social action, or community development. Planning with regard to these objectives that does not take into account the role and functions of related institutions and support factors is not likely to be very successful. The increasingly revealed complexity of the situation, in turn, leaves little room for simplistic linear models of cause and effect. (p. 275)

"The introduction and growing acceptance of a sociological perspective," Halloran concluded, "represents the most important development for communication over the last twenty years" (p. 275). Our choice of research topics in the present situation, Halloran says, should be determined by our "ideas about worthwhileness" (p. 278). He mentions a few of what he considers "worthwhile questions": Is there sufficient diversity in the media's presentation of news and current affairs? Are we satisfied with the present control, organization, and structure of media and communication systems? Are there alternatives that would make possible greater access and participation? What is the influence on violence in society, of advertising, and "the media, with their emphasis on negativity, confrontation, sensation, and events and persons?" (p. 277). Privately owned media are not heroes to present-day researchers like Halloran.

How should one study questions like these? "It is more important to be important than to be impeccable," says Halloran (1983, p. 278).

A Countermovement From Critical Researchers

The changes in viewpoint since midcentury that we described under the headings of "The Challenges to Simplicity," "Doubts About Some Old Models," and "Communication as a Study of Culture" might be described as *revisionism*. The viewpoints we are about to describe might more properly be called *revolutionary*. The exponents of these latter points of view are not great in number, but they are vocal and some of them are very able. Their approach has attracted a number of converts, especially in Europe and in the Third World nations of Latin America, Africa, and Asia. Most of the converts are politically oriented, and almost all of them are committed to a critique of what capitalistic countries like the United States, capitalist owned and controlled communication institutions like the Western press and television, and the international news agencies (which are also capitalistic) are doing to international communication.

I do not know whether Halloran considers himself a "critical" researcher or not, but what he has written about communication study in UNESCO has that tone. For example, the following paragraph of Halloran's was quoted by Herbert I. Schiller, the best-known and most influential critical communication researcher in the United States: "In general, prior to 1969," wrote Halloran, "the research projects sponsored by UNESCO [deficient in theories, models, concepts, and methods] tended to legitimate and reinforce the existing system and the established order, and in the Third World, it tended to strengthen economic and cultural dependence rather than promote independence" (in Schiller, 1983, p. 253).

Schiller (1983) says that this statement is "on the mark," and no other critical researcher is likely to dispute that judgment. Although admitting the "remarkable eclecticism" (p. 253) among critical researchers, Schiller mentions a few characteristics that are common among them. For one thing, instead of "focusing on individual *consumption* [and impact] of media products, critical researchers address the *production* of informational outputs." Secondly, "this research makes an effort to understand the sources and exercises of power, especially as they relate to communication processes and information flow." This approach, Schiller noted, is in contrast to "a mainstream belief in pluralist decision-making." Third, said Schiller, "this research demonstrates an awareness of continuous change in social processes and institutions, or, put differently, a strong sense of history" (p. 253).

Dallas Smythe, one of the most outspoken critical researchers in Canada, contrasts *critical* with *administrative* research (Smythe & van Dinh, 1983). The latter is a dirty word for critical researchers. The problems chosen for study, write Smythe and van Dinh, and the research methods used are commonly thought to be the basis for distinguishing between the two approaches (see p. 118). But they propose that a third factor is also involved: the ideological orientation of the researcher. "All of us have our predispositions, either to criticize and try to change the existing political-economic order, or to defend and strengthen it. The frequent pretense of scientific 'neutrality' on this score is a delusion" (p. 117). The importance of this ideological orientation to Smythe and van Dinh can be judged by reading further into their exegesis of the differences between critical and administrative research. They distinguish the two approaches in terms of the types of problems researchers select, the research methods employed, and the ideology of the researcher.

Smythe and van Dinh (1983) say,

> By "administrative" researchable problems we mean how to make an organization's actions more efficient, e.g., how best to advertise a brand of toothpaste, how most profitably to innovate word-processors and video display terminals within a corporation, etc. By "critical" researchable problems, we mean how to reshape or invent institutions to meet the collective needs of the relevant social community, through devices such as direct broadcast satellites, terrestrial broadcast stations and networks, and cable TV, or, at a "micro" level, how to conduct psychotherapy and how to study rumors. By "administrative" tools, we refer to applications of neopositivist, behavioral theory to the end of divining effects on *individuals*. By "critical" tools, we refer to historical, materialist analysis of the contradictory process in the real world. By "administrative" ideology, we mean the linking of administrative-type problems and tools, with interpretation of results that support, or do not seriously disturb, the status quo. By "critical" researchable problems and critical tools, we mean interpretations that involve radical changes in the established order. (p. 118)

This clear, candid statement is worth analyzing in terms of the value of words that are put in juxtaposition to each other. If a researcher who is not of the "critical" school reads it and objects that this description does not characterize the research that *he or she* does (for example, studying "how best to advertise a brand of toothpaste"), it might be well to review what William Melody, formerly Smyth's colleague at Simon Fraser University, had to say about critical researchers: "The great difficulty with 'critical' research is that, far too often, its major target has not been society's problems, but rather administrative research" (Melody & Mansell, 1983, p. 110).

Challenge of the Information Age

I have probably overemphasized the divisions and disagreements in the field of communication study, and have therefore made it seem more fractious than it actually is. But a symptom of newness and liveliness in a field is just as likely to be the appearance of a number of contrary theorems and interpretations as it is to be a coalescing of the field behind some equivalent of Newton's laws. The latter situation requires a Newton, which makes it more unlikely for communication.

Not all present-day communication researchers agree with each other or even speak pleasantly about each other's work. But they have succeeded in maintaining a lively, flourishing field of study that has not faded out since the midcentury years when the field was in its springtime. Gerald R. Miller, who, from a speech communication viewpoint, is less than completely satisfied with the developments in present communication study, says that he discerns the field

> moving toward greater scholarly maturity and respectability. Although I am more sympathetic with some of these trends than with others, each reflects the kinds of questions we should be asking ourselves. A field in ferment is not something to be feared; rather, scholarly conflict, if constructively channeled, offers an opportunity for further growth and development. (Miller, 1983, p. 41)

Furthermore, there may now be especially good reason to rethink our pattern of communication study in the direction of greater coherence and cohesiveness. We apparently stand at the door of a new age, which is being called variously the Age of Information, or the Age of Communication, or the Communication Revolution, or the Information Society. Daniel Bell (1973) forecast this new era in *The Coming of Post-Industrial Society* and Alvin Toffler (1980) described just such a development in some detail in his *The Third Wave.* In this period that we have now entered, microelectronics, automation, and sophisticated uses of communication show every sign of creating a new age on our Earth.

Schiller (1983) described it this way: "Capitalism," he says, "is undergoing a structural transformation. An information component is being inserted into, when it is not replacing, the older industrial base, making the communication process a critical element in the overall system of production" (p. 251). He continued,

> The visible, although still not fully matured, characteristics of these momentous changes are everywhere. Foremost is the shift in the economy and in the labor force, from production to service activities, in which information is a leading and still-growing component. Plus there is the astonishing growth of the information industry itself—equipment, programming, processing, transmission, distribution, storage, and retrieval.

All of these information-based or related activities are being facilitated, and are themselves facilitating, the rapid transformation of information into a commodity. This parallels, in many respects, the commoditization of labor in an earlier time and, still earlier, the breakdown of the commons and the commoditization of the land.

The factors that will decide whether these trends open up or block the long road to humanization are themselves determined by the character and the degree of flexibility of the social institutions *now in place*. Can a labor force, displaced by robots and computers, for example, be shifted humanely to meaningful and compensated activity? And who will be making these vital decisions?

In the face of these transcendental changes, there is need for inquiry and analysis. Some of the basic though still-unanswered questions include: What kind of goods and services are needed, and what will be produced? How large a work force is required, and what should be its training? What will be the mode of governance in an electronically-organized society? Will the international system evolve into an integrated world community of equal participants, or will it shatter into a disunited chaos? Finally, though not exhaustively, what happens to the individual confronted with uncertain opportunities and unknown perils? (pp. 251-253)

Finally, it may be well to quote a commentary from one of the non-Western sources that expressed their opinions on the expected age-to-come. The National Institute for Research Advancement in Japan circulated the following forecast to its members and clients:

The new world brought about by the development of an advanced information society . . . is expected to generate major transformations comparable to those caused by the industrial revolution and completely change the world as we know it. In particular the basic value system that guides society will shift from one based on goods to one where information is the dynamic that propels society.

There is little reason, therefore, to believe that the century we have described in this book may be a final chapter in communication study. Rather, we may expect to be challenged to do more than we have so far done with communication and to find more efficient and more innovative ways to do it.

Notes

1. Editors' Note: Schramm wrote this as the final chapter to this book. It was to have followed the material that appears here as Chapter 8, which Schramm had outlined but not written, before he died.

2. Editors' Note: Schramm wrote a rejoinder that was published in the same issue of *Public Opinion Quarterly* in which Berelson's article appears (Schramm, 1959a). Twenty-five years later the *Journal of Communication* devoted an entire issue to retrospective responses to Berelson's 1959 paper. See *Journal of Communication* (1983), Volume 3, "Ferment in the Field: Communication Scholars Address Critical Issues and Research Tasks of the Discipline." Many of Schramm's descriptions of new viewpoints in the present chapter are taken from this special issue of the journal.

3. Editors' Note: At this writing, about 250 doctoral degrees in all fields of communication are awarded per year by U.S. universities.

4. Editors' Note: Approximately 2,000 U.S. university departments today offer degrees in various fields of communication (Rogers, 1994).

5. See, for example, Innis (1951), McLuhan (1962, 1965), and Salomon (1979).

6. In this essay, Berelson stressed the variable nature of media effects. For instance, he said that the more personal the medium, the more effective in persuasion; particular channels geared to the person's predispositions are more effective than generalized channels; emotional content is more effective than rational content. He also noted that nonpurposive media exposure is more influential than is purposeful media use.

7. See the studies done by the Center for Contemporary Cultural Studies, University of Birmingham, for example, Hall (1980).

PART II

The Establishment of Communication Study in America

Steven H. Chaffee
Everett M. Rogers

Wilbur Schramm

The Founder[1]

People wonder how Wilbur was able to carry on so many different careers at the same time, and where he found the energy. He drew it from many directions—athletics, nutrition, aspiration and inspiration. But his career in the scholarly life began when he dropped everything at Harvard but his classes. The choice of that road, in the words of his friend Robert Frost, "made all the difference—and way led on to way."

—Elizabeth Schramm[2]

Bringing him to Stanford was the most important contribution I have ever made to communication research. He has had great world impact. . . . I don't know of *any* field in which one man stands out so dominantly.

—Chilton R. ("Chick") Bush[3]

I t was entirely in character for Wilbur Schramm, author of the first six chapters of this volume, to have left himself almost completely out of his story of the beginnings of communication study in America. From his account, one might conclude that Schramm had been a mere observer and sometime conversation partner of Lasswell, Lazarsfeld, Lewin, and Hovland,

Wilbur Schramm

someone whose lifetime and career simply overlapped with these forefathers. To the contrary, Wilbur Schramm was *the* founder of communication study, not only in America but in the world. Our purpose here is to describe, based on our own recollections as well as the work of others, how Wilbur Schramm came to found the field he called communication study.

Founders Versus Forefathers

What is a founder? The *founder* of a new academic field might be the author of the first books to define the field; or the creator of the first university departments in the new field; or the teacher of the first generation of new scholars in the field (who then start new departments at other universities). Schramm was the founder of communication study in each of these ways. His professorial career took him to three major research universities: the University of Iowa from 1934 to 1947, the University of Illinois from 1947 to 1955, and Stanford University from 1955 until his age-mandated retirement in 1973. Well before he completed this academic sojourn, communication study was deeply institutionalized at these schools, Schramm's disciples had started dozens of successful programs elsewhere, and throughout the field his textbooks and research monographs were standard fare.

How does his founder role differ from that of the "forefathers" (we might better call them "forerunners") to whom he devoted this final memoir? A *forefather* conducts early, seminal research that establishes the original content of a new academic field. But, as in the four examples here, a forefather does not necessarily identify institutionally with the new field, nor do the forefather's doctoral students. A forefather does not leave the security of a parent discipline to pioneer in creating the new field. Previous chapters in the present volume detailed how the four forefathers remained in their departments of political science, sociology, and psychology, respectively, while they conducted their communication research. Several of them established research institutes or programs, but these were temporary organizations that no longer exist; these units did not award academic degrees, certainly not in communication. In short, without a founder, there would be no new field, and therefore no forefathers to recall. Without Schramm, the research of the earlier four would have remained intellectually disconnected from its common core in communication.

What is required for the founding of a new field? Obviously, timing is important. Wilbur Schramm founded communication study at the end of

World War II, a period when U.S. universities were beginning a tremendous expansion, often doubling or even tripling their student enrollments in a decade. So resources were available. Wilbur Schramm was particularly adept at gaining control of such resources. He was a legendary fund-raiser, often bringing in several hundred thousand dollars in research grants annually to the communication research institutes that he directed. He leveraged this "soft money" into new faculty slots and other types of resources. Schramm was an institution-builder, not an isolated scholar.

To take the risks of a midcareer switch from an established discipline to create a new field, a founder must have a solid self-concept, coupled with considerable interpersonal skills. Wilbur Schramm had a strong ego. He was proud of what he accomplished and he was constantly accomplishing more. To be sure, he presented himself in everyday life as a self-effacing kind of fellow, very humble about what he achieved. More that one colleague will swear that Wilbur literally said "aw shucks" in response to compliments and honors.

Schramm worked long, hard hours, and was deeply involved in his research, teaching, and administrative duties. He often expressed regret that he could not do more. For example, when the National Institute of Mental Health (NIMH) sought a proposal from him for its project on television and children in 1969, he turned down their request, saying he had "too many other projects going on." As author of the first major American study of the topic (Schramm, Lyle, & Parker, 1961), Schramm would have added luster to the eventual Surgeon General's report (NIMH, 1972). He was much in demand throughout his later career, and no one could have complied with half the invitations directed toward him.

Schramm projected the image of a gentlemanly scholar, always with adequate time for consideration of others' problems. People were instantly drawn to Wilbur Schramm and they felt confident of his capacities. That was one dimension of his ability to attract outstanding doctoral students and large research grants, and to maintain solid interpersonal relationships with deans and university presidents. Schramm had a vision of where communication study should go, and he was determined to take it there, carrying it along with his considerable competencies.

So Wilbur Schramm possessed a unique set of personal qualities and interpersonal skills to found communication study. Still, other people were also present at about the same time, possessing some of these same qualities; we mention some of these individuals in the coming pages. But Schramm was without peer or rival, and no one who was aware of the field of communication study in its formative decades would question his preeminence.

Sociologists of science have investigated the role a new intellectual paradigm plays in creating a scientific revolution (that is, a new form for research in an established field), and how an "invisible college" of scholars in an ongoing field is attracted to the new paradigm (Crane, 1972; Kuhn, 1962). Strangely, however, sociologists and historians of science have given little attention to the process of founding a new scientific field. Perhaps this lacuna exists because such an event is so extremely rare. Since about 1900, the era when the five conventional social sciences (economics, psychology, political science, sociology, and anthropology) became established, U.S. universities have seen very few new academic fields develop. There are new departments of linguistics, computer science (a recent spin-off from electrical engineering), area studies (for example, Latin American Studies), ethnic studies, and feminist studies. But these are typically interdisciplinary programs and do not claim to be a new field or discipline. Communication study may in fact be the most widely accepted new field in American universities over the period of the past 80 or 90 years. As we shall see, however, its introduction is far from complete even today. It is organized in many different ways at different institutions and there is as yet no standard curriculum. Thus we could not tell the whole story here, even if that were our purpose; this book is concerned only with the beginnings of communication study.

The present chapter chronicles the role of Wilbur Schramm in this unusual process of the founding and diffusion of the new field of communication study, detailing certain of the conflicts that occurred as institutional and professional resistances were overcome. It is a tale that has largely overlapped with our own careers, and our telling of it is as much a personal memoir as is Schramm's remembrance of the forefathers in the first six chapters of this book.

A Renaissance Man

The admiring term *Renaissance Man* most often evokes Leonardo da Vinci, the Florentine architect-engineer-anatomist-sculptor-painter who typified the period that we call the Renaissance (roughly 1450-1600), when European civilization was being literally reborn. Leonardo excelled in several different fields, and it is this versatility that we honor in applying the term Renaissance Man.

Wilbur Schramm clearly wanted to become, and surely was, a Renaissance Man. Anyone describing Wilbur Schramm begins by listing a remarkable collection of competencies. He was an athlete, good enough to be offered a tryout at third base with the Columbus (Ohio) Red Birds, a AAA professional baseball club. While he was a graduate student at Harvard University, he played the flute with the Boston Symphony (at the same time holding down five other part-time jobs). Schramm won an O. Henry Prize for Fiction for one of his short stories, and another was made into a Hollywood movie segment. He founded the Iowa Writers' Workshop, one of the most important fiction-writing graduate programs in the United States. He was a licensed airplane pilot. As one year's self-improvement project while a senior faculty member at Stanford, Schramm bought a self-instruction manual so that he could learn computer programming in the FORTRAN language. A colleague recalls that Schramm wrote so profusely during his years at Stanford that he wore out several electric typewriters (Nelson, 1977). Everyone who knew him well begins by describing Schramm in terms of these and many other indicators of his protean skills. He had a "can-do" spirit, an important quality for the founder of a new academic field. And he wanted to do great and unusual things.

After his death, we asked a number of former colleagues how tall they thought Schramm was. Estimates ranged from 5'11" to 6'2"; Schramm had at 36 described himself in a university memo as 5'11", and he probably lost some height in later years. Our point is that no one recalled Wilbur Schramm as of lesser stature than he was.

The Beginnings of Wilbur Schramm

Schramm was born in Marietta, Ohio in 1907. This small midwestern town sits below the extended Mason-Dixon Line, just across the Ohio River from the Old South. In his youth, Schramm also lived at times in Virginia, West Virginia, and Kentucky. Not surprisingly, then, there was a touch of Southern gentility in Schramm's manner and diction. For example, he usually referred to his wife as "Miss Betty," in a courtly Southern fashion.

An unfortunate event that was to shape Schramm's career occurred at age 5 when a botched tonsillectomy operation left him with a pronounced stammer. This impediment was to last throughout his life, although he learned many ways to employ it to positive effect. For the young Wilbur Schramm, a speech defect meant that he could not plan on a career in law, his father's occupation. He grew up playing sports and excelling in his academic studies. Schramm graduated at the top of his class both from Marietta High School (where he played a piece on the flute, rather than give a valedictory address) and from Marietta College (where he *did* speak as valedictorian of the class of '28). He was elected to Phi Beta Kappa despite working his way through school as a part-time reporter for the local Marietta newspaper and as a stringer for the Associated Press. Through these jobs he was also honing the writing skills that would be the key to his career.

In 1930 Schramm went to Harvard University for a master's degree in American literature. He also studied philosophy with Alfred North Whitehead, who in later years he said was the person who had influenced him most. (Whitehead too had a stutter but overcame it; see Cartier, 1980, p. 69.) Schramm struggled to pay the steep Harvard tuition, and after earning his MA degree in 1930, he went to the State University of Iowa to pursue a PhD in English. He completed his dissertation concerning Henry Wadsworth Longfellow's poem, *Hiawatha,* in 1932 (Schramm, 1932).

Why did Schramm choose Iowa? In addition to charging much lower tuition than Harvard, Iowa in the 1930s was a promising university, an institution that was definitely on the rise despite the Great Depression. Its liberal arts faculty was gaining a high reputation in both the humanities and the social sciences. A special attraction for Schramm was the University of Iowa's highly regarded speech clinic, directed by Professor Lee Edward Travis. Schramm wanted the best help he could get for his chronic disability.

Travis at that time theorized that stuttering was caused by wrong-handedness, so he strapped Schramm's right hand into a leather sling, immobilizing it. This cure failed. Wendell Johnson, another therapist in the Iowa speech clinic, maintained instead that stuttering was a socially-determined problem that could be cured by changing the individual's self-perceptions. Johnson helped Schramm somewhat, although the speech problem continued. Schramm's stammer, then, brought him into contact with human communication theory, a field in which Johnson, an early general semanticist, was writing (Johnson, 1946). The stammer may also explain why Schramm, later in his career, preferred teaching small seminars rather than large lecture classes. He developed an intimate and personalized style of teaching at Iowa, a pattern that he continued in the three communication doctoral programs that he established. Even when his courses attracted large enrollments, Schramm's classroom style remained personalized, folksy, and anecdotal. Although his writing was highly analytical, carefully outlined, and rigorously edited, in class sessions he would often digress into storytelling—another form of communication at which he excelled.

After completing his PhD, Schramm spent two years of postdoctoral study at the University of Iowa, working with the physiological psychologist Carl E. Seashore on a series of laboratory experiments in audiology. Schramm investigated the rhythm of poetry reading, publishing an article on this topic in 1934 (Seashore & Schramm, 1934). This choice of research problem suggests Schramm's continuing interest in the psychology of speech, perhaps influenced by his stammer and the therapy that he obtained to attempt to cure it as well as a continuation of his literary background. Why did Schramm do postdoctoral study, and why in psychology (seemingly far from English literature)? First, academic positions were very scarce in the Depression year of 1932. Furthermore, Seashore was one of Iowa's most esteemed scholars of that time. Schramm was attracted to great minds throughout his career. But his choice of psychology also illustrates Schramm's optimistic belief that behavioral science methods could be applied to humanistic problems. This refusal to accept the "two cultures" assumption of his fellow literature professors was already setting him apart. He would always consider himself both a humanist and a social scientist. Even earlier, he had merged social and literary research in a monograph on the price of books in Chaucer's time and how it had affected the length of the classic *Canterbury Tales* (Schramm, 1933).

During this period at Iowa, Schramm also became acquainted with an emigré German scholar, Kurt Lewin (see Chapter 4), who was conducting field experiments on group communication and behavior change. Lewin came to Iowa in 1935 through the efforts of an educational psychologist, George Stoddard, who directed the Iowa Child Welfare Research Station where the behavior of normal children was studied. Schramm participated in Lewin's weekly discussion group, known by Iowa students as "the Hot Air Club."[4] It met in a local restaurant near the University of Iowa campus and featured presentations and discussions of Lewin's field theory. Lewin theorized that individual behavior was a product both of an individual's drives or needs and of the individual's environment, a viewpoint that meshed with Schramm's eclectic approach.

From Lewin, Schramm absorbed further theoretical perspectives and methodological skills of behavioral science as well as Lewin's stimulative approach to research questions. Schramm often recounted a conversation in which Lewin asked him how many people had read his recent published research article. Maybe a few hundred, Schramm admitted. Then Lewin asked Schramm how many people had read his newest short story, which had appeared in the popular magazine *The Saturday Evening Post*. Several hundred thousand, Schramm estimated. "Why?" Lewin asked. "Do you know *why*?"

In 1934, Schramm was appointed an assistant professor in the Department of English at Iowa. He taught courses on the great 19th century

American writers, such as Herman Melville, Walt Whitman, and Mark Twain. Five years later, upon the sudden death of the professor who was teaching a course in fiction writing, Schramm took over this course, called the Iowa Writers' Workshop, and expanded it into a graduate-level program. The workshop staff consisted of Schramm plus a half dozen part-time faculty. They taught intensive, hands-on courses in fiction writing. Each of the dozen students met individually with Schramm once a week. When he felt a piece of writing was ready, the student was asked to present it in the weekly seminar that often met in Schramm's home. Schramm brought in accomplished writers to talk to his students, such as Archibald MacLeish, later a Pulitzer Prize-winning poet. Schramm was developing a close apprenticeship mode for teaching a few prize pupils.

Schramm not only taught fiction writing, he did it. During the period 1939-1941, Schramm published a dozen magazine stories in large-circulation magazines.[5] Schramm's stories were "tall tales" about such subjects as Grandpa Hopewell and his flying tractor; Jones, the horse that played third base for the Brooklyn Dodgers; and Windwagon Smith, whose prairie schooner got blown all the way back to where it had started. The latter yarn even got Schramm to Hollywood, as it became a segment in a Walt Disney film.[6] These stories brought in added (and needed) income, and Schramm might easily have continued his comfortable if busy lifestyle as a literature professor and fiction writer in Iowa City. But World War II intervened.

Washington at War

Shortly after the United States entered World War II on December 7, 1941, Schramm volunteered by contacting MacLeish, then U.S. Librarian of Congress and also newly appointed as Director of the Office of Facts and Figures (OFF), the central propaganda agency for the U.S. government. A month later, in January, 1942, Schramm was at work in Washington, D.C. Among other duties, he had a hand in drafting President Franklin D. Roosevelt's "fireside chats" that were broadcast by radio to the American people. Schramm, always highly patriotic, also was responsible for liaison work with U.S. universities, encouraging them to aid in the war effort. The Office of Facts and Figures gauged public opinion, created radio spots and other patriotic messages, censored U.S. media content, and monitored foreign broadcasts and other media messages. Among other academics who were recruited to the OFF when the war broke out was Ralph O. Nafziger, a journalism professor from the University of Minnesota, whose career was to parallel, and occasionally intersect with, Schramm's over the next 25 years (see Rogers & Chaffee, 1994, especially pp. 20-24, see also chapter 8, pp. 165-167).

During the war, Schramm collaborated with many social and behavioral scientists in Washington, D.C. One was George Stoddard, his former colleague at the University of Iowa. Another was the methodologist Rensis Likert, who conducted survey research on public attitudes toward the war as an extension of his Farm Survey work for the U.S. Department of Agriculture. Consultants to the OFF included Harold Lasswell (see Chapter 2) and Ralph Casey, who had collaborated with Lasswell on analyses of propaganda and public opinion during the 1930s (Lasswell, Casey, & Smith, 1935; see Rogers & Chaffee, 1994, pp. 17-20 on Casey and Schramm). Casey was director of the journalism school at the University of Minnesota. At the OFF Schramm also had contact with Ernest R. ("Jack") Hilgard, a psychologist of learning from Stanford University. Paul Lazarsfeld (see Chapter 3), who was not an American citizen, served as a consultant (several days a week) for the unit in the OFF where Schramm worked, and was also a consultant to Samuel Stouffer's Research Branch in the U.S. Army's Information and Education Division in the Pentagon. The Research Branch employed several dozen sociologists, psychologists, and other social scientists to (a) conduct surveys of the morale, racial attitudes, and other attitudes of U.S. troops and (b) carry out experiments on the effects of military training films. The latter experimental research was directed by Carl Hovland (see Chapter 5), on leave from Yale University.

Schramm lived in a suburb of Washington, D.C., and commuted to his office in a carpool with, among others, political scientist Gabriel Almond and Margaret Mead, the famous anthropologist. Mead directed a research program on nutrition behavior for the National Research Council that funded Kurt Lewin's field experiments at Iowa on changing food habits, such as persuading housewives to serve their families glandular meats (e.g., tripe, heart, liver).[7] Mead, Hilgard, Likert, and Schramm were part of a group that met monthly in a Washington hotel for dinner and discussions about interdisciplinary social science work. Schramm normally chaired these meetings.

During World War II, Washington was the place to be for a social scientist. America's enemies seemed to represent such an unmitigated evil that few if any social scientists opposed the war. America's war aims united these scholars in a common cause and brought them together in one place where they formed a network of relationships that endured for the rest of their careers. The war effort demanded an interdisciplinary approach to problems, often closely related to communication study because in so many ways it was seen as "a war of words." Communication was also viewed as the basic tool for mobilization of the American people to volunteer, conserve, and in other ways aid in concentrating the nation's resources on winning the war. In important ways, then, World War II created the conditions for the founding of the communication field, a point that Schramm often stressed to his students in later years.

Just prior to the war, from 1934 to 1940, John Marshall, an official of the Rockefeller Foundation in New York, had convened a monthly seminar of a dozen scholars to explore the emerging field of communication. The Rockefeller Communication Seminar, as it was called, included Lazarsfeld (whose Radio Research Project at Columbia University was funded by the Foundation) and Lasswell (whose Wartime Communication Project in the U.S. Library of Congress was also funded by the Foundation), along with other noted scholars. At one of these monthly seminars, Lasswell presented his five-questions model for communication research: *"Who* says *what* to *whom* via *what channel* with *what effect?"* (Lasswell, 1948).[8] This simple framework dominated the yearlong series of discussions and was featured as an organizing principle in the seminar's final report that was circulated to government officials in Washington in 1940.

It was evident by this time that the United States would become involved in World War II, which had begun in 1939 in Europe. The Rockefeller Communication Seminar report argued that the United States should use mass communication to prepare for the approaching emergency: to encourage patriotic sacrifices by the U.S. public, to explain the nation's war aims, and to counteract enemy propaganda. Communication research was needed, said the report, to improve the effectiveness of the government's public communication programs. Because John Marshall funded research on radio effects, content analyses of newspapers and magazines, and investigations of the impacts of film, he needed a rubric broad enough to include all of these media. Marshall used (and probably created) the term *mass communication* in his letters inviting scholars to participate in the 1939-1940 Rockefeller Communication Seminar.[9]

After less than 2 years in Washington, Schramm decided to return to Iowa City. The OFF had been reorganized into the Office of War Information (OWI), which later became the U.S. Information Agency (USIA). The U.S. Congress had second thoughts about the role of a propaganda agency in a democracy and slashed the OWI budget in 1942-1943. Morale in the agency sank, including Schramm's. He returned to Iowa City in mid-1943, bringing with him the germ of an idea for a field of mass communication and a set of academic contacts that he could use in bringing it into being.

Officials at the University of Iowa regarded Schramm as a promising scholar and administrator. The success of his Iowa Writers' Workshop had continued during his Washington years (and in fact continues to this day). But Schramm's replacement, Professor Paul Engle, was doing a fine job of directing the workshop. Also, Schramm's Washington experiences made him doubt that he would again be happy to teach students at Iowa about Melville and Chaucer. He was 36 years old when he returned to Iowa City in 1943. The university administration sounded him out about directing the University of Iowa Library. He declined. Then Frank Luther Mott, Director of the School of Journalism, resigned to become dean at the University of Missouri. Despite the fact that Schramm had only limited (part-time) newspaper experience, the background then considered necessary to becoming a journalism professor, he was offered the position of director.

Schramm submitted a plan for the school's development that called for broadening the journalism major from how-to-do-it journalism classes to also include social sciences courses: sociology, psychology, economics, and so on. Schramm also proposed creation of a PhD program in mass communication,[10] and the founding of a bureau of newspaper readership as one component of the School of Journalism. The doctoral program would be interdisciplinary, according to his outline, involving various social science departments and the speech department, as well as journalism. Clearly, Schramm had been transformed during his 15 months in Washington. (In Minneapolis, Casey and Nafziger were making similar changes in the University of Minnesota's J-School.) Schramm had left Iowa as a professor of English literature, but he came back with a vision for communication study. He was to face various difficulties in implementing this vision in the years ahead, and his proposals at Iowa mainly served as a dry run for his later, larger-scale innovations at the University of Illinois.

Schools of Journalism

In 1943, the School of Journalism at Iowa was mainly providing a vocational type of higher education preparing undergraduate students to enter jobs as newspaper reporters. Professors of journalism in U.S. universities themselves were mostly schooled via practical experience as newspaper journalists; many held a master's degree in some field, but very few were PhDs. This picture of a school of journalism as professional (rather than scholarly) in orientation characterized not only Iowa but almost all of the several hundred journalism programs then in existence.

The major exception was at the University of Wisconsin in Madison, where an unusually academic brand of journalism education had been pioneered by Willard G. ("Daddy") Bleyer (1873-1935).[11] A PhD in English with a background in newspaper work, Bleyer started a course in journalism in 1904. Early on, he placed emphasis on research as part of education for journalism. If schools of journalism were to guide rather than merely follow professional practice, he considered that social science could help by answering practical questions about newsworthiness, editing decisions, and determinants of readership. Bleyer and his faculty pioneered in press history, law, and management. He instituted a journalism minor for social science PhD students, which ex-newspapermen could pursue while teaching professional skills courses in the J-School. He offered them a graduate seminar in public opinion, a topic that not only constituted a new kind of news but also provided clues to newspapers' effects on readers and on the moral and political order generally (Bleyer, 1931).

A midwestern Progressive, Bleyer took a dim view of the sensationalist press; he wanted the J-School to represent the profession at its best. Undergraduate journalism majors at Wisconsin took courses in sociology, political science, and economics as a means of understanding the society on which they were to report, while their instructors completed PhDs in those same departments. Over the three decades of Bleyer's unique leadership, the journalism program instilled the University of Wisconsin's social progressivism into the press of the state. It also provided other universities with journalism professors who saw research as a natural part of their career responsibilities. The schools they came to lead in the ensuing decades provided good soil for Schramm's germinating idea of a new field of communication study.

In the 1940s, both in Washington, D.C., and later back in the Midwest, Wilbur Schramm was exposed to the Wisconsin idea for journalism education by two of Bleyer's leading disciples, Ralph Casey and Ralph Nafziger of the University of Minnesota.[12] Their vision meshed, in a way Schramm saw more readily than others, with the image of mass communication as a field of study that had been outlined in the Rockefeller Communication Seminar report. But Bleyer's viewpoint was not widely accepted among journalism professors in the United States, nor was it part of most university administrators' notions of education for journalism when Wilbur Schramm returned to Iowa as director of the School of Journalism.

In the 1940s owners and editors of newspapers stressed that journalists mainly needed to know the basics—how to write and how to spell. The profession was resistant to college graduates of any stripe. Most editors viewed social science as irrelevant to everyday newspaper work, which they insisted was best learned as they had learned it—on the job. The idea of journalism professors with PhD degrees in social science seemed a foolish, possibly dangerous, trend. Newspaper publishers and editors had a good deal of influence on the schools of journalism. After all, they hired (or refused to hire) the graduates of a journalism school, and they were the most likely sources of donations for student scholarships.

Wilbur Schramm's plan for the J-School at Iowa placed him without question on the opposite side of this divide. In arguing that his school of journalism should not only conduct research but also award doctoral degrees, Schramm went one big step beyond Bleyer's innovative journalism minor for the PhD. Schramm established the first doctoral program in mass communication. This new curriculum at Iowa included J-School courses in communication theory, research methods, public opinion, propaganda analysis, and other social scientific topics, buttressed by outside courses in psychology, sociology, economics, and political science. Not many students were attracted to Schramm's rigorous new PhD program, though; by 1947, when Schramm left Iowa City for the University of Illinois, only two doctoral candidates were nearing completion of their degrees.

Schramm also established a research institute at Iowa, patterned after Lazarsfeld's Office of Radio Research at Columbia University. The Iowa research institute obtained modest funding for audience studies from Iowa newspapers and from a Cedar Rapids radio station. These companies wanted to know how large their audience was, and who was in it.[13] Schramm also obtained a grant from the Young and Rubicam advertising agency in New York through its research director, Dr. George ("Ted") Gallup. Gallup had been one of Iowa's first journalism students; after taking his BA in the J-School, he taught there while doing MA and PhD work in applied psychology. Gallup had based his dissertation on readership surveys for various Iowa newspapers. Now he was in a position to repay his alma mater for the start it had given him in his highly successful career in advertising research and public opinion polling.

By starting the world's first mass communication doctoral program in a school of journalism, Schramm had created a general model for mass communication study in universities. A more dramatic development was soon to help the new field of communication study take off. And Wilbur Schramm was to make it happen, too.

Mass Communication at Illinois

During the 1946-1947 academic year, Schramm decided that he needed more resources at the University of Iowa if his experiment in mass communication education was to flourish. He asked the university administration to guarantee him $130,000 per year for 10 years. They refused, and Schramm began to look elsewhere. His old friend George Stoddard had become president of the University of Illinois and was trying to get that university moving. Partly at the suggestion of Fred Siebert (another Bleyer student), Stoddard offered Schramm a position as a member of his inner circle of advisers (see Rogers & Chaffee, 1994, p. 5). Schramm insisted that he also wanted to implement his Iowa program in mass communication on a larger scale at Illinois. Stoddard was receptive.

So Schramm went to Illinois as Director of the Institute of Communications Research (essentially, the interdisciplinary doctoral program in communication plus a soft-money research program) and as Professor of Communication (the first individual in the world to be appointed to a faculty position so named). Stoddard also placed Schramm in charge of the University of Illinois Press, the radio and television stations, veterans affairs, a conference center, and a host of other activities. Wags at the Illinois Faculty Club called Schramm "The Communication Czar" and "The Duke of Allerton" (Allerton Park was the name of the conference center).

The Institute of Communications Research was the jewel of Schramm's administrative crown at Illinois. It was eventually funded with about 15 hard-money faculty positions. Approximately a dozen new doctoral students were admitted each fall. They gained apprenticeship research experience by working with faculty members on studies funded by soft money that Schramm brought in. Schramm attracted several hundred thousand dollars in research grants per year.[14] The Illinois doctoral students took courses in social science departments, plus core courses in communication that were taught in the Institute. The first graduates of the Illinois doctoral program went out to start similar units at other universities eager to build communication study, such as Michigan State (see Chapter 8).

One problem at Illinois was that no textbooks were available for the new communication research courses. Schramm organized a conference, held at Allerton Park and funded by the Rockefeller Foundation, to advise him on his new institute and its doctoral program. Papers were presented by Lazarsfeld, Hovland, Nafziger, Casey, and other leading communication scholars. Schramm edited these conference papers into a book, *Communication in*

Modern Society (1948), which became in effect the first textbook for the new field. It was soon supplanted by a wide-ranging collection of articles and excerpts, edited by Schramm and titled *Mass Communications* (1949/ 1960). Schramm dedicated this influential volume to Lazarsfeld, Lasswell, and Hovland for bringing the social sciences to bear on communication.[15]

Schramm's most important book was undoubtedly *Process and Effects of Mass Communication,* originally a U.S. Information Agency training manual composed of papers by various scholars. The reader was published in 1954 by the University of Illinois Press (as were all of Schramm's early books, about one per year while he was at Illinois).[16] Schramm was, of course, editor of the press, but these were all best-sellers by university press standards. For many students (and future professors) of communication, the Schramm books, especially his 1954 reader, were their introduction to the new field of communication study.[17]

In addition to his own books, Schramm arranged for the Press to publish *The Mathematical Theory of Communication* by Claude E. Shannon, together with an explanatory paper by Warren Weaver (1949). This important and much-cited volume laid out the original conception of what came to be called Information Theory. It began with a simple source-message-channel-receiver model of communication, defined the "bit" (binary digit) as a standard unit of the amount of information, and set forth a series of propositions about communication flows. This brilliant conceptualization by Shannon, originally a technical paper written for Bell Telephone Laboratories that grew out of his cryptographic research during World War II, was incorporated into communication study by Schramm (1955) and his doctoral students, such as David K. Berlo (1960) and Wilson Taylor (1953).[18]

During the Illinois years another war, this time in Korea, played a key role in Schramm's intellectual evolution—and therefore in the field's. In 1951, Schramm, a thoroughly patriotic Cold Warrior, was invited by the USIA to conduct a survey of public opinion in Seoul that examined the appeal that Communism held during the invasions from North Korea; the city changed hands several times in a period of months. The research report, published a few years later, was republished in several languages; it brought Schramm's name to attention in the capitals of many other countries concerned about Communist incursions (Riley & Schramm, 1951; Schramm & Riley, 1951).

The Korea project marked the beginning of Schramm's role as an adviser to other nations' governments and of his interest in comparisons between Western and Soviet-Communist theories of the press (Schramm, 1956).

(Only later would his Cold War orientation give way to a concern for the problems of economic and social development in Third World nations.) Mass communication programs around the United States began in the late 1950s offering courses in comparative press systems and in international communication flows, and, a decade later, on the role of communication in development. Schramm produced many of the standard readings for such courses and led the way in conducting research on these topics.

Illinois was thus the place where communication research in the pro-grammatic sense was first established, although its roots could be traced to Schramm at Iowa and even to Bleyer at Wisconsin. Schramm's personal relationship with Illinois President Stoddard was crucial throughout, and when in 1954 Schramm's "angel" resigned the presidency of the university, Schramm's position as "Communication Czar" at Illinois was equally threatened. He was sounded out about administrative positions as dean of a school of communication at one university and decided he was not interested. But when in 1955 Chick Bush, another Bleyer protégé, who was head of the journalism department at Stanford University, invited Schramm to consider coming west, he accepted. Two years later, Schramm replaced Bush as director of Stanford's Institute for Communication Research.

Stanford as the Seed Institution for Communication Study

Schramm may have thought it would be easier to establish a new academic field when headquartered at a prestigious private university, but in the mid-1950s Stanford had not yet climbed into the top ranks of U.S. universities. Hiring Schramm was part of its process of ascent. Stanford's Department of Journalism (the unit in which Schramm was appointed) was small and mostly professional in orientation. Bush, imbued with Bleyer's vision, highly valued what Schramm had built at Illinois. He was pushing journalism at Stanford toward a social science perspective, and he counted on Schramm to pull it much farther in that direction.[19] Bush felt this was the only way his department could survive in a research university such as Stanford, whose leaders disdained vocational training and expected their professors to publish original research papers.

The university administration was enthusiastic about recruiting Schramm. Jack Hilgard, who had known Schramm in Washington during World War II, was dean of Stanford's Graduate School. He controlled some $50,000 per year of special monies to be used to strengthen the social sciences at

Stanford. Hilgard provided the funding for Schramm's initial appointment, although when Schramm arrived at Stanford in 1955 he brought along a large grant from the Ford Foundation that paid half of his salary for the next 4 years. Under Schramm, the Institute for Communication Research always seemed awash in research funds. In 1973, his final contribution when he retired was to leave his colleagues a million-dollar grant from the U.S. Agency for International Development for research and training in development communication.

During his Stanford years, Schramm eschewed administrative positions. He had learned his lesson at Illinois. Although he was director of Stanford's Institute for Communication Research, this role was entrepreneurial and the title honorific. The Institute was incorporated into the Department of Communication when that unit was formed by a merger of Journalism with portions of a dismantled Speech and Drama Department. The communication department head had the day-to-day administrative responsibilities, leaving Schramm free to conduct research, teach, and direct the doctoral program. On more than one occasion over the years, Schramm was invited to become department head, but he steadfastly refused. When higher administrators at Stanford sought counsel from the communication department, however, they usually called on Schramm.[20] It was he, after all, who was responsible for most of the research money in the department and the lion's share of the academic prestige that it earned as well.

Schramm's program at Stanford soon became famous for the doctoral students that it produced. Almost every traditional school of journalism in a major university wanted to hire "a Stanford type." Well-trained in quantitative methods, and usually entering academics as a second career after at least a few years in media work, many of these new communication scholars had fast-track careers. Within a few years several held prominent administrative positions or pioneered new research specialties. Both patterns are exemplified by two of Schramm's (and Bush's) Stanford PhDs: Wayne Danielson and Maxwell McCombs.

Wayne Danielson (born 1929) grew up in Burlington, Iowa, and attended the University of Iowa, completing his BA degree in journalism in 1952. He then earned his MA degree at Stanford in 1953. Danielson applied to continue for his doctorate but was advised by Bush that he would first need newspaper experience so that he would be employable in a school of journalism after graduation. So he worked for the San Jose Mercury News for a year and then in 1954 enrolled in Stanford's interdisciplinary doctoral program in communication. This was a year before Schramm arrived. In addition to taking courses in the Institute for Communication Research,

Danielson enrolled in courses in psychology from Hilgard on learning theory, from Leon Festinger (a Lewin protégé) in social psychology, and in statistics from Quinn McNemar. These psychology courses were standard for early Stanford PhD students, a decision Bush had made even before Schramm's arrival. Danielson and another doctoral student, Paul Deutschmann, conducted one of the first studies of how a major news story spread to the mass public (Deutschmann & Danielson, 1960). It became a widely cited classic and led to many other such news diffusion investigations (Rosengren, 1987). Deutschmann and Danielson applied the general model of innovation diffusion (Rogers, 1983) to a major news story, finding that the media played a much more dominant role than is the case with technological innovations. The study of news diffusion rapidly became a staple form of research in journalism and an important exception to the usual social pattern of diffusion (in which interpersonal channels tend to predominate). Mass and interpersonal channels were, they found, complementary; an individual typically hears of a presidential assassination, a disaster, or other breaking news event from the media, and then discusses it with friends, relatives, or work associates.

Danielson received his PhD in Mass Communication Research in 1957 and taught for one year at the University of Wisconsin, then moved to the University of North Carolina in Chapel Hill for 10 years. He rose rapidly through the academic ranks, becoming dean of the School of Journalism. Then Danielson moved to the University of Texas at Austin as dean of the College of Communication for a decade (1969-1979). Texas's College of Communication has more student majors in communication than any other academic unit in the United States and perhaps in the world. Danielson presided over UT's explosive growth in communication. Since stepping down as dean, Danielson has continued as professor of journalism and computer science at Texas.

Another exemplary product from Schramm's Stanford doctoral program is Maxwell E. McCombs, currently a colleague of Danielson's in Austin. McCombs was born in 1938 in Birmingham, Alabama, and attended Tulane University, graduating in 1960. One of his teachers, Walter Wilcox, a former newspaper publisher who had earned his PhD at Iowa, recommended that McCombs continue for a master's degree at Stanford. When McCombs arrived in Palo Alto, Bush handed him his first quarter schedule of courses for journalism MA work: statistical methods, learning theory, content analysis, and communication theory. McCombs finished his master's, worked as a reporter for the *New Orleans Times-Picayune* for 2 years, and then returned to Stanford for his PhD in Communication (completed in 1966). He taught journalism at UCLA (where Wilcox was chairman) for a year and then took a faculty position at North Carolina, remaining until 1973. There he collaborated with Donald Shaw, a recent Wisconsin PhD, in a ground-breaking study of "the agenda-setting function" of the news media during the 1968 presidential election campaign (McCombs & Shaw, 1972). Funded with a small grant from the National Association of Broadcasters, McCombs and Shaw interviewed 100 undecided North Carolina voters about what they thought were the main issues in the election. Concurrent newspaper coverage was content-analyzed to see which issues were being emphasized. McCombs and Shaw found a near-perfect rank order correlation between the press's agenda and the public's agenda, which they interpreted as an effect of the media.

This innovative little study launched an important research tradition in communication research. Since 1972, more than 350 agenda-setting studies have been published, and the term McCombs and Shaw coined, "agenda-setting," has become part of the general lexicon of American politics (Rogers & Dearing, 1988; Rogers, Dearing, & Bregman, 1993). McCombs went on to hold endowed professorships in communication at Syracuse University and then at the University of Texas at Austin, where he also chaired the Department of Journalism (1986-1991).

The careers of Danielson and McCombs illustrate the path of the model Schramm protégé. Early on, they applied their quantitative methods and social science theories to real-world problems that the news media set in motion. News diffusion and agenda-setting are not the avowed purposes of newspapers, and they were certainly not the stuff of traditional journalistic skills training. Schramm's students saw that an understanding of how these indirect effects of the news operate in society was an essential part of a journalist's professional education. Both scholars prepared for their academic careers by interrupting advanced graduate work to become newspaper reporters for a time and then returned to finish their PhDs.[21] They were hired at top universities, in journalism programs, and rose rapidly—Danielson principally in administration, McCombs mainly in research and doctoral education. Schramm often spoke of both of them with an obvious pride of authorship.

How Schramm Worked

During his Stanford years (1955-1973), Wilbur Schramm developed a remarkable ability to highlight socially significant problems of communication study. For example, in the late 1950s, Schramm conducted surveys of schoolchildren's use of the then-new mass medium of television in more than 10 communities in the United States and Canada. In 1961, Schramm and two of his PhD students synthesized the findings in a landmark book, *Television in the Lives of Our Children* (Schramm, Lyle, & Parker, 1961). A few years later, the issue of children and television violence became an important policy debate in the United States and the U.S. Surgeon General funded a major research program on this issue. The 1961 Schramm book became a standard reference, and in reports of the Surgeon General's project, research by Stanford people on television violence was referred to more often than that from any other institution. Of the five volumes of technical reports published by NIMH in 1972, the overview papers for four were written by former Schramm students and postdoctoral fellows; the fifth was by a Stanford psychology PhD (NIMH, 1972). Thousands of studies have since been completed on television's effects on children, carried out by communication scholars, psychologists, psychiatrists, sociologists, and education scholars. Schramm's students remain among the leading figures in that literature. The same is true in several other areas where he paved the academic way.

Schramm's social views evolved throughout his life, from a rather traditional Christian white American ethnocentrism early on, to that of an ecumenical and respectful collaborator with people from around the world in his later years. Gender issues were another matter. Schramm seemed never to adapt to the feminist movement that enveloped U.S. higher education in the 1960s and 1970s. Perhaps it is understandable, given the world in which he was raised, that his writings in the 1950s betrayed sex role stereotyping in its various manifestations. Traces of gender inequality persisted to his death. In the mid-1970s, for example, he recommended one of his Stanford PhDs for a faculty position at another university with the private observation (mentioned on at least two separate occasions) that she was "the purtiest little thing." This woman scholar, who stood almost exactly the same height as Schramm, was a strong feminist who would not have appreciated hearing what he doubtless intended as a compliment. Schramm's 1973 book, *Men, Messages, and Media: A Look at Human Communication,* created a storm over its title, and was changed for the second edition to the cumbersome *Men, Women, Messages, and Media.*

Anyone who writes as much as Schramm did spends endless hours alone. Family life inevitably suffers, and he was not close to his children during their growing years. Although he had many coworkers and admirers, he had few close friends. To some extent, this may have been a matter of self-protection. Schramm was, as the person holding the purse strings and power in his research institutes, an obvious target for people seeking his help in advancing their careers. He did not share confidences with his students or even with many of his colleagues. When he made a decision, it was enforced politely but firmly. As one junior colleague put it, "There's a fist of steel in that velvet glove."

Schramm was a seemingly tireless worker, as one of the present authors observed vividly one sunny Sunday afternoon in Palo Alto in 1964. Schramm had put together funding, participants, and a program for a summerlong conference on communication and development to be held in Honolulu. He was to cochair this event with Daniel Lerner of the Massachusetts Institute of Technology, author of a classic study of development in the Middle East (Lerner, 1958). Schramm's own research contribution to the conference proceedings was to be a worldwide test of Lerner's theory (which had been based on only six countries in one region). The statistical test that Schramm concocted involved correlations over time between indicators of mass media development and such related factors as urbanization, literacy, industrialization, and per capita income (Schramm & Ruggels, 1967). On the Sunday afternoon before he and Miss Betty were to depart on a 6 a.m. plane to Honolulu, Schramm was hard at work in his bedroom, poring over volumes of UNESCO data and computing cross-lagged correlations on a mechanical calculator. To one side was his typewriter, where numbers for detailed tables were being painstakingly entered one by one.

Although an advocate and skilled practitioner of social science, Schramm made his greatest academic contribution as a synthesizer of other people's work. His most quoted writings were not reports of primary research findings but organizing schemes. One of his favorites was an adaptation of Lasswell's highly abstract typology of communication functions,[22] which had been elaborated for sociologists by Charles Wright in 1960.[23] Schramm used the general scheme analogically, to liken modern mass communication to parallel functions in traditional society. He found this comparative model useful in understanding both settings. Here is the way he explained it in his moralistic book *Responsibility in Mass Communication,* written for the Federal Council of Churches of Christ in America and published in 1957:

> The traditional public functions of communication . . . are the same now as they were when the first tribes assembled on the beaches and in front of the caves.

Thus, mass communication *helps us correlate our response* to the challenges and opportunities which appear on the horizon, and *reach consensus* on social actions to be taken. We used to do this through tribal councils or town meetings. Now we turn to mass communications to read the rival arguments, see the rival candidates, and have the alternative course of action explained to us.

Mass communication *helps us transmit the culture* of our society to new members of the society. We have always had teaching at mother's knee, and imitation of the father—and still have. For thousands of years we have had schools of some sort or other. But mass communication enters into this assignment by supplying textbooks, teaching films and programs, and a constant picturing of the roles and accepted mores of our society.

Mass communication *helps entertain us.* The ballad singer, the dancer, and the traveling theater (even the pitch man) of older times have now gone on television, radio, and films.

Finally, mass communication *helps sell goods for us* and thus keeps our economic system healthy. We used to listen for the town crier's advertisements, the word-of-mouth tidings of bargains to be had, the bells of the traveling store-wagon. Now we read the ads in the papers or the magazines, see the ads on television, or hear them on radio. (pp. 33-34)

In later years, when Schramm was championing the potential role of mass media in development, this set of analogies would be repeated but in a manner designed for readers in settings where traditional society was still the dominant form (Schramm, 1964).

Schramm was particularly adept at synthesizing and converting others' findings into useful generalizations. He summarized, for example, hundreds of studies comparing the relative effectiveness of instructional television versus in-person lecturing (he concluded that neither channel was consistently more effective) (Schramm & Chu, 1967). On another occasion, Schramm compared the relative effectiveness of "big media" (television and film) versus "little media" (such as radio) in development communication (Schramm, 1977). In many local settings, he pointed out, little media could be much more efficient.

Schramm's move to Stanford in 1955 led to a stronger focus on international communication, which came to represent about half of his total effort during the latter half of his career. He produced widely read books about international communication, such as *One Day in the World's Press* (1959b)[24] and *Mass Media and National Development* (1964).[25] Schramm and his doctoral students carried out evaluations of instructional television systems in Colombia, El Salvador, American Samoa, and the Ivory Coast (e.g., Hornik, Mayo, & McAnany, 1976; Schramm, Nelson, & Bethan, 1981). In 1962, Schramm was appointed the Janet M. Peck Professor of International Communication at Stanford, a chair created for him and named for a donor with a strong interest in improving international relations. In this capacity, he was probably the first person to hold an endowed professorship in communication.

Why was Schramm so interested in international communication? One underlying reason may have been his desire to spread communication study outside the United States. He formed a strong link to European scholarship through the French Press Institute at the University of Paris and through his work for UNESCO, which was headquartered in Paris. He recruited international students to study communication at Stanford and urged them to return to their home countries and become professors of communication too. Often this return of the sojourning student was not feasible because suitable academic positions were not yet available in many countries. So Schramm became active in establishing new units abroad. He helped to found the Indian Institute for Mass Communication in Delhi and the East-West Communication Institute at the University of Hawaii, for example. In these ways, Schramm promoted communication study not only in the United States but around the world, a story that could fill yet another chapter. But that is not within the literal boundaries of the present volume.

Winding Down in Hawaii

Wilbur Schramm was too energetic and too full of plans to spread the new field of communication, to retire at the age of 65. But that was Stanford's mandatory retirement age in 1973, so reluctantly he moved to Honolulu where he was soon appointed Director of the East-West Institute for Communication, one part of the East-West Center on the University of Hawaii's Manoa campus. His goal, he wrote to friends, was "to build one more institution." The East-West Center had been established by the U.S. Congress and was funded by a federal appropriation through the U.S. Department of State. Its mission was to conduct research and to provide training on problems of the Pacific region. Other units in the East-West Center, in addition to the Communication Institute (at the time Schramm arrived), dealt with agriculture and food, population, and culture.

As director of the East-West Communication Institute, Schramm had to deal with the usual amount of petty administrative details, which were abhorrent to him. On one occasion, he invited a famous Japanese scholar to come and work at the Institute for six months. But then Schramm was told by higher officials in the East-West Center that he could not have an office for the visiting scholar. So Schramm gave the Japanese scholar his own office and moved his desk outside of the building, where he directed the affairs of his institute sitting in the sun and rain. After a few days, the East-West Center administration relented and soon the Japanese visitor was ensconced in a suitable space. Schramm had shamed them into his point of view using his formidable reputation to move the bureaucracy.

In 1978, at age 70, Schramm retired from the East-West Communication Institute but continued to play an active role in its affairs. It would be more accurate to say that "Schramm was retired" than "Schramm retired." He never stopped working, including both library and field research, and of course he never stopped writing. He published eight books after he left Stanford in 1973, four of them after he reached age 70. He taught for a year in Hong Kong as the Aw Boon Haw Professor of International Communication at the Chinese University of Hong Kong (a position created for him) and was a guest scholar for a term at the University of Michigan. He carried out demonstration research projects in American Samoa and in Indonesia. He revised earlier books, such as *Responsibility in Mass Communication* (Rivers & Schramm, 1969). He organized and chaired numerous academic conferences, especially for communication specialists from the Pacific Rim nations. He was honored by academic organizations for his career contributions to the field. He wrote poetry, turning particularly to the Japanese *haiku,* which he admired for its spare form. He treated his friends to wistful verses celebrating the island life on his annual Christmas cards. He was continually sought out for advice on academic appointments and publications by colleagues on the U.S. mainland. He served as consulting editor for the *International Encyclopedia of Communications* (Barnouw, 1989) and wrote several of the entries himself.

But after Stanford, Schramm no longer headed a combined teaching and research unit with PhD students and a faculty to lead. Visitors to Hawaii who had known him in the Iowa, Illinois, and Stanford days quickly sensed his frustration with what he viewed as an enforced, and not especially welcome, retirement. Literally, to have retired from his lifetime of work would have been unthinkable to Wilbur Schramm.

He was attracted to the East-West Center because part of its mission was to help establish applied research institutions in the Pacific and Asian nations and to carry out research and demonstration projects in those settings. To Schramm, this meant communication research, and he had already written the book on what mass communication could accomplish for developing countries. But history, which had meshed with his goals so well in the 1950s, conspired against him at this juncture.

The Vietnam war era produced a pronounced shift in academic circles away from many of the presumptions on which Schramm had built communication as a social science. In particular, Schramm's vision of modernization through communication came under attack. In his 1964 *Mass Communication and National Development* and subsequent writings, Schramm had painted a future for the Third World built around optimistic national development goals modeled on the United States and grounded in the empirical tradition in social science.

In the 1970s, though, Schramm found himself the target of polemical "critical theory" scholars, often in the very countries that he had hoped to help. Many Third World eyes turned away from American quantitative behavioral scientists, among whom Schramm's name remained most prominent even in his retirement, finding their intellectual heroes instead in European philosophers and literary critics of neo-Marxist and Freudian persuasions. Schramm's parables of the communication process and mass communication functions were denounced as "top-down" and "linear" prescriptions, designed to ensure U.S. "domination" of Third World nations trapped by "media imperialism" in a relationship of "dependency" to the metropolitan powers. Schramm's connections to the U.S. government, from World War II to the East-West Center itself, became a focus for criticism, as did his consulting work for central planning ministries in many developing countries.

This controversy provided the academic climate in which Schramm worked through his final years, and it took a toll on his spirit as much as did his advancing age. Characteristically, he responded with work rather than with counterrhetoric. For research, he turned in two directions. One was to the past, including both the history of the field (as in the present book) and that of human communication broadly construed, in *The Story of Human Communication* (1988). His other research direction was to become the champion of "little media" projects.

In place of his grand vision of national economic development systems energized by advanced communication media that can stimulate large-scale social change (exemplified by his 1964 book, *Mass Media and National Development*), Schramm in *Big Media, Little Media* (1977) became the advocate of finite, localized instructional media projects with specific, attainable goals. In these educational media programs, directing modern technologies at agricultural and semiliterate populations, Schramm pointed out, for example, that pictures can sometimes be more effective than thousands of words—perhaps a difficult conclusion to reach for a man whose career had been formed so much around words.

Behavioral science work could be built into little-media projects, but it would be science of a more modest, less macroscopic character than he had in mind when he first imagined what communication could accomplish for society in general or in the developing world. Early in a development program, there would be needs assessments and formative evaluations of alternative message designs directed at literacy or health or a specific agricultural practice. Later on, there would be summative evaluation to determine how well the project's goals had been achieved. Larger lessons would be sought from the findings, but each study was itself pragmatic, focused, and adapted to local needs. For Schramm, this did not seem like a retreat from a loftier plane. He remarked that he enjoyed "getting my hands dirty," and observed that he was learning as much from each country's indigenous educators and students as they were from him.

Making communication programs work for economic and social development proved more challenging in practice than an earlier Schramm might have predicted. One major undertaking was an attempt to conduct elementary education in American Samoa via television. In that country of dispersed islands, he reasoned, a television signal could cross the water and bring learning to students in remote schoolrooms. But it did not work very well, as he was forced to conclude after some years of trial, because students (and adults) welcomed television more for its entertainment value than for the knowledge it could bring them. A satellite broadcasting campaign in Indonesia produced similarly modest education gains—while advertising for cigarettes and soft drinks had such an impact that the Indonesian government banned it.

In these final, missionary efforts, Schramm took his place alongside the dozens of other communication researchers that he had inspired with his vision and he found just as much frustration out in the field as any of them. Still, those who talked with Schramm about these development communication projects in his last years often noted a kind of satisfaction with his own work that he had not shown in his earlier career. He loved Hawaii, where he could take his daily swim and gaze down from his condominium on the city, the beach, the island, and especially the vast ocean. At the end he considered himself a citizen of the Pacific, or at least as much of it as could be reached via communication media.

* * * *

Our last contact with Wilbur Schramm occurred in August, 1987, at a 2-week conference on Communication and Development held at the East-

West Center in Honolulu. Schramm gave the keynote address and attended most of the sessions. Some of his theories were attacked during the conference, especially by communication scholars from Third World nations. But he was unflappable, a true gentleman, and friendly even to his critics.

This is how we remember him.

Notes

1. The present chapter draws on several previous publications, including Cartier (1988), Chaffee, Chu, Lyle, and Danielson (1974), Delia (1987), McAnany (1988), Rogers (1994), Rogers and Chaffee (1994), Tankard (1990).

2. Elizabeth (Mrs. Wilbur) Schramm, quoted in MacElwain (1985).

3. Quoted from a June 29, 1970, personal interview by David Grey, Archives Reading Room, State Historical Society of Wisconsin, Madison, WI. On Bush's relationship to Schramm, see Rogers and Chaffee (1994), especially pp. 24-27.

4. Lewin's *Quasselstrippe,* or "rambling string"; see Chapter 4.

5. One of this chapter's authors, then growing up on an Iowa farm, avidly consumed Schramm's articles in the *Saturday Evening Post.* The other author first encountered Schramm's byline in a collection of classic articles and stories about baseball.

6. Schramm's fiction stories were collected in book form as Schramm (1941).

7. This research was reported in Lewin (1942, 1943). Lewin's concept of "gatekeeping," later a metaphor for news editing, was originally applied to the process by which food gets selected for a family's table (see Shoemaker, 1991).

8. Virtually the same formulation also appeared in Smith, Lasswell, and Casey (1946) and in various writings by Lazarsfeld and others in the same era.

9. The Rockefeller Foundation at various times funded the communication research of Lazarsfeld, Lewin, Lasswell, and Hovland, as well as Schramm.

10. In some internal documents, Schramm referred to the PhD field simply as "Communication."

11. The seminal role of Bleyer and his students is described more fully in Chapter 8 and in Rogers and Chaffee (1994).

12. Influences on Schramm via Bleyer's students is analyzed more fully in Rogers and Chaffee (1994).

13. Schramm was of course interested in *effects* of these media as well and developed the model of converting "administrative research" projects to academic purposes that go beyond the immediate goals of the sponsors. In this respect, he followed Hovland's example from World War II (see Chapter 5).

14. One major source of research support was the U.S. Information Agency, which was the postwar name given to the Office of War Information, where Schramm had worked during World War II (see Simpson, 1994).

15. The situation might have been characterized in the reverse. Schramm was incorporating these social scientists into his newly identified field of communication study.

16. As head of the university press, Schramm was in a good position to collect high-quality papers, get them reviewed approvingly for their academic content, and publish them without much concern for market factors.

17. This was true of both authors of the present chapter, for example.

18. Taylor created the "cloze procedure," a measure of readability, based on Shannon's theory (see Taylor, 1953).

19. Even before World War II, Bush had taught a course in research methods, including elementary statistics, for his journalism students (Lindley, 1976).

20. Until Bush retired in 1962, he and Schramm tended to be treated as co-equals. Thereafter, Schramm effectively spoke on behalf of the department as well as the institute in university political contexts.

21. Bush was insistent, whereas Schramm was not, on professional media experience as background for a career in journalism education. Both Danielson and McCombs later said they considered themselves Bush's students first, Schramm's second.

22. Lasswell, in Bryson (1948), proposed three general functions that he called surveillance, correlation, and transmission. See Chapter 2.

23. Wright (1960) added a fourth function, entertainment, to Lasswell's list.

24. This book represented one approach to comparative study of news coverage of important international events by reproducing newspaper front pages of the day following the Soviet invasion of Hungary, and the French/British/Israeli invasion of the Suez Canal.

25. This book laid out the new specialty of development communication, which soon came to be a recognized subfield of communication study.

8

Institutionalization of Advanced Communication Study in American Universities

And the world will be better for this,
That one man, scorned and covered with scars,
Still strove, with his last ounce of courage,
To reach the unreachable stars.

*—From Man of La Mancha, recited by
Wayne Danielson in tribute to Wilbur Schramm*[1]

Why aren't we [in communication] asking those kinds of questions? I wanted to do that so bad it hurt.

*—Wilbur Schramm, recalling in 1983 his reaction
40 years earlier to wartime research by the forefathers*[2]

Communication differs from other social sciences in that an industry—the mass media—stands behind the academic field. The rise of the mass media in the 20th century provided the impetus for growth of communication research by presenting society with both problems and opportunities

155

of unprecedented scope. Lasswell's career was spurred by concern about propaganda, for example, and Hovland's by the hope that mass communication could be harnessed in support of the war effort. Wilbur Schramm concerned himself with the ways that television might affect children's lives, and with the application of communication technologies in education and national development. But most of these research themes would not have taken root in the American university were it not for a large enrollment base consisting of students aspiring to jobs in the media and other glamorous careers in the expanding world of professional communication.

Job opportunities in print, film, and broadcasting, and in related fields such as advertising, public relations, and public information, are plentiful. Newspaper and magazine publishers have been among higher education's most generous donors, endowing scholarships, professorships, and even schools to ensure a steady supply of graduates educated for mass communication work. Students have poured into communication programs in ever-increasing numbers.[3] At many highly respected universities, communication students outnumber majors in any other discipline. As a result, PhDs who aspire to become communication professors have excellent job prospects in comparison with most academic fields.[4] The numbers are there.

More is needed to establish a new field of study in American higher education, though, than jobs, money, and willing students. What is demanded first is a body of knowledge. Wilbur Schramm saw the raw material for the field emerging from the work of the four forefathers whose careers he highlights in Part I of this book. Theory and research, the hallmarks of academic development, were the elements that Schramm first put together, as we noted in Chapter 7. Beyond development of a body of knowledge, and of theories and methods with which to build it, communication study needed a unified vision of itself and it needed places to grow. Schramm offered the first of these requisites, as we have seen. The present chapter considers the second, that is, the problem of establishing communication study beyond the particular schools—Iowa, Illinois, and Stanford—to which Schramm's own career took him. To prove its long-range viability, the field had to depend on other institutions, and other people.

The Schramm Plan

Wilbur Schramm foresaw an integrated social science of human communication.[5] This subject would become part of the standard university curriculum, at least at the graduate level. Advanced programs would be supported by undergraduate teaching of entry-level skills for communication professions such as print journalism, persuasion, and broadcasting. Existing departments of journalism and speech would be merged into a single unit that would offer professional training for bachelor's and master's students, topped off by doctoral study of communication processes and effects. This scholarly work would treat communication generically; such a department could include advanced study of interpersonal communication and of innovative media technologies, for example (Schramm, 1963). These new kinds of communication knowledge would eventually supplant—or at least supplement—the traditional skills-centered curricula. Schramm imagined something akin to the history of other scientific disciplines, which that had gradually upgraded and differentiated themselves by building a specialized knowledge base.

The process that Schramm envisioned was approximately what took place at Stanford University during his tenure there (from 1955 to 1973) as his communication research institute and the journalism department merged with the broadcasting and film components of the speech and drama department to form the department of communication. This merger was effected administratively around the time that Chilton Bush, longtime head of the journalism department, retired in 1962.[6] But neither Schramm's vision nor Stanford's implementation of it became a popular model for other major research universities of that time. Nor was it widely adopted as a blueprint for institutions whose basic mission is undergraduate instruction, which is to say the great bulk of American colleges and universities.

Diversity in Institutionalization

What organizational template has been followed in institutionalizing communication study? There is no single dominant pattern. Communication units in American higher education, viewed as a group, present a seemingly hopeless confusion of idiosyncratic structures.[7] Each university has dealt with this new field in ways suitable to its particular history and mission, as interpreted by its own strong intellectual personalities.

We presume that this variety represents an early stage in the field's development and that eventually some single model will come to characterize the field of communication study at most institutions. That has been the historical pattern within most disciplines. Meanwhile, though, what has happened to communication study around the country tends to undercut

Schramm's vision of a unified academic field.[8] Vocational skills instruction still dominates in undergraduate communication study at most colleges and universities. A homogenized graduate department where, for example, interpersonal communication and mass communication processes are studied in relation to one another is scarcely to be found. Students of new information technologies have difficulty finding an academic home; communication units have accommodated those interests in only limited ways. Communication study has not yet come to be considered a standard discipline within higher education (Levy & Gurevitch, 1994; Rogers & Chaffee, 1983).

Academic concern with communication as an abstract process traditionally focused on rhetoric, a school of thought that dates back to Aristotle. In the late 19th century, rhetoric along with logic and grammar formed the academic "trivium," part of the "seven liberal arts" that constituted the idealized university curriculum. In Schramm's time, though, long-accepted principles of rhetoric were being tested by the brash new behavioral sciences. Schramm's colleague Nathan Maccoby even called Hovland's empirical approach to persuasion " 'scientific' rhetoric" (Maccoby, 1963). But several thousand professors of rhetoric were not about to hand over their established place in American higher education to a few dozen social psychologists. Speech departments, most of them headed by rhetoricians teaching their traditional discipline, were firmly established in most universities when advanced communication study arrived on the scene. Behavioral science would have to prove itself a superior approach to understanding persuasion, not just an alternative one, if it were to gain a significant position in speech. When radio emerged in the 1920s, broadcasting skills instruction was inserted in the curriculum alongside the "orality" tradition of speech performance courses; television later followed where radio had gone. Meanwhile, education for journalism was developing on a separate track. Mass media instruction was therefore split apart before the concept of mass communication as a unified field occurred to people.

Journalism was by midcentury almost as ubiquitous in American higher education as speech, but it was identified less with an academic tradition and more with a profession. Almost all college journalism instructors offered as their "teaching credential" a substantial number of years of professional experience. It was not the PhD but a successful first career as a journalist that qualified one to teach this craft in a university.[9] The typical school of journalism each year produced hundreds of budding reporters; a few would eventually become publishers, and therefore potential university benefactors. In most institutions, the journalism unit remained a department (often nominally a "school") in a liberal arts college governed by a humanities and sciences faculty. But many of the best state institutions of higher education were becoming research universities, not simply over-sized liberal arts colleges. In the graduate schools that burgeoned following World War II, academic administrators expected their departments to produce research as well as instruction (Chaffee, 1988, pp. 132-134).[10] The kind of research that was valued depended on whether the communication-related unit was governed within the social studies or the humanities. Where social science was the expectation, this helped pave the way for acceptance of Schramm's model. A journalism school that did not generate communication research of some type could find itself in a precarious position in the post-war research university.[11]

Resistance to advanced communication study was eased in the 1950s by the fact that higher education was expanding rapidly.[12] The new PhDs—sometimes derided as "communicologists" but seen by colleagues as po-tential sources of research prestige and income—were more easily ac-cepted as an addition, rather than a substitution, within a department faculty. But speech and journalism faculties were not going to sacrifice their traditional missions or their established modes of inquiry.

In a university where no speech or journalism unit existed, there might be less resistance to advanced communication study but there was also less reason to institutionalize it. A top-ranked university, for example in the prestigious Ivy League, did not feel a need to *add* a new social science to its roster of departments. An institution aspiring to become a research university, on the other hand, might see advanced communication study as a fast track toward greater academic respectability—and toward extramural research grants such as those Schramm had brought to Illinois and Stan-ford. Given these conflicting factors, it is not surprising that the entry of communication study into academia did not follow a singular pattern and did not result in any predictable new structure.

Three Kinds of Universities

We might group U.S. universities into three categories regarding ad-vanced communication study. First, some of the oldest and most famous universities, especially in the New England region, have no unit devoted to communication study in Schramm's sense.[13] Some of them have profes-sional communication programs, but these produce only a very minor portion of the field's scholarship. Communication research at Columbia or Yale, for example, never progressed much beyond Lazarsfeld's, Lasswell's, and Hovland's projects of 40 years ago, and those programs do not exist today. Communication study did not become institutionalized in its own right.

A second group of schools includes many of the large and dynamic state universities, especially in the Midwest. In these "multiversities,"[14] communication study was added to the missions of speech, journalism, and similar preprofessional teaching units, which remain separate departments. Schramm's original institution, the University of Iowa, is a good example. The Speech Department was not much interested in a doctoral-level merger with the Journalism School when Schramm proposed this in 1944. Today's School of Journalism and Mass Communication remains wholly separate from the Department of Communication Studies (formerly Speech), and different kinds of communication research programs are housed in each. Roughly the same thing happened at Illinois, despite Schramm, and at Minnesota, Wisconsin, Indiana, and kindred state research universities. This multidepartmental model has proven quite viable; these institutions have produced the bulk of communication research in the four decades since Schramm left Illinois.

Finally, some universities newer to graduate social science research have established unified communication departments "from scratch," or nearly so. Partly because this third group of universities is the youngest and least traditional, it is also the least prestigious in overall university rankings by faculty peers. Departments called Communication (or Mass Communication) are being created most often at smaller universities where graduate work and research are not stressed (Dickson, 1995). Often "Communication" is simply a convenient administrative rubric for lumping together several small skills programs that at bigger universities would be large enough to sustain separate departments.[15]

Communication study, then, although a thriving academic enterprise when viewed as a whole, is, from the Ivy League perspective (which controls thinking at the top of American higher education), stereotyped as a less-than-legitimate field. Communication study is strongest in the large state universities of the nation's heartland, but even there it is still struggling for academic respectability. It is growing mainly in up-and-coming institutions, but in many cases what is called a Department of Communication is a far cry from the research-intensive academic entity that Schramm envisioned.

Leading Examples: Michigan State and Wisconsin

The full story of the institutionalization of communication study in America is beyond the scope of this book. Our concern here is with the beginnings of the field, and this story can best be explained by recounting in some detail how communication as a social science took early root in a few prototypic universities. For that purpose we focus on two institutions, the University of Wisconsin, in Madison, and Michigan State University, in East Lansing. This choice extends the "personal memoir" principle of the present book, as each of us joined the faculty at one of these schools in the 1960s—Chaffee at Wisconsin and Rogers at MSU. But there are better reasons for focusing on these two Big Ten universities. For years these schools have stood at the top of the field, with very few peer institutions, in terms of faculty and PhD productivity in communication research. Yet they differ markedly in their institutional structures. We use them to illustrate how communication study was established in universities of, respectively, our second and third categories, whereas it failed to emerge in the older institutions of our first category.

We shall reserve for other writings the longer story of how communication study transformed the fields of speech and journalism, and how it was itself transformed from a social science to an even more eclectic, multidisciplinary activity (Rogers, 1994). Schramm, however, in his outline for the present volume, felt that something should be added here about the initial process, including the changes in academic unit names that marked deeper substantive changes in communication study. We do not follow Schramm's chapter outline precisely, as this chapter has become our story; but we will touch on all of the points he had listed for the final chapter that he intended to write for this book.

Michigan State: The First
Department of Communication

When Wilbur Schramm introduced his ideas for a new field of study at Iowa and Illinois in the late 1940s, the neighboring institution in East Lansing was called Michigan State College (MSC), and it was not considered an academic (or yet an athletic) power. In the early 1950s the state of Michigan decided to upgrade the East Lansing campus in all respects, calling it a "University" and expanding its funding and mission so it could take its place alongside the other leading state universities of the Big Ten

(Dressel, 1987).[16] At Michigan State this rising tide lifted the boat of communication, the newest field on the national academic scene. Michigan State was a university on-the-make, and it adopted the field of communication study as a welcome innovation. As the state's land-grant university, Michigan State was founded to serve the agricultural and engineering interests of Michigan through teaching, applied research, and extension. Its practical and vocational character extended to other university programs, such as the School of Education. Communication fit into this pragmatic mission and was a natural target for build-up in the expansive 1950s (Dressel, 1987).

The situation in East Lansing was inherently different from that in, say, Madison or Urbana-Champaign, where the state university and the land-grant university were one and the same. In Michigan, the mission of developing high academic distinction on a par with the older Ivy League institutions was reserved for the University of Michigan in Ann Arbor. In the 1950s, however, Michigan State was upgraded to the level of, in effect, a second major state university. The state of Michigan's model was obviously California, where UCLA had rapidly emerged as a state university second only to the original University of California at Berkeley. Although this expansion involved strengthening the liberal arts, MSU could not hope to compete with the outstanding academic departments in Ann Arbor, generally ranked behind only Berkeley among U.S. public universities. Wisely, MSU's administration decided to build from strength, which meant investing in the academic side of their pragmatically oriented schools.

In 1955, MSC decided to establish a School of Communication Arts; when the institution's title was upgraded from "College" to "University" later that year, the Communication Arts unit was in turn promoted from "School" to "College" (E. Bettinghaus, personal communication, February 8, 1995). Gordon Sabine was appointed the first dean (Troldahl, 1968). The original structure of this new college included a school of journalism and a department of speech.[17] Each had broken off from the English department earlier in the century, but by 1950 they were housed in separate schools on the East Lansing campus, under different deans. The mission of the newly integrated College of Communication Arts was only partly spelled out in the legislation creating it. It included instruction in journalism, radio skills, television skills, audiovisual aids, "et cetera." The skills instruction implicit in the "et cetera" was initially honored in the immediate creation of separate departments of advertising and of television, radio, and film.

Soon though, the idea of communication was insinuated into MSU's structure more thoroughly. A PhD program in communication, emphasizing the study of language, was approved by the university's graduate school in 1957-1958 (Bain, ca. 1984). A division of mass communication was formed to house the journalism, advertising, and television-radio-film programs. Fred Siebert, Schramm's erstwhile colleague at Illinois and director of MSU's J-School, was appointed director of this division, which lasted until 1958. A core curriculum in communication arts, common to all departmental majors in the college, had evolved into a Department of Communication Arts by 1957.[18] After Siebert became dean of the college in 1962, this title was shortened to "Communication," and thus MSU housed the nation's first major university department so named.[19] The title of the overarching unit was in turn broadened, consistent with Schramm's vision; in 1974 it became the College of Communication Arts and Sciences.

Wilbur Schramm had no direct hand in this thoroughgoing institutionalization of communication at Michigan State, but his influence is easy to trace. Fred Siebert, Sabine's successor as dean of the college, was a Bleyer protégé from Wisconsin who had been Schramm's colleague and coauthor at Illinois (Siebert, Peterson, & Schramm, 1956). When Michigan State set about to recruit assistant professors for its new department of communication, its administrators looked mainly for Schramm-oriented PhDs. David K. Berlo and Hideya Kumata, who had been Schramm's research assistant on a study of propaganda, were hired out of the Illinois doctoral program in 1956, the same year Malcolm MacLean, an early Wisconsin PhD in mass communication, came to MSU. Erwin P. Bettinghaus, who had been a student in the last course Schramm taught at Illinois, was added to the MSU faculty in 1958. These budding scholars brought Schramm's perspectives with them. At Stanford, Chilton ("Chick") Bush was already producing PhDs, and in 1956 MSU hired one of his stars, Paul J. Deutschmann. Deutschmann, a former newspaper city editor, was originally brought to head the school of journalism but soon became instead director of MSU's Communication Research Center, an attempt to replicate Stanford's Institute for Communication Research. Deutschmann, a workaholic to rival Schramm, died of a heart attack in 1962. In this period, leadership settled firmly into the department of communication.

David Berlo, whose background included psychology, mathematics, and speech, was appointed to chair the department of communication while still in his 20s. Over the next few years, Berlo's unit outshone any other in the university in terms of national and international eminence within its field. Among the future luminaries added to its faculty roster in those early years were Gerald R. Miller, a speech and social psychology PhD from Iowa, who was to do much toward establishing the study of interpersonal communication as a social science field; mass communication scholar Bradley S. Greenberg, a Wisconsin PhD fresh from a postdoctoral stint at Stanford; Verling C. ("Pete") Troldahl, a mass communication PhD from Minnesota; and R. Vincent Farace, an Iowa PhD who along with Everett M. Rogers helped established organizational communication as a viable academic specialty at MSU. Kumata and Rogers developed Michigan State's strength in international communication, and Bettinghaus (a future dean at MSU) became a leading figure in persuasion studies.

Berlo was a leader of great energy and vision. He had completed his PhD at Illinois in just 2 years, while serving part of this time on active duty in the U.S. Air Force and also working at a radio station. He saw in his department's title and very existence an opportunity to make an instant mark in the academic world. "No one knows what a department of communication looks like," he challenged his faculty, "it's up to us to invent it." For most of them, this evoked a vision they had absorbed from the teachings and writings of Wilbur Schramm.

Berlo, like Schramm, invested much of his thinking in conceptualizing the new field. His introductory textbook *The Process of Communication* (1960) began with many of the same models that Schramm had collected in his *Process and Effects* reader. But there was one important difference in approach: Berlo's book was aimed at freshmen rather than doctoral students. Unlike Schramm, he saw the future of communication in undergraduate, rather than graduate, education. MSU's Communication 100 course was required of students majoring in any communication field and in the School of Education as well. Classes were, of course, huge, and serving as a teaching assistant in Comm. 100 became the training ground for a long line of future professors who apprenticed under Berlo and his colleagues.

At MSU, then, "communication" was the central organizing title for both the college and its showcase academic department. Thousands of Spartan students studied Berlo (in person, or at least in print) each year. Many hundreds of majors in the several communication departments were poring over Schramm's works in advanced courses and graduate seminars. As expanding universities around the country began catering to the rising student demand for communication courses in the early 1970s, Michigan State's integrated Department of Communication provided the organizational model. A new professor from MSU's rigorous doctoral program was in many ways the ideal addition to a faculty constructing a unit for communication study.[20] Quite often, though, MSU's PhDs found their academic employment where positions already existed in large numbers, in well-established journalism and speech departments.

Wisconsin: Modifying Established Units

The rapid, even startling, developments at Stanford and Michigan State did not go unnoticed in peer institutions—particularly at Wisconsin, where the school of journalism followed the Bleyer tradition while across campus the department of speech held to the rhetorical perspective. Wisconsin, as both a state university with a renowned history department and a land grant university distinguished in the life sciences, stood high among American public universities. Its first course in rhetoric was taught in 1887 and its first course in journalism in 1905. These communication skills curricula had by the first decade of the present century evolved into wholly independent departments, each under strong, stable leadership. When Ralph O. Nafziger returned to Madison from the University of Minnesota in 1948, he became only the third director in the Wisconsin J-School's history. In 1954, Frederick W. Haberman became just the fourth chairman of the Department of Speech. They were to serve 18 and 23 years, respectively, in these positions. During their administrative tenures, the social scientific approach to communication study arrived at Wisconsin but it was received quite differently in the two departments.

Journalism and Mass Communication

Nafziger was the key figure at Wisconsin in making a place for communication study within an enduring administrative structure. An experienced newspaperman before he began teaching journalism, Nafziger was devoted first to strengthening the profession; the one new faculty member who accompanied him from Minnesota to Wisconsin in 1948 was Graham Hovey, a topflight professional newsman. But Nafziger was also a leading exponent of quantitative research methods. As a graduate student, he had published one of the first newspaper readership studies (Nafziger, 1930) and took statistics from the young sociological methodologist Samuel Stouffer.[21] Nafziger specialized in studies of the foreign press, and in 1942-1943 he, like Schramm, worked at the U.S. Office of Facts and Figures, the nation's wartime propaganda agency. Nafziger's knowledge of German, and of the German press, made him an invaluable content analyst for the OFF. Back at Minnesota in 1944, Nafziger established the first research division within a J-School. It was linked with the Minnesota Poll, a collaborative news research agency, which provided field experience and support for Nafziger's graduate students.

In the process of accepting the Wisconsin position as director of the School of Journalism, Nafziger negotiated a number of changes. He agreed to accept the university's instructional program in advertising from the business school. To teach advertising in the J-School was consonant with advice Nafziger was getting from newspaper publishers around the state, but advertising was also a field that was coming alive to the implications of behavioral science. Nafziger received commitments of support for two additional entities that would make Wisconsin parallel with Minnesota, Iowa, and Illinois: an interdepartmental PhD program in mass communication and a mass communication research center housed in the school of journalism.

Nafziger's approach to creating these new academic entities was incremental in terms of personnel but radical with respect to intellectual discipline. He encouraged junior faculty who lacked the PhD, such as newspaper editing instructors Scott Cutlip and Bruce Westley, to develop scholarly specializations. As faculty teaching slots opened in the 1950s, Nafziger mostly hired PhDs, including S. Watson Dunn, a marketing PhD who headed advertising; Charles Higbie, an experienced journalist with a political science doctorate from the London School of Economics; and Harold L. ("Bud") Nelson, the first PhD from Minnesota's doctoral program in mass communication. These teacher-scholars were added to a faculty roster that already included Frank Thayer (1944), author of a best-selling textbook, *Legal Control of the Press,* and leading press historian Henry Ladd Smith.[22]

But Nafziger observed that "a new breed of cat" was also needed if the J-School was to establish a respected doctoral program while continuing to carry out its teaching and service missions in journalism, advertising, and public relations. The PhD program was set up jointly with the Department of Agricultural Journalism (where Nafziger had received his bachelor's degree). He enlisted the cooperation of social scientists elsewhere in the university, notably methodologist Burton Fisher in Sociology, statistician Chester Harris in Educational Psychology, and social psychologist Leonard Berkowitz, known for early experiments on effects of film violence. Dissertation committees regularly included faculty from such "outside" social science departments.

To establish his mass communication research center, Nafziger in 1956 brought to Madison Percy H. Tannenbaum, an Illinois PhD in communication. Tannenbaum's mentor had been Charles Osgood, an experimental psychologist who had succeeded Schramm as director of the research institute at Illinois; Osgood and Tannenbaum had coauthored several prominent publications exploring theoretical implications of a new research technique, the semantic differential (Osgood, Suci, & Tannenbaum, 1957; Osgood & Tannenbaum, 1955). Under Tannenbaum, the research center, and soon the Wisconsin

PhD program, focused on a more microscopic level of analysis than Nafziger or others in the J-School were accustomed to.

If it is to Nafziger's credit that he sought out this new and different kind of research, it is equally to the credit of Tannenbaum that he suggested in the late 1950s that the PhD program be expanded to include legal and historical scholarship alongside applied psychological and social science.[23] Nafziger continued to recruit new faculty with PhDs, mostly sociobehavioral scientists and mostly from the new doctoral programs: Wayne Danielson from Stanford, William Hachten (a legal and international scholar) from Minnesota, Jack McLeod (a Wisconsin J-School graduate with a Michigan PhD in social psychology), Richard F. Carter (a 1957 Wisconsin PhD who had been teaching at Stanford), and Steven Chaffee from Stanford. Nafziger also kept on several of Wisconsin's own quantitatively oriented PhDs, including Malcolm S. MacLean, Jr. (an erstwhile instructor in photojournalism), James A. Fosdick (also teaching photojournalism), and Vernon A. Stone, who taught broadcast journalism. By the time Nafziger retired in 1966 all his hires[24] except Danielson and MacLean were still at Madison and the Wisconsin faculty and PhD program had become the most productive in journalism and mass communication research.[25]

Speech, a.k.a. Communication Arts

Several blocks across the Madison campus was a well-established Department of Speech. From its origins in rhetoric and public address, this department had grown to include subunits devoted to theater and drama, speech disorders, and skills instruction in radio, television, and film. When Haberman succeeded Andrew T. Weaver (who had served for 27 years) as chairman in 1954, the Speech department displayed no inclination toward the social sciences; the department, about twice the size of the Journalism School, was firmly tied to the humanities division of the UW faculty. Although speech disorders entailed some psychological research, the overall department's predominant intellectual tradition was rhetoric, the disciplinary specialty of both Weaver and Haberman; mass communication was taught in the speech department as skills, not as a research area. Through the 1950s, while Nafziger was bringing a string of social and behavioral scientists into the mass communication program in the J-School, Speech did not join this movement. The two departments remained almost totally unconnected, although speech PhD students were included in Malcolm MacLean's mass communication research seminar in the J-School in the mid-1950s (R. F. Carter, personal communication, April 20, 1995).

The first Wisconsin speech professor hired to teach behavioral theory and quantitative methods was Theodore Clevenger, who came from the Illinois faculty in 1959 and stayed at UW for 3 years.[26] As a PhD student at Florida State University, Clevenger had majored in public address but with an unusual minor: experimental design. He combined these specialties in experiments on factors that induce stage fright and in comparisons of different ways of teaching the course in oral interpretation. Haberman viewed Clevenger's addition to the faculty as a continuity more than as a departure because these research topics were central concerns in speech, even though Clevenger's way of studying them was different (F. Haberman, personal communication, August 11, 1994).

Clevenger left Wisconsin in 1962 in a dispute over laboratory space; his replacement was Frederick Williams, a new speech PhD from the University of Southern California who had done research on hearing and on broadcasting. Williams soon began collaborating with Tannenbaum over in the mass communications research center. This was one of a very few intellectual connections between these two units during the 1960s.[27] After Tannenbaum left Wisconsin in 1968, Williams moved his research program to the UW Institute for Research on Poverty for a year and then left for the University of Texas.

In 1968, Wisconsin's Speech department hired its first Michigan State PhD in Communication, Gordon Whiting; two others, John McNelly and Ivan Preston, had already been hired in Journalism. Like Clevenger and Williams, Whiting had done undergraduate and graduate work in speech. His interests, though, lay primarily in international communication and development, and in speech factors in social stratification. He found his research collaborators in Wisconsin's Land Tenure Center rather than in the Speech Department. Another empirical scholar, C. David Mortensen, joined the speech faculty in 1970, studying language and persuasion in small groups.

Fred Haberman was not resistant to behavioral science, he simply didn't feel his department needed much of it. He opened the door to experimental research because his colleagues saw this as a way of strengthening what they were already doing.[28] But there were new forms of communication study afoot at Michigan State and similarly structured programs.[29] Interpersonal communication was one, but not until 1974 did Wisconsin hire its first specialist in this area, Joseph Cappella. Although he started graduate school in physics, Cappella had read in rhetoric and philosophy while a Michigan State doctoral student, a comforting background for Haberman and other senior rhetoricians in what had been renamed the Department of

Communication Arts.[30] Cappella specialized from the start in quantitative research on interpersonal processes, rapidly becoming a leading scholar and mentor in that field. He and Dean Hewes, another interpersonal communication scholar, were the first tenure candidates that Speech put through the UW's social studies, rather than humanities, divisional committee.

Joanne Cantor, an experimentalist who had studied under Dolf Zillmann at Indiana University, became in 1975 the first behavioral scientist of mass communication to be hired in Communication Arts at Wisconsin. Her arrival closed a circle of sorts, as Zillmann had been a doctoral advisee of Tannenbaum, whom Nafziger had brought into the J-School nearly 20 years earlier. Cantor was the department's first quantitative empiricist with no background in traditional speech and rhetorical studies.

Communication as a social science at Wisconsin developed almost entirely in parallel, rather than in collaboration, between the two major departments in the College of Letters and Science. It developed at least a decade later in Speech rather than in Journalism because of different kinds of leaders, different intellectual traditions, and structural barriers such as the separation of the university faculty into divisions of humanities and social studies. Communication never became the title of any one department; when Speech and Journalism prepared in the late 1960s to move into one building, a series of summit meetings resulted in new unit labels that included the word *communication*, but only the building itself was given that generic title in unadulterated form.[31] And yet Wisconsin became, like Michigan State, one of the nation's leading centers of advanced communication study.

Institutionalizing the Name

The term communication has gradually been insinuated into higher education in countless ways over the years. Many speech departments (and in the mid-1970s the Speech Association of America) adopted the name "Speech Communication"—a have-your-cake-and-eat-it-too solution. Schools of journalism have in some cases added "and Mass Communication" to their titles; this compromise was adopted by the Association for Education in Journalism (now AEJMC) in 1976. Rarely, in the early decades, was the Stanford approach of merging speech and journalism into a single communication unit followed. At some institutions, though, either journalism or speech renamed itself communication, whereas the other retained its traditional title and separate departmental identity.

Some universities, following the Illinois and Michigan State example, combined several departments into schools of communication (often with "arts" and/or "sciences" added). At the University of Texas today, for example, this unit includes departments of advertising, radio-TV-film, journalism, and speech communication, with some 4,000 students and more than 80 professors. At Michigan State, the college includes the departments of communication, telecommunications, journalism, advertising, and audiology. At Illinois, Schramm's erstwhile college includes the Institute of Communications Research, departments of journalism and advertising, and a division of broadcasting. Speech, though, remains outside this unit, as the Department of Speech Communication in the liberal arts college. Within the Big Ten, the only unified communication unit at this writing is the merged department at the University of Michigan.[32] At Northwestern, a smaller, private institution, there are separate departments of film, radio-TV, and communication studies in the School of Speech, plus the independent Medill School of Journalism. Merger is today in the air elsewhere in the country and may enhance the institutionalization of communication study that Schramm put into motion a half-century ago. Standing against this prospect are not only traditional self-concepts of speech and journalism units but also a resurgent resistance to social and behavioral science itself; humanistic study of mass communication has regained the momentum that the social sciences had seized in Schramm's time. That story too must remain for another telling.

NSSC: An Association and a Journal

Speech was the academic field of origin for a separate form of institutionalization of communication study, the first organization bearing that title. This development occurred independently of Wilbur Schramm and most of the universities, seminal researchers, and academic statesman whose stories have been recounted to this point in this book. Two of the essential characteristics of a scholarly field are the formation of an academic association and the publication of a research journal. Because academic careers, including tenure and other quality control judgments, are built on peer review, one of the early steps in establishing a field is to create venues for the sharing of research with colleagues elsewhere.

Communication was not quick to undertake this kind of professional organization, partly because Wilbur Schramm put his energies into university curricula, schools, and research institutes, and published books more often than journal articles or convention papers. The need for an interuniversity entity to represent communication study as a whole was filled, gradually and almost inadvertently, by other scholars. Around 1950, the National Society for the Study of Communication (NSSC) was formed; NSSC's scholarly organ, the *Journal of Communication,* began publication in 1951.[33] As part of a reorganization in 1968, NSSC decided to rename itself and became the International Communication Association (ICA). Its conventions and journals constitute a major gathering place for scholars of communication today.

NSSC began as a dissident movement within the Speech Association of America, an organization composed mostly of the nation's thousands of teachers of rhetoric, argumentation and debate, forensics, and public address.[34] After World War II, several new fields of oral presentation, such as speech disabilities and broadcasting, began breaking off from speech to become separate (and quite viable) departments on their own. Some speech professors, viewing this trend with dismay, began to see communication as the unifying umbrella, a discipline that would analyze generic communication behaviors, rather than teach formal declamation. Their emphasis in founding NSSC was on the *study* of communication, as represented by such new intellectual traditions as general semantics, clinical methods, empirical research on reading and listening, and abstract models of the communication process. This was intended as a reform movement within speech, with the concrete aim of establishing a broadly conceptual introductory course to replace the speech performance courses that most schools offered for entry to the major.

The fledgling NSSC struggled throughout its early years, meeting annually in conjunction with the SAA convention; for a time it seemed little more than a special interest group within the much larger organization. The organization reached a temporary peak membership of slightly more than 500 in 1957, but this dropped to some 300 the next year when its officers decided to hold the NSSC annual conference at a time and place separate from that of SAA. NSSC's first three presidents were Paul D. Bagwell of Michigan State, Ralph G. Nichols of the University of Minnesota, and Elwood Murray of the University of Denver. The *Journal* was originally edited (1951-1952) by Thomas Lewis of Florida State University, who had trouble finding enough publishable manuscripts to fill more than two small issues per year. All of these leaders, and indeed almost all of NSSC's members, were SAA regulars with backgrounds in traditional speech and rhetoric but with a more generic notion of the place communication study could hold in the modern university. Among their hopes was that an introductory course in communication would become a requirement across the university curriculum, not just in speech.[35]

The emergence of NSSC paralleled, but involved little contact with, the events in which Wilbur Schramm played such a central role in pulling together the field of communication study. At both Iowa and Illinois, the speech faculties had in the 1940s steered clear of Schramm's social scientific doctoral ventures. The only apparent connection between Schramm and NSSC in its founding years seems to have been Wendell Johnson, a general semanticist who had been one of Schramm's speech therapists at Iowa and who served on one of NSSCs original governing committees in 1951—several years after Schramm had left Iowa. Of the research programs initiated by the four forefathers whose careers Schramm details in the earlier chapters of this book, the closest connection with NSSC was probably Franklin Knower of Ohio State University, whose early classroom experiments on persuasion techniques were cited by Carl Hovland in his World War II studies (Hovland et al., 1953; Hovland et al., 1949). Knower was a charter member of NSSC but does not appear to have taken an active organizational role in it.

Not only were NSSC and its *Journal* independent of Schramm's expanding orbit, for its first decade or more the organization operated in relative isolation by almost any standard. Fifteen years after its founding, it still had only about 500 members. Its efforts were diffused in many directions, including local speakers bureaus, centrally contrived research projects, and industry training programs. Then in about 1965, the organization gelled around a central mission of fostering member research through convention presentations and publication in the *Journal*. By 1968, membership had doubled and it would double again in the next dozen years. ICA was created in 1967-1969 by reconstituting NSSC as an independent (of SAA) organization of scholars, mostly social and behavioral scientists, with little administrative superstructure and a streamlined set of academic divisions. The major functions of ICA were to publish the *Journal* (and several other academic journals it was to create in the coming years), and to hold an annual convention at which the dominant activity would be sessions devoted to summaries and discussion of original research and theoretical papers. These activities filled the need for professional review and publication of career academics in research universities. The concomitant relabeling of the society from "National" to "International" was more apparent than real, however; more than 90% of the members were U.S. citizens, and the next largest group was Canadian. Not until its meeting in West Berlin in 1977 would ICA hold a convention outside the North American continent.[36]

The reinvention of NSSC as ICA in 1968 is a useful historical marker in the process of the institutionalization of communication study. The association's original identification with speech became diluted, as did the emphases on introductory instruction and service activities. Four broad divisions were created: information systems, interpersonal communication, organizational communication, and mass communication. The presidency, which in NSSC had been held almost exclusively by speech professors of one persuasion or another, began to rotate among scholars representing these more generic areas of study.

The organizational group was particularly strong. It was led by W. Charles Redding of Purdue University, who had been active in NSSC from its inception and its president in 1963. Interpersonal communication, which in the 1950s scarcely existed as an identifiable field of academic study, developed rapidly in the 1970s and became ICA's largest division. Although cross-membership with SAA continued to be the rule, significant numbers were also recruited from the ranks of the Association for Education in Journalism and other mass communication groups—people for whom "communication" meant what they had read in the books of Wilbur Schramm rather than what had been in the minds of the founders of NSSC.

The first clear connection to the Schramm tradition was signaled by the election in 1971 of Malcolm S. MacLean, Jr., of the University of Iowa as president-elect of ICA.[37] MacLean was the first ICA president with a background in journalism and mass communication. He was, however, by no means the first behavioral scientist from outside speech to head the organization; as early as 1953 the president of NSSC had been Herold Lillywhite, a speech therapist. Industry connections were important too, although commercial consultant C. J. ("Mickey") Dover, NSSC president in 1965, was the only nonacademic to head the organization. Schramm's erstwhile Stanford colleague Nathan Maccoby was ICA president from 1974-1975. In other words, as the organization grew, it diversified and, to a considerable extent, came to embody Schramm's vision of a multidisciplinary research field of communication.

The *Journal of Communication* evolved in parallel with the organization's expanding membership through 1974. When Francis A. Cartier became editor in 1953 he solicited enough papers to fill at least a thin quarterly. Over the next two decades, under a succession of editors serving 3-year terms, a standard academic review system was established, processing papers through a varied editorial board. The *Journal* offered NSSC/ICA members a miscellany of empirical studies, literature reviews, theoretical analyses, reports on the organization itself, advice on how to communicate or teach, and metaphorical entertainments (e.g., Darnell's 1967 article, "How Much Wood Would a Woodchuck Chuck").

ICA's publications program was radically restructured in 1974 to reflect the disciplinary lines that had developed within the organization. Editorship of the *Journal of Communication* was assigned on a long-term basis to George Gerbner, dean of the Annenberg School for Communication at Penn. Under a unique contract, the *Journal* was operated jointly by the Annenberg School and ICA for the 18 years of Gerbner's editorship[38] (after which time it reverted to ICA ownership). Gerbner adopted a more magazine-like format, emphasizing shorter articles and often dealing with cultural and policy aspects of mass communication institutions. Both the size and the circulation of the *Journal* more than doubled under Gerbner, due mainly to subscribers abroad who were attracted by the new format and the mass media focus.[39]

To service its large constituency of behavioral researchers, ICA in 1974 created a second journal, *Human Communication Research*. The first editor, Gerald R. Miller, attracted mostly theory-testing empirical studies related to his specialty, interpersonal communication. Another empirically oriented journal, *Communication Research,* was also established in 1974 as an independent venture by Sage Publications. Its founding editor was F. Gerald Kline, who continued in this capacity for 10 years. As a leader in journalism and mass communication at the Universities of Michigan and Minnesota, Kline attracted mainly mass communication manuscripts close to the Schramm tradition; Kline's journal took on his academic coloration, mainly due to the kinds of authors who submitted articles to him. Although *HCR*'s title was virtually identical to that of *CR,* its editors, beginning with Miller, were mainly interpersonal scholars, and that became its established character. So the new journals, despite generic "communication" labels, rapidly came to reflect the new structure of the field, replacing the universities' speech-journalism instructional dichotomy with the researchers' interpersonal-mass communication dichotomy.

The empirical emphasis of these new journals in turn neglected scholars of a philosophical (and rhetorical) bent, and in 1991 ICA initiated yet another journal, *Communication Theory*. Its first editor, Robert T. Craig, established it as mainly a venue for conceptual essays and metatheoretical overviews. These journals took their place alongside the longstanding research outlets *Journalism Quarterly* and the *Quarterly Journal of Speech,* published respectively by AEJMC and SCA, in addition to a host of newer periodicals.

This emergence of the field at the transinstitutional level can be said to have occurred abruptly with the creation of NSSC in the early 1950s, or perhaps with its reorganization into ICA in the late 1960s, or more gradually throughout the entire quarter-century from 1950 to 1974. The process was, of course, very much intertwined with what was going on contemporaneously within universities such as Wisconsin and Michigan State, which housed many of the scholars who contributed papers to the academic conventions and articles to the journals of ICA and other associations. Although we have emphasized Wilbur Schramm's role throughout this chapter, it is clear that communication study would have come to exist without him, albeit perhaps in a lesser form and at a later time.

The Fate of Research Institutes and Centers

Wilbur Schramm was a strong advocate of the research institute model as the vehicle for institutionalizing advanced communication study in the American university. He recognized that preexisting departments would hold to their traditional missions, and he was confident that communication study could win its academic spurs on the strength of research alone. Consequently, everywhere he went he established centers devoted to communication research separated from traditional departments: the Research Center in Iowa's J-School when he was its director; the Institute of Communications Research at Illinois as part of the College of Communication when he was its dean; the interdepartmental Institute for Communication Research at Stanford; and the East-West Communication Institute within the East-West Center in Hawaii. We repeat this list to make a point: Not one of those institutes long survived Schramm's tenure in it as an independent, nondepartmental entity. At Iowa, the center became essentially an emphasis within the J-School and not the dominant scholarly approach in the school. At Illinois, the institute acquired doctoral teaching responsibilities and tenure-line appointments, functioning much like a department. Stanford's Institute became a component of the Department of Communication (alongside journalism and documentary film production). At the East-West Center, Schramm's institute gradually disappeared through successive reorganizations as indicated by the evolution of titles: first Communication, then Communication and Culture, then Culture and Communication, and at this writing an imperiled Institute of Culture.

Early in the effort to institutionalize advanced communication study, it was conventional to segregate the research function in such an "institute" or "center." Schramm was following what he took to be the successful model of German universities (from which the idea of the research university came to America) and of Lazarsfeld's Bureau of Applied Social Research at Columbia. Other scholars of communication study were following Schramm. But these seemingly segregated research components today rarely amount to more than a couple of professors and some distinctive stationery. As faculty research has become the norm within American higher education, and as communication doctoral programs have diversified to include historical, legal, critical, and cultural studies as well as sociobehavioral science, these institutes mostly stand as reminders of an idea whose time is past.

Meanwhile, the centers of early advanced communication study "founded" by Ivy League luminaries such as Lazarsfeld at Columbia University and Hovland at Yale University were disbanded—and there is no successor unit devoted to advanced communication study today at those universities. (Professional journalism units can be found at Columbia and some other Ivy League schools, but they house little that Schramm would have called advanced communication study.) The early research programs at Columbia and Yale were indeed the basis on which Schramm's vision was founded, but the institutions themselves turned out not to be foundational. That remained to Schramm and like-minded colleagues at newer universities that seized on communication study to enhance their academic reputations.

The "department" and the "school" have, for all the confusion they present to us today, succeeded where the "institute" and the "center" largely failed in the task that Schramm envisioned for them—that of institutionalizing advanced communication study. In the modern university, the department is the basic unit representing a discipline. Departments hire professors to teach and conduct research, and reward them with tenure and raises if they perform these tasks well. Universities refer to departmental faculties for quality control judgments: who should be hired or promoted, what courses should be taught and by whom, where is the discipline heading, and what should the institution do about it? Departments may be cumbersome devices for some of these purposes, but by and large they are the units that persist. Advanced communication study has found its place in American higher education primarily in established instructional departments that made a place for it and in new departments in expanding universities, but as of this writing communication has gained little ground in older, prestigious universities that are neither expanding nor feeling a need for new areas of inquiry.

The position of communication study cannot, at this writing, be called a wholly secure one. Although some in communication study may consider it a social science field, older established fields do not. Citation analyses of journal articles show, for example, that communication scholars frequently cite findings from psychology, sociology, anthropology, political science, and economics but that this is not reciprocated (Reeves & Borgman, 1983; Rice, Borgman, & Reeves, 1988; So, 1988). Nor is there a study group representing communication study alongside these traditional disciplines within the National Science Foundation, to cite another indicator of the field's precarious status. University organizational charts are as likely to classify communication as a stand-alone school, parallel to a school of education or nursing, as to treat is as an academic department in the more usual sense.

We cannot, therefore, conclude that institutionalization of the field has been fully realized. But certainly the first steps have been made by Wilbur Schramm and others who built on the forefathers he describes in the first section of the book—and by many others working through university structures, organizational efforts, and diligent research. A great deal more is known about generic communication processes today than was the case half a century ago. Communication study, for all its present limitations, is one of the very few new academic fields to become established in the 20th century in American higher education. Having made our own careers in communication study, we regret that we lack the space and resources here to extend our recounting of those to whom this field is indebted.

The Future

What, then, is the future of communication study? Wilbur Schramm left his prediction on the hard disk of his computer when he died, in the form of a conclusion he had drafted for this book. In the near term, that is, the next several decades, he expected that academic departments would consolidate around the name "communication," meaning by it approximately what we have been describing in this chapter. In the longer term, perhaps 30 to 50 years out, Schramm foresaw a further intellectual integration in which communication study would merge with anthropology, psychology, sociology, economics, and political science—and perhaps other disciplines—to form a science of human behavior. Schramm expected that communication study would lead this drive toward unification of the behavioral sciences. Whether this scenario, the unification of all behavioral sciences around a communication core, will be realized remains for readers of this book, among others, to determine.

Notes

1. The occasion was the presentation to Schramm of the third Paul J. Deutschmann Award for outstanding contributions to mass communication research, at the convention of the Association for Education in Journalism, Fort Collins, Colorado, in August, 1973.

2. Quoted in Cartier (1988, p. 174).

3. In higher education for journalism, where a careful survey is conducted each year, enrollment increased approximately tenfold (from 14,600 to 148,000) in the period 1967-1990 (cf. Becker, 1991; Peterson, 1973). By 1990, approximately 50,000 bachelor's degrees in all communication fields were being awarded (about 5% of the 1 million degrees bestowed annually by U.S. universities), according to data from the U.S. Department of Education (Rogers, 1994). This estimate had approximately doubled in the decade 1979 to 1989.

4. See Chaffee and Clarke (1975). DeFleur (1992) has estimated that 500 new PhDs are needed annually to fill communication faculty positions, as compared to about 250 PhDs currently being produced in the field. These figures may overstate the case, as communication faculty positions are sometimes filled by PhDs from other disciplines.

5. Schramm often used the term *behavioral science* when that term was in vogue during the 1950s; in this chapter we use *social science* for simplicity, recognizing that this is the more popular current category in academia. As Richard Carter, a faculty colleague of Schramm's at Stanford, observes, "Although mass communication is profoundly social, it is essentially behavioral" (1995, pp. 5-6). He calls for a return to the behavioral viewpoint.

6. Substantively, Stanford's several communication programs remained essentially separate despite their formal unification into a single department. Thirty years after the merger, separate master's degree programs in journalism and in documentary film production continued to exist, neither with any curricular overlap with the other nor with the PhD program housed in the Institute for Communication Research.

7. Many universities have two or more departments devoted to communication study of some sort. Sometimes they are in different colleges, under different deans.

8. Empirical analyses indicate that communication scholars divide along three dimensions: mass communication versus interpersonal communication, humanistic versus scientific methods, and theoretical versus applied research (Barnett & Danowski, 1992; see also Reeves & Borgman, 1983; Rice, Borgman, & Reeves, 1988; So, 1988).

9. The master's degree was the standard terminal educational attainment within journalism faculties through the 1950s, although there were some BAs, alongside a few PhDs and law school graduates.

10. A research university puts great emphasis on graduate education and faculty research. This model was adopted in the United States from the German university system beginning with Johns Hopkins University in about 1880. Today there are about 60 research universities in the United States.

11. For example, a department of journalism that offered only a master's degree was created in 1950 at the University of California at Los Angeles—and then was abolished when program cutbacks began under Governor Ronald Reagan some 20 years later.

12. After World War II, there was a tremendous expansion in U.S. higher education enrollments, both because of funding for ex-servicemen via the GI Bill of Rights and because this raised the standard of education for career advancement for everyone else.

13. A notable exception in the Ivy League is the Annenberg School for Communication at the University of Pennsylvania that was funded by massive gifts from Philadelphia publisher

Walter Annenberg. Established in the 1960s, it attained high academic standing in the years following the period we are describing in this chapter.

14. The term *multiversity* was popularized by Clark Kerr when he was chancellor of the University of California system in the early 1960s.

15. Dickson's (1995) survey found that the unit in which journalism is taught is most often called Communication or Mass Communication. Use of this title is negatively correlated with faculty size, enrollment, doctoral education, and other indicators of academic prestige.

16. The term *Big Ten* refers to the football conference of major midwestern universities that was originally called the Western Conference. It had ceased to have 10 members when the University of Chicago dropped its football program in the late 1930s, so the addition of Michigan State in the early 1950s brought the conference back to full complement. With the further addition of Pennsylvania State University in the early 1990s, the Big Ten now has eleven member schools. In addition to athletics, these schools are connected by various interinstitutional arrangements and generally compare themselves to one another for academic standards.

17. The speech department was dissolved in 1968 and its resources shifted to communication.

18. It was originally called the Department of General Communication Arts and known as GCA on campus (E. Bettinghaus, personal communication, February 8, 1995).

19. A "communication" division existed at Stephens College as early as 1939 (Weaver, 1977).

20. In 1973, the departments of advertising, journalism, and telecommunication initiated a second PhD program, in mass media. It became a major source of policy, economics, and historical scholars of mass communication.

21. Stouffer, who had been editor of his family's newspaper in Sac City, Iowa, for 2 years after finishing his BA, later studied at the University of Chicago with William Ogburn and L. L. Thurstone. Before joining the Wisconsin faculty, he spent a postdoctoral year in England working with Ronald Fisher and Karl Pearson, the leading statistical methodologists of the time.

22. Nelson was hired to replace Smith, who left the Wisconsin faculty in 1955 for the University of Washington.

23. Tannenbaum's role in broadening the PhD program was emphasized by Harold L. Nelson in an interview with Steven Chaffee on August 10, 1994. As the leading historical and legal scholar on the Wisconsin J-School faculty, Nelson had been a principal beneficiary of this effort on Tannenbaum's part.

24. It is generally accurate to call these appointments Nafziger's. In that time, longstanding unit administrators exercised broad authority, including selection of junior faculty, following consultation with trusted colleagues. Nafziger took the position that the time for the full faculty to consider an appointment would be the tenure review.

25. In a detailed analysis of publications in research journals of the journalism and mass communication field for the period 1962 to 1971, Wisconsin ranked first in faculty productivity by more than 50% over second-place Stanford. Wisconsin graduates (highest degree earned) ranked first as well, by more than 30% over second-place Minnesota (Cole & Bowers, 1973).

26. Clevenger was the sole behavioral scientist, apart from the speech pathologists, in a speech faculty of 36 members. At this time, by contrast, nearly one-third of Nafziger's Journalism professors had done graduate work, primarily in some field of social or behavioral science.

27. Clevenger had also collaborated to some extent with Tannenbaum.

28. Haberman (during interview of Aug. 11, 1994) said he attempted to interest Iowa's Samuel Becker, who was successfully integrating rhetorical study with quantitative research on television effects, in moving to Wisconsin. Failing this, Haberman's department added an Iowa PhD, Lloyd Bitzer, in 1961. Bitzer's interests, however, lay in rhetorical rather than behavioral studies.

29. One such program was Florida State University in Tallahassee, where Clevenger went a few years after leaving Wisconsin and which also initiated an important PhD program in communication.

30. After a 2-year hiatus to complete a research project, Haberman served as chairman of the Speech Department again from 1972 to 1979 (F. Haberman personal communication, August 11, 1994).

31. Speech became Communication Arts, whereas Journalism became Journalism and Mass Communication. They were housed in Vilas Communication Hall, the Vilas Family Trust having provided the final million dollars for construction after the state legislature balked at an increase over the original cost estimate.

32. In 1995, a Department of Communication Studies was created at Michigan. It includes neither journalism nor film studies, which were among the principal programs that had been merged in the mid-1970s to form the Department of Communication.

33. This section is based heavily on information provided in Weaver (1977).

34. On the origins of communication study within the field of speech in the first half of this century see Cohen (1994). Cohen defines "communication" quite differently from Schramm, and there is little overlap beyond their terminological coincidence (Craig, 1995).

35. Berlo's introductory course at Michigan State was one that realized this goal to some extent, being required of all education majors as well as throughout the College of Communication.

36. ICA thereafter adopted the policy of holding every fifth annual convention abroad. Its membership remains overwhelmingly North American.

37. MacLean, as noted earlier here, had been a leading exponent of quantitative communication studies at both Wisconsin and Michigan State before he joined the Iowa faculty.

38. During the last 10 years of Gerbner's leadership, day-to-day editorial work was supervised by his chief assistant, Marsha Seifert.

39. In 1992, Gerbner retired as editor, but the mass media emphasis was retained under the new editor, Mark Levy.

References

American Psychological Association. (1958). Distinguished scientific contribution awards, 1957. *American Psychologist, 13*(4), 155-168

Bain, J. M. (ca. 1984). *Three decades of planning and progress: A brief history of the Department of Communication at Michigan State University.* Unpublished manuscript.

Bandura, A. (1977). *Social learning theory.* Englewood Cliffs, NJ: Prentice Hall.

Barker, R., Dembo, T., & Lewin, K. (1941). Frustration and regression: An experiment with young children. *University of Iowa Studies in Child Welfare, 18*(1), 1-314.

Barnett, G. A., & Danowski, J. A. (1992). The structure of communication: A network analysis of the International Communication Association. *Human Communication Research, 19*(2), 264-285.

Barnouw, E. (Ed.). (1989). *International encyclopedia of communications.* New York: Oxford University Press.

Bavelas, A. (1949). A mathematical model for group structures. *Applied Anthropology, 7,* 16-30.

Becker, L. B. (1991). Annual enrollment census: Comparisons and projections. *Journalism Educator, 46*(3), 50-60.

Bell, D. (1973). *The coming of post-industrial society: A venture in social forecasting.* New York: Basic Books.

Berelson, B. (1948). Communications and public opinion. In W. Schramm (Ed.), *Communications in modern society.* Urbana: University of Illinois Press.

Berelson, B. (1959). The state of communication research. *Public Opinion Quarterly, 23,* 1-5.

181

Berelson, B., Lazarsfeld, P. F., & McPhee, W. N. (1954). *Voting: A study of opinion formation in a presidential campaign.* Chicago: University of Chicago Press.

Berlo, D. K. (1960). *The process of communication.* New York: Holt, Rinehart & Winston.

Bleyer, W. G. (1931). What schools of journalism are trying to do. *Journalism Quarterly, 8,* 35-44.

Blumer, H. (1933). *Movies and conduct.* New York: Macmillan.

Blumer, H., & Hauser, P. (1933). *Movies, delinquency and crime.* New York: Macmillan.

Blumler, J. G. (1983). Communication and democracy: The crisis beyond and the ferment within. *Journal of Communication, 33*(3), 166-173.

Brown, J. F. (1929). The methods of Kurt Lewin in the psychology of action and affect. *Psychological Review, 36,* 200-221.

Bryce, J. (1921). *Modern democracies.* New York: Macmillan.

Bryce, J. (1987). *The American commonwealth* (3rd ed.). New York: Macmillan. (Original work published 1900)

Bryson, L. (Ed.). (1948). *The communication of ideas: A series of addresses.* New York: Harper.

Cantril, H., Gaudet, H., & Herzog, H. (1940). *The invasion from Mars: A study in the psychology of panic with the complete script of the famous Orson Welles broadcast.* Princeton, NJ: Princeton University Press.

Carey, J. W. (1977). Mass communication research and cultural studies. In J. Curran, M. Gurevitch, & J. Woollacott (Eds.), *Mass communication and society.* London: Edward Arnold.

Carroll, J. B. (Ed.). (1956). *Language, thought, and reality: Selected writings of Benjamin Lee Whorf.* Cambridge, MA: Technology Press of the Massachusetts Institute of Technology.

Carter, R. F. (1995). On the essential contributions of mass communication programs. *Journalism Educator, 49*(4), 4-10.

Cartier, J. M. (1988). *Wilbur Schramm and the beginnings of American communication theory: A history of ideas.* Unpublished doctoral dissertation, University of Iowa, Iowa City.

Chaffee, S., & Clarke, P. (1975). Training and employment of PhDs in mass communication. *Journalism Monographs, 42.*

Chaffee, S. H. (1988). Research as an academic necessity. In N. W. Sharp (Ed.), *Communication research: The challenge of the Information Age.* Syracuse, NY: Syracuse University Press.

Chaffee, S. H., Chu, G. C., Lyle, J., & Danielson, W. (1974). Contributions of Wilbur Schramm to mass communication research. *Journalism Monographs, 36.*

Charters, W. W. (1933). *Motion pictures and youth.* New York: Macmillan.

Cohen, H. (1994). *The history of speech communication: The emergence of a discipline, 1914-1945.* Annandale, VA: Speech Communication Association.

Cole, R. R., & Bowers, T. A. (1973). Research article productivity of U.S. journalism faculties. *Journalism Quarterly, 50,* 246-254.

Coleman, J. S. (1980). Paul Lazarsfeld: The substance and style of his work. In R. K. Merton & M. W. Riley (Eds.), *Sociological traditions from generation to generation: Glimpses of the American experience.* Norwood, NJ: Ablex.

Commission on Freedom of the Press. (1947a). *A free responsible press: A general report on mass communication: Newspapers, radio, motion pictures, magazines and books.* Chicago: University of Chicago Press.

Commission on Freedom of the Press. (1947b). *Government and mass communication.* Chicago: University of Chicago Press.

Cooley, C. H. (1983). *Social organization: A study of the large mind.* New Brunswick, NJ: Transaction Books. (Original work published 1909)

Craig, R. T. (1995). [Book review of Cohen (1994) and of Rogers (1994)]. *Communication Theory, 5,* 178-184.

Crane, D. (1972). *Invisible colleges: Diffusion of knowledge in scientific communities.* Chicago: University of Chicago Press.

Dale, E. (1935a). *The content of motion pictures.* New York: Macmillan.

Dale, E. (1935b). *How to appreciate motion pictures.* New York: Macmillan.

Dale, E. (1937). Need for study of the newsreel. *Public Opinion Quarterly, 1*(3), 122-125.

Danielson, W. (1974, October). Wilbur Schramm and the unreachable stars: The technological papers. *Journalism Monographs, 36.*

Danielson, W. (1989). How to write like Wilbur Schramm. *Journalism Quarterly, 66,* 519-521.

Darion, J. (1966). *Man of La Mancha.* New York: Random House.

Darnell, D. K. (1967). How much wood would a woodchuck chuck. *Journal of Communication, 17*(1), 63-65.

DeFleur, M. (1992). *The forthcoming shortage of communications PhDs: Trends that will influence recruiting.* New York: Freedom Forum Media Studies Center.

Delia, J. G. (1987). Communication research: A history. In C. R. Berger & S. H. Chaffee (Eds.), *Handbook of communication science* (pp. 20-98). Newbury Park, CA: Sage.

Dembo, T. (1931). *Der Anger als dynamisches Problem. Psychologische Forschung, 15,* 1-144.

de Sola Pool, I. (1969). Content analysis and the intelligence function. In A. A. Rogow (Ed.), *Politics, personality, and social science in the twentieth century: Essays in honor of Harold D. Lasswell.* Chicago: University of Chicago Press.

de Sola Pool, I., Lasswell, H. D., Lerner, D., Chapman, M., Conner, B., Lamb, B., Marshall, B., Meyer, E., Schueller, E., & Tinkoff, M. S. (1951). *Symbols of internationalism.* Stanford, CA: Stanford University Press.

Deutschmann, P. J., & Danielson, W. A. (1960). Diffusion of the major news story. *Journalism Quarterly, 37,* 345-355.

Dickson, T. (1995, August). *Final report of the AEJMC Task Force on Curriculum.* Paper presented at the annual conference of the Association for Education in Journalism and Mass Communication, Washington, DC.

Dollard, J., Miller, N. E., Doob, L. W., Mowrer, O. H., & Sears, R. R. (1939). *Frustration and aggression.* New Haven, CT: Yale University Press.

Donohue, G. A., Tichenor, P. J., & Olien, C. N. (1972). Gatekeeping: Mass media systems and information control. In F. G. Kline & P. J. Tichenor (Eds.), *Current perspectives in mass communication research* (pp. 41-69). Beverly Hills, CA: Sage.

Dressel, P. A. (1987). *College to university: The Hannah years at Michigan State, 1935-1969.* East Lansing: Michigan State University Publications.

Dulles, F. R. (1968). Review of *Propaganda Technique in the World War. The Bookman, 67.*

Dysinger, W. S., & Ruckmick, C. A. (1935). *The emotional responses of children to the motion picture situation.* New York: Macmillan.

Ember, C. R. (1988). *Guide to cross-cultural research using the HRAF archive.* New Haven, CT: Human Relations Area Files.

Ennis, T. W. (1978, December 20). Harold D. Lasswell, dead at 76; was top U.S. political scientist: An obituary. *New York Times,* p. B-11.

Eulau, H. (1968). The behavioral movement in political science: A personal document. *Social Research, 35,* 1-29.

Festinger, L. (1950). Informal social communication. *Psychological Review, 57,* 271-282.

Festinger, L. (1957). *A theory of cognitive dissonance.* Stanford, CA: Stanford University Press.

Festinger, L., Cartright. D., Barber, K., Fleischl, J., Gottsdanker, J., Keysen, A., & Leavitt, G. (1948). A study of a rumor: Its origin and spread. *Human Relations, 1,* 464-486.

Festinger, L., Reicken, H. W., Jr., & Schacter, S. (1956). *When prophecy fails.* Minneapolis: University of Minnesota Press.

Festinger, L., Schachter, S., & Back, K. (1950). *Social pressures in informal groups: A study of a housing project.* New York: Harper.

French, J. R. P., Jr. (1950). Field experiments: Changing group productivity. In J. G. Miller (Ed.), *Experiments in social process.* New York: McGraw-Hill.

French, J. R. P., Jr., & Coch, L. (1948). Overcoming resistance to change. *Human Relations, 1,* 512-532.

French, J. R. P., Jr., & Marrow, A. J. (1945). Changing a stereotype in industry. *Journal of Social Issues, 1*(3), 33-37.

Greffrath, M. (1979). *Die Zerstörung einer Zukunft: Gespräche mit emigirerten Sozialwissenschaftlern.* Germany: Reinbek.

Hall, S. (1980). Cultural studies and the centre: Some problematics and problems. In S. Hall, D. Hobson, A. Lowe, & P. Willis (Eds.), *Culture, media, language: Working papers in cultural studies, 1972-1979.* London: Hutchinson.

Halloran, J. D. (1983). A case for critical eclecticism. *Journal of Communication, 33*(3), 270-278.

Holaday, P. W., & Stoddard, G. D. (1933). *Motion pictures and standards of morality.* New York: Macmillan.

Hornik, R. C., Mayo, J. K., & McAnany, E. G. (1976). *Television and educational reform in El Salvador.* Stanford, CA: Stanford University Press.

Hovland, C. I. (1936). *The generalization of conditioned responses.* Unpublished doctoral dissertation, Yale University, New Haven, CT.

Hovland, C. I. (1952). A "communication analysis" of concept learning. *Psychological Review, 59,* 461-472.

Hovland, C. I. (Ed.). (1957). *The order of presentation in persuasion.* New Haven, CT: Institute of Human Relations/Yale University Press.

Hovland, C. I. (1959). Reconciling conflicting results derived from experimental and survey studies of attitude change. *The American Psychologist, 14,* 8-17.

Hovland, C. I. (1960). Computer simulation of thinking. *The American Psychologist, 15*(11), 687-693.

Hovland, C. I., & Janis, I. L. (Eds.). (1962). *Personality and persuasibility.* New Haven, CT: Yale University Press.

Hovland, C. I., & Janis, I. L., & Kelley, H. H. (1953). *Communication and persuasion: Psychological studies of opinion change.* New Haven, CT: Yale University Press.

Hovland, C. I., Lumsdaine, A. A., & Sheffield, F. D. (1949). *Experiments on mass communication: Studies in social psychology in World War II* (Vol. III). Princeton, NJ: Princeton University Press.

Hovland, C. I., & Weiss, W. (1951). The influence of source credibility on communication effectiveness. *Public Opinion Quarterly, 15,* 635-650.

Hull, C. L., Hovland, C. I., Ross, R. T., Hall, M., Donald, T. P., & Fitch, F. B. (1940). *Mathematico-deductive theory of rote learning: A study in scientific methodology* (Institute of Human Relations). New Haven, CT: Yale University Press.

Innis, H. A. (1951). *The bias of communication.* Toronto: University of Toronto Press.

Janis, I. L., & Feshbach, S. (1953). Effects of fear-arousing communications. *Journal of Abnormal and Social Psychology, 48,* 78-92.

Janowitz, M. (1969). Content analysis and the study of the "symbolic environment." In A. A. Rogow (Ed.), *Politics, personality, and social science in the twentieth century: Essays in honor of Harold D. Lasswell.* Chicago: University of Chicago Press.

Johnson, W. (1946). *People in quandaries: The semantics of personal adjustment.* New York: Harper & Row.

Katz, E. (1983). The return of the humanities and sociology. *Journal of Communication, 33*(3), 51-52.

Katz, E., & Lazarsfeld, P. F. (1955). *Personal influence: The part played by people in the flow of mass communications.* New York: Free Press.

Kelley, H. H. (1952). Two functions of reference groups. In G. E. Swanson, T. M. Newcomb, & E. L. Hartley (Eds.), *Readings in social psychology* (Rev. ed.). New York: Holt.

Kelley, H. H., & Volkart, E. H. (1952). The resistance to change of group-anchored attitudes. *American Sociological Review, 17,* 453-465.

Kelman, H. C., & Hovland, C. I. (1953). "Reinstatement" of the communicator in delayed measurement of opinion change. *Journal of Abnormal and Social Psychology, 48,* 327-335.

Klapper, J. T. (1960). *The effects of mass communication.* New York: Free Press.

Kuhn, T. S. (1962). *The structure of scientific revolutions.* Chicago: University of Chicago Press.

Lang, K., & Lang, G. E. (1953). The unique perspective of television and its effect. *American Sociological Review, 18,* 3-12.

Lang, K., & Lang, G. E. (1983). The "new" rhetoric of mass communication: A longer view. *Journal of Communication, 33*(3), 128-140.

Lasswell, H. D. (1923a). Chicago's old first ward: A case study in political behavior. *National Municipal Review, 12,* 127-131.

Lasswell, H. D. (1923b). Political policies and the international investment market. *Journal of Political Economy, 31,* 380-400.

Lasswell, H. D. (1925). Prussian schoolbooks and international amity. *Journal of Social Forces, 3,* 718-722.

Lasswell, H. D. (1935). *World politics and personal insecurity.* New York: McGraw-Hill.

Lasswell, H. D. (1936a). Encyclopedia of the social sciences in review. *International Journal of Ethics, 46,* 388-396.

Lasswell, H. D. (1936b). *Politics: Who gets what, when, how.* New York: Whitlesey House.

Lasswell, H. D. (1937). Relation of skill politics to class politics and national politics. *Chinese Social and Political Science Review, 21,* 298-313. [This article is abridged and reprinted as Chapter 6 in D. Marvick (Ed.), *Harold D. Lasswell: On political sociology* (pp. 152-164). Chicago: University of Chicago Press.]

Lasswell, H. D. (1941a). The garrison state and the specialists on violence. *American Journal of Sociology, 46,* 455-468.

Lasswell, H. D. (1941b). World attention survey. *Public Opinion Quarterly, 5,* 456-462.

Lasswell, H. D. (1948). The structure and function of communication in society. In L. Bryson (Ed.), *The communication of ideas: A series of addresses.* New York: Harper.

Lasswell, H. D. (1949). Why be quantitative? In H. D. Lassell & N. C. Leites (Eds.), *Language of politics: Studies in quantitative semantics* (pp. 40-52). New York: George Stewart.

Lasswell, H. D. (1951). *The world revolution of our time: A framework for basic policy research.*

Lasswell, H. D. (1960). *Psychopathology and politics.* New York: Viking. (Original work published 1930)

Lasswell, H. D. (1971). *Propaganda technique in the World War.* New York: Knopf. (Original work published 1927)

Lasswell, H. D. (1972). Communication research and public policy. *Public Opinion Quarterly, 36,* 301-310.

Lasswell, H. D. (1977a). The garrison state and the specialists on violence. In D. Marvick (Ed.), *Harold D. Lasswell on political sociology.* Chicago: University of Chicago Press.

Lasswell, H. D. (1977b). Skill politics and skill revolution. In D. Marvick (Ed.), *Harold D. Lasswell: On political sociology.* Chicago: University of Chicago Press.

Lasswell, H. D., Casey, R. D., & Smith, B. L. (1935). *Propaganda and promotional activities.* Minneapolis: University of Minnesota Press.

Lasswell, H. D., Casey, R. D., & Smith, B. L. (Eds.). (1946). *Propaganda, communication, and public opinion: A comprehensive reference guide.* Princeton, NJ: Princeton University Press.

Lasswell, H. D., & Jones, D. B. (1939). *World revolutionary propaganda.* New York: Knopf.

Lasswell, H. D., Lerner, D., & de Sola Pool, I. (1952). *The comparative study of symbols.* Stanford, CA: Stanford University Press.

Lasswell, H. D., Lerner, D., & Rothwell, C. E. (1952). *The comparative study of elites.* Stanford, CA: Stanford University Press.

Lasswell, H. D., Lerner, D., & Speier, H. (1980a). *Emergence of public opinion in the West: Propaganda and communication in world history* (Vol. 2). Honolulu: University Press of Hawaii.

Lasswell, H. D., Lerner, D., & Speier, H. (1980b). *A pluralizing world of information: Propaganda and communication in world history* (Vol. 3). Honolulu: University Press of Hawaii.

Lasswell, H. D., Lerner, D., & Speier, H. (1980c). *The symbolic instrument in early times: Propaganda and communication in world history* (Vol. 1). Honolulu: University Press of Hawaii.

Lazarsfeld, P. F. (1925). Über die Perihlbewegung des Merkur aus der Einsteinschen Gravitationstheorie. *Zeitschrift für Physik, 35,* 119-128.

Lazarsfeld, P. F. (1933). An unemployed village. *Character and Personality, 1,* 147-151.

Lazarsfeld, P. F. (1969). An episode in the history of social research: A memoir. In D. Fleming & B. Bailyn (Eds.), *The intellectual migration: Europe and America 1930-1960.* Cambridge, MA: Belknap.

Lazarsfeld, P. F., Berelson, B., & Gaudet, H. (1944). *The people's choice: How the voter makes up his mind in a presidential campaign.* New York: Duell, Sloan, & Pearce.

Lazarsfeld, P. F., Bühler, C., Biegeleisen, B., Hetzer, H., & Reininger, K. (1931). *Jugend und Beruf: Kritik und Material.* Jena, Austria: Gustav Fisher.

Lazarsfeld, P. F., Jahoda, M., & Zeisel, H. (1933). *Die Arbeitslosen von Marienthal: Ein soziographischer Versuch über die Wirkungen langdauernder Arbeitslosigkeit.* Leipzig: S. Hirzel.

Lazarsfeld, P. F., Jahoda, M., & Zeisel, H. (1960). *Die Arbeitslosen von Marienthal: Ein soziographischer Versuch über die Wirkungen langdauernder Arbeitslosigkeit* (2nd ed.). Allensbach und Bonn: Verlag für Demoskopie.

Lazarsfeld, P. F., Jahoda, M., & Zeisel, H. (1971). *Marienthal: The sociography of an unemployed community.* Chicago: Aldine-Atherton.

Lazarsfeld, P. F., Klein, L. R., & Tyler, R. W. (1964). Some problems of organized social research. In *The behavioral science: Problems and prospects.* Boulder, CO: University of Colorado, Institute of Behavioral Science.

Lazarsfeld, P. F., & Stanton, F. N. (Eds.). (1944). *Radio research, 1942-1943.* New York: Duell, Sloan & Pearce.

Lazarsfeld, P. F., & Stanton, F. N. (Eds.). (1949). *Communication research, 1948-49.* New York: Harper & Brothers.

Lerner, D. (1958). *The passing of traditional society: Modernizing the Middle East.* New York: Free Press.

Lerner, D., & Lasswell, H. D. (Eds.). (1951). *The policy sciences: Recent developments in scope and method.* Palo Alto, CA: Stanford University Press.

Levinson, D. (1988). *Instructor and librarian's guide to the HRAF archive.* New Haven, CT: Human Relations Area Files.

Levy, M. R., & Gurevitch, M. (Eds.). (1994). *Defining media studies: Reflections on the future of the field.* New York: Oxford University Press.

Lewin, K. (1929). Die Auswirking von Umweltkräften. *Proceedings of the 9th International Congress of Psychology,* pp. 286-288.

Lewin, K. (1931). The conflict between Aristotelian and Galilean modes of thought in contemporary psychology. *Journal of Genetic Psychology, 5,* 141-177.

Lewin, K. (1940). Formalization and progress in psychology. *University of Iowa Studies in Child Welfare, 16*(3).

Lewin, K. (1942). *The relative effectiveness of a lecture method and a method of group decision for changing food habits.* Washington, DC: Committee on Food Habits, National Research Council.

Lewin, K. (1943). Forces behind food habits and methods of change. *Bulletin of the National Research Council, 58,* 35-65.

Lewin, K. (Ed.). (1951). *Field theory in social science: Selected theoretical papers.* New York: Harper & Row.

Lewin, K., Barker, R., & Dembo, T. (1937). Experiments on frustration and regression in children. *Psychological Bulletin, 34,* 754-755.

Lewin, K., & Bavelas, A. (1942). Training in democratic leadership. *Journal of Abnormal and Social Psychology, 37,* 115-119.

Lewin, K., Lippitt, R., & White, R. (1939). Patterns of aggressive behavior in experimentally created "social climates." *Journal of Social Psychology, 10,* 271-299.

Lindley, W. L. (1976). Chilton Bush: The great innovator. *Journalism Educator, 31,* 18-23.

Lippitt, R. (1940). An experimental study of authoritarian and democratic group atmospheres. In Studies in topological and vector psychology. *University of Iowa Studies in Child Welfare, 1,* 16.

Lippitt, R., & White, R. (1940). An experimental study of authoritarian and democratic group atmosphere. In *Studies in topological and vector psychology, University of Iowa Studies in Child Welfare, 16*(3), 45-193.

Lippitt, R., & White, R. (1943). The "social climate" of children's groups. In R. Lippitt & R. White (Eds.), *Autocracy and democracy: An experimental inquiry.* New York: Harper & Row.

Lippmann, W. (1965). *Public opinion.* New York: Free Press. (Original work published 1922)

Lynd, R. S., & Lynd, H. M. (1929). *Middletown: A study in American culture.* New York: Harcourt, Brace.

Maccoby, E. E., & Jacklin, C. N. (1974). *The psychology of sex differences.* Stanford, CA: Stanford University Press.

Maccoby, N. (1963). The new "scientific" rhetoric. In W. Schramm (Ed.), *The science of human communication: New directions and new findings in communication research.* New York: Basic Books.

MacElwain, M. (1985, April). Meet Wilbur Schramm. *Saturday Evening Post,* pp. 25, 50.

Marrow, A. J. (1969). *The practical theorist: The life and work of Kurt Lewin.* New York: Basic Books.

Marvick, D. (1977). Introduction: Context, problems, and methods. In D. Marvick (Ed.), *Harold D. Lasswell: On political sociology.* Chicago: University of Chicago Press.

McAnany, E. G. (1988). Wilbur Schramm, 1907-1987: Roots of the past, seeds of the present. *Journal of Communication, 38*(4), 109-122.

McCombs, M. E., & Shaw, D. L. (1972). The agenda-setting function of mass media. *Public Opinion Quarterly, 36,* 176-187.

McDougall, D. (1984). *Harold D. Lasswell and the study of international relations.* Washington, DC: University Press of America.

McGuire, W. J. (1973). The YIN and YANG of progress in social psychology: Seven koan. *Journal of Personality and Social Psychology, 26,* 446-456.

McGuire, W. J. (1985). Attitudes and attitude change. In G. Lindzey & E. Aronson (Eds.), *Handbook of social psychology* (Vol. 2: Special Fields and Applications). New York: Random House.

McLuhan, M. (1962). *The Gutenberg galaxy: The making of typographic man.* Toronto: University of Toronto Press.

McLuhan, M. (1965). *Understanding media.* New York: McGraw-Hill.

Melody, W. H., & Mansell, R. E. (1983). The debate over critical vs. administrative research: Circularity or challenge. *Journal of Communication, 33*(3), 103-116.

Merriam, C. E. (1925). *New aspects of politics.* Chicago: University of Chicago Press.

Merton, R. K. (1979). Remembering Paul Lazarsfeld. In R. K. Merton, J. S. Coleman, & P. H. Rossi (Eds.), *Qualitative and quantitative social research: Papers in honor of Paul F. Lazarsfeld.* New York: Free Press.

Merton, R. K., Fiske, M., & Curtis, A. (1946). *Mass persuasion: The social psychology of a war bond drive.* New York: Harper & Row.

Merton, R., & Lazarsfeld, P. F. (Eds.). (1950). *Continuities in social research: Studies on the scope and method of "The American Soldier."* New York: Free Press.

Miller, G. R. (1983). Taking stock of a discipline. *Journal of Communication, 33*(3), 31-41.

Nafziger, R. O. (1930). A reader interest survey of Madison, Wisconsin. *Journalism Quarterly, 2*(1), 128-141.

National Institute of Mental Health. (1972). *Television and growing up: The impact of televised violence* (Report to the Surgeon General, U.S. Public Health Service, from the Surgeon General's Scientific Advisory Committee on Television and Social Behavior). Rockville, MD: Author.

Nelson, L. M. (1977). The Stanford years. In D. Lerner & L. M. Nelson (Eds.), *Communication research: A half-century appraisal.* Honolulu: University Press of Hawaii.

Neurath, P. (1960). *Radio farm forum in India.* Paris: United Nations Educational, Scientific and Cultural Organization.

Neurath, P. (1983). In memoriam Paul F. Lazarsfeld: Paul F. Lazarsfeld and the institutionalization of empirical social research. In B. Holzner, K. D. Knorr & H. Strasser (Eds.), *Realizing social science knowledge.* Vienna: Physica-Verlag.

Noelle-Neumann, E. (1983). The effects of media on media effects research. *Journal of Communication, 33*(3), 157-165.

Osgood, C. E., Suci, G. J., & Tannenbaum, P. H. (1957). *The measurement of meaning.* Urbana: University of Illinois Press.

Osgood, C. E., & Tannenbaum, P. H. (1955). The principle of congruity in the prediction of attitude change. *Psychological Review, 62,* 42-55.

Park, R. E. (1922). *The immigrant press and its control.* New York: Harper.

Park, R. E. (1940). News as a form of knowledge: A chapter in the sociology of knowledge. *American Journal of Sociology, 45,* 669-686.

Park, R. E. (1955). News as a form of knowledge. In R. E. Park (Ed.), *Society: Collective behavior, news and opinion, sociology and modern society.* Chicago: University of Chicago Press.

Park, R. E. (1972). The crowd and the public (C. Elsner, Trans.). In H. Elsner, Jr. (Ed.), *The crowd and the public and other essays.* Chicago: University of Chicago Press. (Original work published 1904)

Park, R. E., & Burgess, E. W. (1969). *Introduction to the science of sociology.* Chicago: University of Chicago Press. (Original work published 1924)

Peterson, P. V. (1973). J-enrollments reach all-time high as some academic disciplines ebb. *Journalism Educator, 27*(4), 4-5.

Peterson, R., & Thurstone, L. L. (1933). *Motion pictures and social attitudes of children.* New York: Macmillan.

Reeves, B., & Borgman, C. (1983). A bibliometric evaluation of core journals in communication research: Networks of communication publications. *Human Communication Research, 10,* 119-136.

Reick, T. (1949). *Listening with the third ear: The inner experience of a psychoanalyst.* New York: Farrar Straus.

Renshaw, S., Miller, V. L., & Marquis, D. P. (1933). *Children's sleep.* New York: Macmillan.

Rice, R., Borgman, C., & Reeves, B. (1988). Citation networks of communication journals, 1977-1985. *Human Communication Research, 15,* 256-283.

Riley, J. W., Jr., & Schramm, W. (1951). *The reds take a city.* New Brunswick, NJ: Rutgers University Press.

Rivers, W. L., & Schramm, W. (1969). *Responsibility in mass communication* (Rev. ed.). New York: Harper & Row.

Rogers, E. M. (1983). *Diffusion of innovations* (3rd ed.). New York: Free Press.

Rogers, E. M. (1994). *A history of communication study: A biographical approach.* New York: Free Press.

Rogers, E. M., & Chaffee, S. H. (1983). Communication as an academic discipline: A dialogue. *Journal of Communication, 33*(3), 18-30.

Rogers, E. M., & Chaffee, S. H. (1994, December). Communication and journalism from "Daddy" Bleyer to Wilbur Schramm: A palimpsest. *Journalism Monographs, 147.*

Rogers, E. M., & Dearing, J. W. (1988). Agenda-setting research: Where has it been, where is it going? In J. A. Anderson (Ed.), *Communication Yearbook 10.* Newbury Park, CA: Sage.

Rogers, E. M., Dearing, J. W., & Bregman, D. (1993). The anatomy of agenda-setting research. *Journal of Communication, 43*(2), 68-84.

Rogow, A. A. (1969). Toward a psychiatry of politics. In A. A. Rogow (Ed.), *Politics, personality, and social science in the twentieth century: Essays in honor of Harold D. Lasswell.* Chicago: University of Chicago Press.

Rosenberg, M. J., & Hovland, C. I. (Eds.). (1960). *Attitude organization and change.* New Haven, CT: Yale University Press.

Rosengren, K. -E. (1987). News diffusion: An overview. *European Journal of Communication, 2,* 135-142.

Ross, L. Q. (1937). *The education of H*Y*M*A*N K*A*P*L*A*N.* New York: Harcourt Brace.

Rosten, L. (1938). *The return of H*Y*M*A*N K*A*P*L*A*N.* New York: Harper & Brothers.

Rosten, L. (1967, April 15). Harold Lasswell: A memoir. *Saturday Review,* pp. 65-67.

Salomon, G. (1979). *Interaction of media, cognition and learning.* San Francisco: Jossey-Bass.

Sapir, E. (1931). Communication. In *Encyclopedia of the Social Sciences* (Vol. 4). New York: Macmillan/Free Press.

Schiller, H. I. (1983). Critical research in the Information Age. *Journal of Communication, 33*(3), 249-257.

Schramm, W. (1932). *Hiawatha and its predecessors.* Unpublished doctoral dissertation, University of Iowa, Iowa City.

Schramm, W. (1933). The cost of books in Chaucer's time. *Bibliography of modern language, 48,* 139-145.

Schramm, W. (1941). *Windwagon Smith and other yarns.* New York: Harcourt Brace.

Schramm, W. (Ed.). (1948). *Communication in modern society.* Urbana: University of Illinois Press.

Schramm, W. (Ed.). (1954). *Process and effects of mass communication.* Urbana: University of Illinois Press.

Schramm, W. (1955). Information theory and mass communications. *Journalism Quarterly, 32,* 131-146.

Schramm, W. (1956). The Soviet-Communist theory of the press. In F. S. Siebert, T. Peterson, & W. Schramm (Eds.), *Four theories of the press.* Urbana: University of Illinois Press.

Schramm, W. (1957). *Responsibility in Mass Communication.* New York: Harper & Row.

Schramm, W. (1959a). Comments on "The state of communication research." *Public Opinion Quarterly, 23,* 6-9.

Schramm, W. (1959b). *One day in the world's press.* Stanford, CA: Stanford University Press.

Schramm, W. (1960). *Mass communications.* Urbana: University of Illinois Press. (Original work published 1949)

Schramm, W. (Ed.). (1963). *The science of human communication: New directions and new findings in communication research.* New York: Basic Books.

Schramm, W. (1964). *Mass media and national development.* Stanford, CA: Stanford University Press.

Schramm, W. (1973). *Men, messages, and media: A look at human communication.* New York: Harper & Row.

Schramm, W. (1977). *Big media, little media: Tools and technologies for instruction.* Beverly Hills, CA: Sage.

Schramm, W. (1988). *The story of human communication.* New York: Harper & Row.

Schramm, W., & Chu, G. C. (1967). *Learning from television: What the research says.* Washington, DC: National Association for Educational Broadcasters.

Schramm, W., Lyle, J., & Parker, E. B. (1961). *Television in the lives of our children.* Stanford, CA: Stanford University Press.

Schramm, W., Nelson, L. M., & Bethan, M. T. (1981). *Bold experiment: The story of educational television in American Samoa.* Stanford, CA: Stanford University Press.

Schramm, W., & Riley, J. W., Jr. (1951). Communication in the Sovietized state, as demonstrated in Korea. *American Sociological Review, 16,* 757-766.

Schramm, W., & Ruggels, W. L. (1967). How mass media systems grow. In W. Schramm & D. Lerner (Eds.), *Communication and change in the developing countries.* Honolulu: East-West Center Press.

Seashore, C. E., & Schramm, W. (1934). Time and intensity in English tetrameter verse. *Philological Quarterly, 13*(1), 65-71.

Sherif, M., & Hovland, C. I. (1960). *Social judgment.* New Haven, CT: Yale University Press.

Shoemaker, P. (1991). *Communication concepts 3: Gatekeeping.* Newbury Park, CA: Sage.

Shuttleworth, F. K., & May, M. A. (1933). *The social conduct and attitude of movie fans.* New York: Macmillan.

Siebert, F. S., Peterson, T., & Schramm, W. (1956). *Four theories of the press.* Urbana: University of Illinois Press.

Simpson, C. (1994). *Science of coercion: Communication research and psychological warfare 1945-1960.* New York: Oxford University Press.

Smith, B. L. (1969). The mystifying intellectual history of Harold D. Lasswell. In A. A. Rogow (Ed.), *Politics, personality, and social science in the twentieth century: Essays in honor of Harold D. Lasswell.* Chicago: University of Chicago Press.

Smith, B. L., Lasswell, H. D., & Casey, R. D. (1946). *Propaganda, communication, and public opinion: A comprehensive reference guide.* Princeton: Princeton University Press.

Smythe, D. W., & van Dinh, T. (1983). On critical and administrative research: A new critical analysis. *Journal of Communication, 33*(3), 117-127.

So, C. Y. K. (1988). Citation patterns of core communication journals: An assessment of the development status of communication. *Human Communication Research, 15,* 236-255.

Stouffer, S. A., Guttman, L., Suchman, E. A., Lazarsfeld, P. F., Star, S. A., & Clausen, J. A. (1950). *Measurement and prediction: Studies in social psychology in World War II* (Vol. IV). Princeton, NJ: Princeton University Press.

Stouffer, S. A., Lumsdaine, A. A., Lumsdaine, M. H., Williams. R. M., Jr. Smith, M. B., Janis, I. L., Star, S. A., & Cottrell, L. S., Jr. (1949). *The American Soldier: Combat and its aftermath: Studies in social psychology in World War II* (Vol. II). Princeton, NJ: Princeton University Press.

Stouffer, S. A., Suchman, E. A., DeVinney, L. C., Star, S. A., & Williams, R. M., Jr. (1949). *The American soldier: Adjustment during army life: Studies in social psychology in World War II* (Vol. I). Princeton, NJ: Princeton University Press.

Tankard, J. W. Jr. (1990). Wilbur Schramm: Definer of a field. In W. D. Sloan (Ed.), *Makers of the media mind: Journalism educators and their ideas.* Hillsdale, NJ: Lawrence Erlbaum.

Tannenbaum, P. H. (1953). *Attitudes towards source and concept as factors in attitude change through communications.* Unpublished doctoral dissertation, University of Illinois at Urbana-Champaign.

Taylor, W. L. (1953). "Cloze procedure": A new tool for measuring readability. *Journalism Quarterly, 30,* 415-453.

Thayer, F. (1944). *Legal control of the press.* Chicago: Foundation Press.

Toffler, A. (1980). *The third wave.* New York: Morrow.

Troldahl, V. C. (1968). *Perspectives in studying communication.* Unpublished paper, East Lansing, Michigan State University, Department of Communication.

Washington, B. T. (1912). *The man farthest down: A record of observation and study in Europe.* New York: Doubleday.

Weaver, C. H. (1977). Appendix: A history of the International Communication Association. In B. D. Ruben (Ed.), *Communication yearbook I: An annual review published by the International Communication Association.* New Brunswick. NJ: Transaction Books.

White, D. M. (1950). The gate-keeper: A case study in the selection of news. *Journalism Quarterly, 27,* 283-290.

Whorf, B. L. (1941). The relation of habitual thought and behavior to language. In L. Spier, A. I. Hollowell, & S. S. Newman (Eds.), *Language, culture, and personality: Essays in memory of Edward Sapir.* Menasha, WI: Sapir Memorial Publication Fund.

Whorf, B. L. (1956). A linguistic consideration of thinking in primitive communities. In J. B. Carroll (Ed.), *Language, thought, and reality: Selected writings of Benjamin Lee Whorf.* Cambridge, MA: Technology Press of the Massachusetts Institute of Technology. (Original work published 1941)

Windelband, W. (1898). *A history of philosophy* (J. H. Tufts, Trans.). New York: Macmillan.

Wright, C. (1960). *Mass communications: A sociological perspective.* New York: Random House.

Zajonc, R. B. (1960). The concepts of balance, congruity, and dissonance. *Public Opinion Quarterly, 24*(2), 280-296.

Zeigarnik, B. (1927). Über Behalten von erledigten und unerledigten Handlungen. *Psychologische Forschung, 9,* 1-85.

Zeisel, H. (1979). The Vienna years. In R. K. Merton, J. S. Coleman, & P. H. Rossi (Eds.), *Qualitative and quantitative social research: Papers in honor of Paul F. Lazarsfeld.* New York: Free Press.

Zimbardo, P. G. (1985, June). Laugh where we must, be candid where we can: PT conversation with Allen Funt. *Psychology Today,* pp. 42-47.

Author Index

193

Subject Index

About the Authors

Wilbur Schramm was Director Emeritus of the East-West Center's Institute for Communication at the time of his death in Honolulu in 1987. He was born in Marietta, Ohio, in 1907 and graduated Phi Beta Kappa from Marietta College in 1929. He then attended Harvard University (MA, 1930) and the State University of Iowa (PhD, English, 1932). After a 2-year postdoctoral appointment in psychology, he taught English at Iowa from 1934 until he left for wartime service in 1942-1943; he returned to Iowa as director of the School of Journalism, where he taught from 1943 to 1947. He was at the University of Illinois from 1947 to 1955 and at Stanford University from 1955 to 1973; after retirement from Stanford, he was at the East-West Center for the remainder of his career, except for teaching terms at the Chinese University of Hong Kong and the University of Michigan. Schramm's many publications include a number of landmark books in the development of the academic field of mass communication, including *Communications in Modern Society* (1948), *Mass Communications* (1949/1960), *Process and Effects of Mass Communication* (1954), *Four Theories of the Press* (with Fred Siebert and Theodore Peterson, 1956), *Responsibility in Mass Communication* (1957), *Television in the*

Lives of Our Children (with others, 1961), *Mass Media and National Development* (1964), *Communication and Change in the Developing Countries* (with Daniel Lerner, 1967), *Men, Messages, and Media* (1973), and *Big Media, Little Media* (1978).

Steven H. Chaffee is Janet M. Peck Professor of International Communication at Stanford University. He was Director of the School of Journalism and Mass Communication at the University of Wisconsin–Madison in 1980-1981 and has chaired the Stanford Department of Communication from 1985 to 1990 and in 1996-1997. He is a Past President and Fellow of the International Communication Association. Born in South Gate, California, in 1935, he attended the University of Redlands (BA, 1957), UCLA (MS, 1962), and Stanford University (PhD, Communication, 1965). His publications include *Political Communication* (1976), *Television and Human Behavior* (with George Comstock and others, 1978), *Handbook of Communication Science* (with Charles Berger, 1986), and *To See Ourselves: Comparing Traditional Chinese and American Cultural Values* (with Zhongdang Pan and others, 1994).

Everett M. Rogers is Professor and Chair, Department of Communication and Journalism, at the University of New Mexico. He has been teaching and conducting communication research for the past 42 years. He has served on the faculty of Ohio State University, Michigan State University, University of Michigan, Stanford University, University of Southern California, and the University of New Mexico. He is particularly known for his book, *Diffusion of Innovations*, published in 1995 in its fourth edition, and for his 1994 book, *A History of Communication Study: A Biographical Approach.*